Charcuterie Boards Cookbook

BY: CYNTHIA C. NIEVES

TABLE OF CONTENTS

Charcuterie Boards Cookbook i
1. Classic French Charsliceerie: 7
2. Vietnamese Bia Hoi and Ca Phe Trung 7
3. Mediterranean Meze Board: 7
4. Spanish Tapas Feast: 7
5. Vegan Charsliceerie Spread: 7
6. Seafood Extravaganza: 8
7. Lover's Delight: 8
8. Sweet and Savory Combo: 8
9. Breakfast Charsliceerie Board: 9
10. Brunch Time Delights: 9
11. Game Day Grazing Platter: 9
12. Holiday Cheer Board: 10
13. Summer Picnic Spread: 10
14. Fall Harvest Feast: 10
15. Winter Wonderland Platter: 11
16. Springtime Garden Spread: 11
17. Valentine's Day Romance: 11
18. Easter Brunch Board: 11
19. Mother's Day Surprise: 12
20. Father's Day BBQ: 12
21. Hleteen Spooktacular: 12
22. Thanksgiving Bounty: 12
23. Christmas Eve Extravaganza: 13
24. New Year's Eve Bash: 13
25. Birthday Celebration Platter: 13
26. Graduation Party Board: 14
27. Anniversary Love Board: 14
28. Bridal Shower Elegance: 14
29. Baby Shower Delights: 15
30. Girls' Night In Fun: 15
31. Guys' Night Charsliceerie: 15
32. Kids' Party Adventure: 15
33. Movie Night Snack Board: 16
34. Book Club Gathering: 16
35. Wine Tasting Pairings 16
36. Craft Beer Tasting Board 17
37. Whisky and Cigars Pairing 17
38. Tropical Island Escape 17
39. Coastal Sea Breeze Platter 17
40. Hawaiian Luau Feast 17
41. Southern Comfort Board 18
42. Tex-Mex Fiesta Fun 18
43. Indian Spice Extravaganza 18
44. Thai Street Food Adventure 18
45. Chinese Dim Sum Delights: 19
46. Korean BBQ Party: 19
47. Vietnamese Street Eats: 19
48. Greek Mythical Feast: 20
49. Israeli Hummus and Pita: 20
50. Lebanese Mezze Medley: 20
51. Egyptian Pharaoh's Platter: 20
52. South African Braai Board: 21
53. Australian BBQ Bonanza: 21
54. Brazilian Churrasco Experience: 21
55. Argentinean Asado Grill: 21
56. Chilean BBQ Extravaganza: 22
57. Peruvian Ceviche Fiesta: 22
58. Colombian Street Food: 23
59. Canadian Maple Syrup Indulgence: 23
60. Mexican Street Corn Fiesta: 23
61. Italian Pizza and Pasta Board: 23
62. French Crepes 24
63. Croissants 24
64. Spanish Paella Party 25
65. Portuguese Tapas Bonanza 25
66. British Fish and Chips 26
67. German Oktoberfest Feast 26
68. Austrian Schnitzel Delight 26
69. Hungarian Goulash Board 27
70. Finnish Fisherman's Platter: 27
71. Danish Smørrebrød Spread: 28

72. Norwegian Gravlax and Aquavit: 28
73. Irish Pub Grub Platter: 28
74. Scottish Haggis and Whisky: 29
75. Welsh Rarebit and Ale: 29
76. American Southern BBQ: 29
77. New Orleans Cajun Creole: 29
78. Texan Steakhouse Board: 30
79. Californian Avocado Dream: 30
80. Hawaiian Poke Paradise 30
81. New England Clambake 31
82. New York Deli Board 31
83. Chicago Deep-Dish Party 31
84. Tex-Mex Nacho Fiesta 32
85. Southwest Chili and Cornbread 32
86. Midwestern Hot Dog Party 33
87. Pacific Northwest Salmon Soiree 33
88. Floridian Citrus Celebration 33
89. Caribbean Rum Punch Party 34
90. Central American Tamales Board: 34
91. South American Empanada Fiesta: 34
92. North African Spice Odyssey: 35
93. West African Jollof Joy: 35
94. East African Safari Platter: 36
95. South African Boerewors Braai: 36
96. Arabian Nights Extravaganza: 36
97. Middle Eastern Shawarma Feast: 37
98. Persian Mezze Magic: 37
99. Indian Tandoori Bonanza: 37
100. South Indian Dosa Delights: 38
101. Southeast Asian Satay Soiree: 38
102. Thai Tom Yum and Pad Thai: 38
103. Japanese Ramen and Tempura: 39
104. Chinese Hot Pot Adventure: 39
105. Korean Kimchi and BBQ: 39
106. Vietnamese Pho and Spring Rolls: 40
107. Mexican Churros and Horchata: 40
108. Spanish Churros and Chocolate 41
109. German Black Forest Feast 41
110. Swiss Chocolate Heaven 42

111. British Sticky Toffee Pudding 42
112. American Apple Pie Delight 43
113. Canadian Maple Pecan Pleasure 43
114. Australian Lamington Love 43
115. Brazilian Brigadeiro Bliss 44
116. Argentinean Alfajores Amor 44
117. Turkish Baklava and Tea 45
118. Greek Baklava and Ouzo 45
119. Moroccan Mint Tea Magic 45
120. Japanese Matcha and Mochi 45
121. Indian Mango Lassi Love 46
122. Thai Mango Sticky Rice 46
123. Caribbean Rum Cake Delight 46
124. Hawaiian Pineapple Paradise 47
125. Swiss Rösti and Rosti 47
126. Italian Panettone Perfection 47
127. French Croissant: 48
128. Café au Lait: 48
129. Spanish Flan: 48
130. Sangria: 49
131. Portuguese Pastel de Nata: 49
132. Eton Mess Melody: 50
133. Mexican Tres Leches Treat: 50
134. Israeli Malabi Marvel: 51
135. South African Milk Tart: 51
136. Indian Kulfi: 52
137. Indian Falooda: 52
138. Korean Bingsu Bliss: 52
139. Turkish Dondurma Delight: 53
140. Greek Loukoumades Love 53
141. Vietnamese Egg Coffee Euphoria 53
142. Japanese Wagashi Wonderland 54
143. Scandinavian Cinnamon Bun Joy 54
144. Mexican Aguas Frescas Fiesta 54
145. Italian Affogato and Amaro 55
146. Spanish Crema Catalana Dream 55
147. Brazilian Caipirinha Carnival 55
148. Turkish Turkish Delight Delight 56
149. Greek Ouzo and Meze Melody 56

150. Russian Vodka and Zakuski: 56
151. Irish Irish Coffee Craze: 56
152. Scottish Whisky and Shortbread: 57
153. American Mint Julep Madness: 57
154. Italian Limoncello Love: 57
155. French Kir Royale EXTRAVAGANZA: 57
156. Spanish Sangria and Tapas: 58
157. Mexican Margarita Fiesta: 58
158. Caribbean Rum Punch Paradise: 58
159. Brazilian Caipirinha Carnival: 58
160. Argentinean Mate: 59
161. Alfajores: 59
162. Turkish Ayran: 59
163. Turkish Kebabs: 59
164. Greek Frappé: 60
165. Greek Baklava: 60
166. Russian Kvass: 60
167. ussian Blini: 61
168. Indian Masala Chai Charm: 61
169. Thai Iced Tea: 61
170. Thai Mango Sticky Rice: 61
171. Japanese Iced Matcha Melody: 62
172. Chinese Bubble Tea Bonanza: 62
173. Korean Iced Coffee Delight: 62
174. Vietnamese Iced Coffee Euphoria: 63
175. Moroccan Mint Tea Marvel 63
176. Hawaiian Pina Colada Paradise 63
177. Swiss Iced Chocolate Dream 63
178. Italian Aperol Spritz Sensation 64
179. French Champagne Soiree 64
180. Spanish Gin and Tonic Extravaganza 64
181. Mexican Paloma and Tacos 64
182. Caribbean Piña Colada Party 64
183. Turkish Raki and Meze Melody 65
184. Greek Ouzo and Tzatziki 65
185. American Craft Beer 65
186. Canadian Caesar and Poutine 65
187. Australian Vegemite and Tim Tams 66
188. Brazilian Caipiroska and Coxinha 66
189. Argentinean Malbec and Asado 66
190. Thai Singha Beer and Pad Thai 67
191. Japanese Sake and Sashimi 67
192. Chinese Baijiu and Dumplings 67
193. Korean Soju and Kimbap 68
194. Vietnamese Bia Hoi 68
195. Vietnamese Banh Mi 68
196. Moroccan Mint Tea 69
197. Moroccan Couscous 69
198. Hawaiian Blue Hawaiian Bliss (Cocktail) 69
199. Swiss Absinthe 69
200. Swiss Fondue 70
201. Italian Negroni (Cocktail) 70
202. Italian Antipasti Platter 70
203. French Kir Breton Bonanza (Cocktail) 70
204. Spanish Tinto de Verano Love 71
205. Mexican Michelada 71
206. Mexican Guacamole 71
207. Caribbean Rum Runner Parade (Cocktail) 71
208. Turkish Sahlep 72
209. Turkish Baklava 72
210. Greek Metaxa and Koulourakia 72
211. Indian Kingfisher Beer and Samosas 73
212. Thai Leo Beer and Satay 73
213. Japanese Whisky Highball Frenzy 73
214. Korean Hite Beer and Bibimbap 74
215. Vietnamese Bia Hoi and Pho 74
216. Moroccan Mint Tea and Harira 74
217. Hawaiian Mai Tai Luau 75
218. Swiss Glacier Martini Magic: 75
219. Italian Bellini and Prosciutto: 75
220. French Pernod and Croque Monsieur: 76
221. Spanish Sherry and Gazpacho: 76
222. Mexican Tequila Sunrise Fiesta: 76
223. Caribbean Painkiller Party: 76
224. Turkish Rakı and Kebabs: 77
225. Greek Metaxa and Taramasalata: 77
226. Russian Moscow Mule Parade: 77
227. Indian Mango Lassi and Samosas: 78

228. Thai Singha Beer and Tom Yum: 78
229. Japanese Suntory Toki and Sushi: 78
230. Chinese Plum Wine and Spring Rolls: 79
231. Korean Makgeolli and Japchae: 79
232. Vietnamese Bia Hoi and Bun Thit Nuong: 79
233. Moroccan Mint Tea and Pastilla: 80
234. Hawaiian Blue Lagoon Luau: 80
235. Swiss Swiss Mule Magic: 81
236. Italian Sgroppino and Bruschetta: 81
237. French Kir Royale Breton Bonanza: 81
238. Spanish Tinto de Verano Love 81
239. Mexican Horchata and Tacos 82
240. Caribbean Rum Swizzle Soiree 82
241. Turkish Salep and Turkish Delight 82
242. Greek Ouzo and Dolmades 82
243. Russian Black Russian and Piroshki 83
244. Indian Kingfisher Beer and Pakoras 83
245. Thai Chang Beer and Green Curry 84
246. Japanese Yamazaki Whisky and Tempura 84
247. Chinese Baijiu and Kung Pao Chicken 84
248. Korean Cass Beer and Bulgogi 85
249. Vietnamese Ca Phe Sua Da and Banh Xeo 85
250. Moroccan Mint Tea and Briouats 86
251. Hawaiian Lava Flow Luau 86
252. Swiss Chocolate Martini Magic 86
253. Italian Limoncello Spritz and Caprese 87
254. French Kir Normand Bonanza 87
255. Spanish Cava and Patatas Bravas 87
256. Mexican Tequila Sunset Fiesta 87
257. Caribbean Hurricane Party 88
258. Turkish Mastic Raki and Turkish Delight 88
259. Greek Tsipouro and Saganaki 88
260. Russian White Russian and Blinchiki 89
261. Indian Kingfisher Beer and Tandoori Chicken 89
262. Thai Singha Beer and Green Papaya Salad.................89
263. Japanese Toki Highball Parade 90
264. Chinese Tsingtao Beer and Dim Sum 90
265. Korean Hite Beer and Korean Fried Chicken 90
266. Vietnamese Bia Hoi and Goi Cuon 90

267. Moroccan Mint Tea and Kefta Tagine 91
268. Hawaiian Blue Hawaii Luau 91
269. Swiss Alpine Negroni Magic 91
270. Italian Aperol Spritz and Carpaccio 92
271. French Lillet Royale Bonanza 92
272. Spanish Kalimotxo Love 92
273. Mexican Mexican Mule Fiesta 92
274. Caribbean Blue Hawaiian Party 92
275. Turkish Bouncea and Baklava 93
276. Greek Tsipouro and Souvlaki 93
277. Russian Moscow Mule Parade 93
278. Indian Mango Lassi 93
279. Indian Bhel Puri 93
280. Thai Singha Beer and Som Tum 94
281. Japanese Hibiki Whisky and Sushi 94
282. Chinese Lychee Martini and Dumplings 94
283. Korean Soju and Jajangmyeon 95
284. Vietnamese Bia Hoi and Ca Phe Trung 95
285. Moroccan Mint Tea and Maakouda 95
286. Hawaiian Piña Colada Luau 96
287. Swiss Glacier Martini Magic 96
288. Italian Bellini and Prosciutto 96
289. French Pernod and Croque Monsieur 97
290. Spanish Sherry and Gazpacho 97
291. Mexican Tequila Sunrise Fiesta 97
292. Caribbean Painkiller Party 97
293. Turkish Rakı and Kebabs 98
294. Greek Metaxa and Taramasalata 98
295. Russian Moscow Mule Parade 98
296. Indian Mango Lassi and Samosas 98
297. Thai Singha Beer and Tom Yum 99
298. Japanese Suntory Toki and Sushi 99
299. Chinese Plum Wine and Spring Rolls 99
300. Korean Makgeolli and Japchae 100
301. Vietnamese Bia Hoi and Bun Thit Nuong 100
302. Moroccan Mint Tea and Pastilla 100
303. Hawaiian Blue Lagoon Luau 101
304. Swiss Swiss Mule Magic 101
305. Italian Sgroppino and Bruschetta 101

306. French Kir Royale Breton Bonanza 102
307. Spanish Tinto de Verano Love 102
308. Mexican Horchata and Tacos 102
309. Caribbean Rum Swizzle Soiree 102
310. Turkish Salep and Turkish Delight 103
311. Greek Ouzo and Dolmades 103
312. Russian Black Russian and Piroshki 103
313. Black Russian Cocktail: 104
314. Indian Kingfisher Beer and Pakoras 104
315. Thai Chang Beer and Green Curry 104
316. Japanese Yamazaki Whisky and Tempura 105
317. Chinese Baijiu and Kung Pao Chicken 105
318. Korean Cass Beer and Bulgogi 105
319. Vietnamese Ca Phe Sua Da and Banh Xeo 106
320. Moroccan Mint Tea and Briouats 106
321. Hawaiian Lava Flow Luau 107
322. Swiss Chocolate Martini Magic 107
323. Italian Limoncello Spritz and Caprese 107
324. French Kir Normand Bonanza 107
325. Spanish Cava and Patatas Bravas 108
326. Mexican Tequila Sunset Fiesta 108
327. Caribbean Hurricane Party 108
328. Turkish Mastic Raki and Turkish Delight 108
329. Greek Tsipouro and Saganaki 109
330. Russian White Russian and Blinchiki 109
331. Indian Kingfisher Beer and Tandoori Chicken 109
332. Thai Singha Beer and Green Papaya Salad 109
333. Japanese Toki Highball Parade 110
334. Chinese Tsingtao Beer and Dim Sum 110
335. Korean Hite Beer and Korean Fried Chicken 110
336. Vietnamese Bia Hoi and Goi Cuon 111
337. Moroccan Mint Tea and Kefta Tagine 111
338. Hawaiian Blue Hawaii Luau 111
339. Swiss Alpine Negroni Magic 112
340. Italian Aperol Spritz and Carpaccio 112
341. French Lillet Royale Bonanza 112
342. Spanish Kalimotxo Love 112
343. Mexican Mexican Mule Fiesta 113
344. Caribbean Blue Hawaiian Party 113
345. Turkish Bouncea and Baklava 113
346. Greek Tsipouro and Souvlaki 113
347. Russian Moscow Mule Parade 114
348. Indian Mango Lassi and Bhel Puri 114
349. Thai Singha Beer and Som Tum 114
350. Japanese Hibiki Whisky and Sushi 114
351. Chinese Lychee Martini and Dumplings 115
352. Korean Soju and Jajangmyeon 115

RECIPES

1. Classic French Charsliceerie:

Time: 20 mins
Servings: 4-6

Ingredients:

- Assorted cured meats (such as prosciutto
- salami
- and pâté)
- French cheeses (like brie
- camembert, and blue cheese)
- baguette slices
- cornichons
- olives
- Dijon mustard.

Instructions:

1. Place the cheeses and cured meats on a platter, surround them with the fixings, and serve with baguette slices and mustard.

2. Vietnamese Bia Hoi and Ca Phe Trung

Time: 10 mins
Servings: 1

Ingredients:

- 6 oz fresh draft beer (Bia Hoi)
- 1 egg yolk
- 1 tbsp sweetened condensed milk
- Ice cubes
- Vietnamese coffee drip filter (phin) for serving

Instructions:

1. Egg yolk and sweetened condensed milk Must be combined thoroughly in a glass.
2. Over a Vietnamese coffee drip filter (phin) set above a glass, pour the egg yolk Mixture.
3. To the glass, add ice cubes.
4. Make a pot of robust Vietnamese coffee with a drip filter.
5. The Mixture of egg yolks and coffee must be stirred.
6. Fill a different glass with fresh draft Bia Hoi.
7. Vietnamese Egg Coffee (Ca Phe Trung) Must be served with Bia Hoi on the side.

NUTRITION INFO (per serving - Ca Phe Trung):
Cals: 200, Carbs: 20g, Fat: 5g, Protein: 5g

3. Mediterranean Meze Board:

Time: 25 mins
Servings: 4-6

Ingredients:

- Hummus
- tzatziki
- pita bread
- falafel
- olives
- feta cheese
- cherry tomatoes
- cucumber slices
- stuffed grape leaves
- roasted red pepper dip.

Instructions:

1. On a tray, arrange the different falafel, dips, and toppings from the Mediterranean region. Pita bread Must be served alongside.

4. Spanish Tapas Feast:

Time: 35 mins
Servings: 4-6

Ingredients:

- Patatas bravas
- Spanish tortilla
- garlic shrimp
- chorizo slices
- olives
- Manchego cheese
- marinated anchovies
- tomato bread.

Instructions:

1. The tapas items Must be ready, and they Must be arranged on a tray with cheese, anchovies, and olives. Add tomato bread to the dish.

5. Vegan Charsliceerie Spread:

Time: 15 mins
Servings: 4-6

Ingredients:

- Assorted vegan cheeses (cashew cheese, almond cheese, etc.)
- Vegan deli slices (tofu-based or seitan-based)
- Hummus and/or vegan tzatziki
- Olives (assorted types)
- Assorted nuts (almonds, walnuts, etc.)
- Grapes and/or split apples
- Assorted crackers and breadsticks
- Cherry tomatoes
- Pickles
- Vegan dark chocolate squares

Instructions:

1. Arrange the vegan cheeses, deli slices, and other ingredients on a Big platter or board.
2. Add mini bowls or containers for hummus and/or vegan tzatziki.
3. Fill in the gaps with olives, nuts, grapes, split apples, cherry tomatoes, and pickles.
4. Add some crackers and breadsticks around the edges.
5. Place some vegan dark chocolate squares as a sweet finishing touch.
6. Serve and enjoy!

NUTRITION INFO (per serving):
Cals: 250-300 kcal, Protein: 8-10g, Fat: 15-20g, Carbs: 20-25g, Fiber: 4-6g

6. Seafood Extravaganza:

Time: 30 mins

Servings: 4-6

Ingredients:

- Cooked shrimp
- Smoked salmon or trout
- Steamed mussels
- Crab claws or imitation crab meat (for a more affordable option)
- Cocktail sauce
- Lemon wedges
- Assorted crackers
- Split baguette or pita bread

Instructions:

1. On a sizable platter or board, arrange the seafood dishes.
2. Over the seafood, arrange dishes with cocktail sauce and lemon wedges for squeezing and dipping.
3. Serve the shellfish surrounded by a variety of crackers, baguette slices, or pita bread.
4. If wanted, garnish with some fresh herbs.
5. Dispense and savor!

NUTRITION INFO (per serving):
Cals: 200-250 kcal, Protein: 15-20g, Fat: 8-12g, Carbs: 15-20g, Fiber: 2-4g, Cheese

7. Lover's Delight:

Time: 20 mins

Servings: 4-6

Ingredients:

- Assorted cheeses (brie, cheddar, gouda, blue cheese, etc.)
- Cheese-stuffed olives
- Split prosciutto or other cured meats
- Dried fruits (figs, apricots, etc.)
- Assorted nuts (pecans, hazelnuts, etc.)
- Crackers and bread slices

Instructions:

1. Place the cheeses and prosciutto slices on a sizable dish or Cutting board.
2. Olives packed with cheese, dried fruit, and a variety of nuts can be used to fill up the gaps.
3. Around the rims, add some bread slices and crackers.
4. Slices of apple or fresh grapes can be added for added flavor and color.
5. Dispense and savor!

NUTRITION INFO (per serving):
Cals: 300-350 kcal, Protein: 15-20g, Fat: 20-25g , Carbs: 15-20g, Fiber: 2-4g

8. Sweet and Savory Combo:

Time: 25 mins

Servings: 4-6

Ingredients:

- Split prosciutto or other cured meats
- Assorted cheeses (brie, goat cheese, etc.)
- Dried apricots and figs
- Honey or maple syrup

- Assorted nuts (pistachios, almonds, etc.)
- Fresh berries (strawberries, blueberries, etc.)
- Split baguette or crackers

Instructions:

1. Place the various cheeses and slice prosciutto on a sizable dish or board.
2. Set up bowls of honey or maple syrup to drizzle over the prosciutto and cheese.
3. Dried apricots, figs, and a variety of nuts can be used to fill up the gaps.
4. For an explosion of color and taste, add fresh berries.
5. Serve with crackers or split bread.
6. Dispense and savor!

NUTRITION INFO (per serving):
Cals: 250-300 kcal, Protein: 10-15g, Fat: 15-20g, Carbs: 20-25g, Fiber: 3-5g

9. Breakfast Charsliceerie Board:

Time: 30 mins
Servings: 4-6

Ingredients:

- Scrambled tofu (seasoned with turmeric, nutritional yeast, and black salt)
- Vegan sausage links or patties
- Split avocado
- Cherry tomatoes
- Assorted fruits (grapes, berries, etc.)
- Vegan yogurt or almond milk chia pudding
- Vegan granola
- Split bread or bagels
- Vegan cream cheese or nut butter

Instructions:

1. Place the vegan sausage and scrambled tofu on one side of the board.
2. On a different side, add cherry tomatoes and split avocado.
3. Assorted fruits and vegan yogurt or chia pudding made with almond milk might fill in the gaps.
4. Vegan granola can be added on top of yogurt or pudding.
5. Serve with vegan cream cheese or nut butter and split bread or bagels.
6. Dispense and savor!

NUTRITION INFO (per serving):
Cals: 300-350 kcal, Protein: 15-20g, Fat: 15-20g, Carbs: 25-30g, Fiber: 6-8g

10. Brunch Time Delights:

Time: 25 mins
Servings: 4-6

Ingredients:

- Scrambled eggs or tofu scramble (for a vegan option)
- Smoked salmon or trout
- Split avocado
- Cherry tomatoes
- Cucumber slices
- Assorted cheeses
- Assorted fruits (grapes, berries, etc.)
- Croissants or mini bagels
- Cream cheese or vegan cream cheese

Instructions:

1. On one side of the board, arrange the scrambled eggs or tofu.
2. Add smoked salmon or trout to the scrambled eggs and tofu.
3. On the other side, arrange cherry tomatoes and split avocado.
4. Slices of cucumber, various cheeses, and various fruits can be used to fill in the blanks.
5. Serve with cream cheese or vegan cream cheese and croissants or mini bagels.
6. Dispense and savor!

NUTRITION INFO (per serving):
Cals: 350-400 kcal, Protein: 15-20g, Fat: 20-25g, Carbs: 25-30g, Fiber: 4-6g

11. Game Day Grazing Platter:

Time: 20 mins
Servings: 6-8

Ingredients:

- Assorted deli meats (salami, pepperoni, etc.)
- Split roast beef or turkey
- Cheddar and pepper jack cheese slices
- Pickles and olives
- Baby carrots and celery sticks
- Cherry tomatoes
- Pretzels and tortilla chips
- Ranch and honey mustard dip

Instructions:

1. Place the split roast beef or turkey and various deli meats on a sizable dish or board.
2. To the dish, add pieces of cheddar and pepper jack cheese.
3. Pickles, olives, mini carrots, and celery sticks can be used to fill up the gaps.
4. The dish Must be covered in cherry tomatoes.
5. Place tortilla chips and pretzels on one side.
6. Place the ranch and honey mustard dips in mini bowls nearby for dipping.
7. Dispense and savor!

NUTRITION INFO (per serving):
Cals: 300-350 kcal, Protein: 15-20g, Fat: 20-25g, Carbs: 15-20g, Fiber: 2-4g

12. Holiday Cheer Board:

Time: 30 mins
Servings: 6-8

Ingredients:

- Split roasted turkey or ham
- Cranberry sauce
- Brie and gouda cheese wedges
- Fresh grapes and pomegranate seeds
- Assorted nuts (pecans, walnuts, etc.)
- Split baguette and crackers
- Rosemary sprigs for garnish

Instructions:

1. On a sizable dish or board, arrange the split roasted turkey or ham.
2. Add cranberry sauce in tiny dishes to the platter.
3. On the board, arrange the wedges of brie and gouda cheese.
4. Fresh grapes and pomegranate seeds can be used to fill in the blanks.
5. Spread a variety of nuts on the board.
6. For serving, include crackers and split bread.
7. Add rosemary sprigs as a garnish.
8. Dispense and savor!

NUTRITION INFO (per serving):
Cals: 350-400 kcal, Protein: 20-25g, Fat: 20-25g, Carbs: 20-25g, Fiber: 2-4g

13. Summer Picnic Spread:

Time: 25 mins
Servings: 4-6

Ingredients:

- Grilled vegetable skewers (bell peppers, zucchini, etc.)
- Watermelon wedges
- Cherry tomatoes
- Fresh mozzarella balls
- Split Italian salami
- Baguette slices
- Basil pesto for dipping

Instructions:

1. The grilled veggie skewers Must be arranged on a sizable plate or board.
2. Add cherry tomatoes and wedges of watermelon to the plate.
3. Italian salami slices and balls of fresh mozzarella Must be placed all over the board.
4. Serve the baguette pieces here.
5. Give the bread and vegetables a mini bowl of basil pesto to dip in.
6. Dispense and savor!

NUTRITION INFO (per serving):
Cals: 250-300 kcal, Protein: 10-15g, Fat: 15-20g, Carbs: 20-25g, Fiber: 3-5g

14. Fall Harvest Feast:

Time: 40 mins
Servings: 6-8

Ingredients:

- Roasted butternut squash slices
- Split roast turkey or chicken
- Caramelized onions
- Baked brie with cranberry sauce
- Assorted nuts (walnuts, pecans, etc.)
- Split apples and pears
- Crackers and baguette slices

Instructions:

1. Slices of roasted butternut squash Must be arranged on a big plate or board.
2. Split roast chicken or turkey Must be added to the plate.
3. On the board, arrange baked brie with cranberry sauce and caramelized onions.

4. Split apples, pears, and various nuts Must be used to fill in the spaces.
5. Serve alongside baguette slices and crackers.
6. Dispense and savor!

NUTRITION INFO (per serving):
Cals: 350-400 kcal, Protein: 15-20g, Fat: 20-25g, Carbs: 30-35g, Fiber: 4-6g

15. Winter Wonderland Platter:

Time: 30 mins
Servings: 6-8

Ingredients:

- Assorted cheeses (Brie, Gouda, Camembert)
- Split cured meats (Salami, Prosciutto)
- Crackers and baguette slices
- Grapes and dried apricots
- Combined nuts (almonds, cashews)
- Honey and fig jam for drizzling

Instructions:

1. Put the cured meats and cheeses on a sizable plate or wooden board.
2. Around the cheeses and meats, arrange the crackers and slices of bread.
3. For a splash of color and sweetness, include clusters of grapes and dried apricots.
4. Distribute combined nuts all over the platter.
5. Serve the cheeses with fig jam on the side and drizzle honey over them.

Nutrition (per serving):
Cals: 250, Protein: 12g, Carbs: 15g, Fat: 16g, Fiber: 2g

16. Springtime Garden Spread:

Time: 40 mins
Servings: 4-6

Ingredients:

- Hummus (store-bought or homemade)
- Baby carrots
- Cucumber slices
- Cherry tomatoes
- Radishes, thinly split
- Sugar snap peas
- Bell pepper strips (assorted colors)
- Pita bread or pita chips

Instructions:

1. On a big dish, distribute the hummus in a circular manner.
2. Around the hummus, place the sugar snap peas, cherry tomatoes, radishes, cucumber slices, and baby carrots in separate pieces.
3. Place the bell pepper strips on a different plate area.
4. Pita chips or pita bread Must be served alongside.

Nutrition (per serving):
Cals: 180, Protein: 6g, Carbs: 30g, Fat: 4g, Fiber: 8g

17. Valentine's Day Romance:

Time: 1 hr
Servings: 2

Ingredients:

- Grilled steak, split
- Roasted asparagus
- Mashed potatoes
- Cherry tomatoes, halved
- Cooked shrimp
- Combined salad greens
- Balsamic vinaigrette dressing

Instructions:

1. Place the grilled steak slices on one side of a dish in the form of a heart.
2. On the opposite side, add a serving of mashed potatoes and the roasted asparagus.
3. Put cooked shrimp and cherry tomatoes in the middle.
4. Combined salad greens tossed in balsamic vinaigrette Must take up the remaining space on the platter.

Nutrition (per serving):
Cals: 450, Protein: 28g, Carbs: 30g, Fat: 24g, Fiber: 6g

18. Easter Brunch Board:

Time: 45 mins
Servings: 8-10

Ingredients:

- Hard-boiled eggs, halved
- Smoked salmon
- Cream cheese
- Split red onion
- Capers
- Assorted bagels
- Fresh dill sprigs
- Combined berries (strawberries, blueberries)

Instructions:
1. A Big platter Must have the hard-boiled eggs halved around the sides.
2. In the middle of the platter, place the smoked salmon.
3. Along with the smoked salmon, place cream cheese in a bowl.
4. Spread capers and thinly split red onion over the fish.
5. Around the salmon and eggs, arrange several bagels and fresh dill sprigs.
6. Place some combined berries in a little bowl on the platter.

Nutrition (per serving):
Cals: 280, Protein: 14g, Carbs: 30g, Fat: 12g, Fiber: 4g

19. Mother's Day Surprise:

Time: 1 hr
Servings: 4-6

Ingredients:
- Spinach and feta stuffed chicken breasts
- Roasted sweet potatoes
- Quinoa salad (quinoa, cucumber, cherry tomatoes, feta cheese)
- Steamed green beans
- Lemon wedges

Instructions:
1. Place the stuffed chicken breasts with spinach and feta on a sizable dish.
2. Set the quinoa salad and roasted sweet potatoes around the chicken.
3. Green beans Must be included as a side dish.
4. For more freshness, serve with wedges of lemon.

Nutrition (per serving):
Cals: 380, Protein: 28g, Carbs: 35g, Fat: 14g, Fiber: 6g

20. Father's Day BBQ:

Time: 2 hrs
Servings: 8-10

Ingredients:
- Grilled burgers (beef or veggie)
- Hot dogs
- BBQ chicken wings
- Corn on the cob
- Coleslaw
- Baked beans
- Potato salad
- BBQ sauce

Instructions:
1. Place the hot dogs and hamburgers that have been grilled on one side of a Big dish.
2. the chicken wings from the barbecue on the opposite side.
3. Place potato salad, coleslaw, baked beans, and corn on the cob in separate areas of the platter.
4. BBQ sauce Must be served on the side.

Nutrition (per serving):
Cals: 480, Protein: 22g, Carbs: 40g, Fat: 26g, Fiber: 8g

21. Hleteen Spooktacular:

Time: 1.5 hrs
Servings: 6-8

Ingredients:
- Jack-o'-lantern stuffed bell peppers (rice, ground meat or tofu, spices)
- Witch's finger breadsticks (store-bought or homemade)
- Deviled eggs (with olive spiders for decoration)
- Crudité platter (carrots, celery, bell peppers, cherry tomatoes) with "bloody" beetroot dip
- Hleteen-themed sugar cookies

Instructions:
1. On one side of a big dish, arrange the bell peppers with the Jack-o'-lantern stuffing.
2. The other side Must have the witch's finger breadsticks.
3. Deviled eggs with olive spiders in the middle Must be added.
4. For the crudité plate, arrange a section with a variety of fresh veggies.
5. Serve alongside a "bloody" beetroot dip.
6. For dessert, include a dish of sugar cookies with a Hleteen theme.

Nutrition (per serving):
Cals: 320, Protein: 14g, Carbs: 40g, Fat: 12g, Fiber: 6g

22. Thanksgiving Bounty:

Time: 3 hrs
Servings: 10-12

Ingredients:
- Roast turkey (or vegetarian alternative)
- Stuffing (traditional or vegetarian)
- Mashed potatoes

- Turkey gravy
- Cranberry sauce
- Roasted Brussels sprouts
- Sweet potato casserole
- Dinner rolls with butter

Instructions:
1. A huge dish Must have the roast turkey in the middle of it.
2. Put mashed potatoes and stuffing all around it.
3. Separate bowls Must be used for the cranberry sauce and turkey gravy.
4. To the plate, add roasted Brussels sprouts and sweet potato casserole.
5. Dinner rolls Must be served alongside butter.

Nutrition (per serving):
Cals: 550, Protein: 30g, Carbs: 45g, Fat: 28g, Fiber: 6g

23. Christmas Eve Extravaganza:

Time: 2.5 hrs
Servings: 8-10

Ingredients:
- Glazed ham
- Garlic roasted potatoes
- Roasted winter vegetables (carrots, parsnips, beets)
- Shrimp cocktail
- Smoked salmon platter with dill and lemon
- Cheese platter (assorted cheeses, grapes, figs)
- Yule log cake (Bûche de Noël)

Instructions:
1. A huge dish Must have the glazed ham in the middle of it.
2. Roasted winter veggies and potatoes with garlic Must be placed all around it.
3. Serve platters of smoked salmon and shrimp cocktail separately.
4. Put figs, grapes, and various cheeses on a separate dish.
5. As the centerpiece of dessert, serve the Yule log cake.

Nutrition (per serving):
Cals: 450, Protein: 26g, Carbs: 35g, Fat: 22g, Fiber: 6g

24. New Year's Eve Bash:

Time: 2 hrs
Servings: 12-15

Ingredients:
- Assorted sushi rolls (salmon, tuna, avocado, cucumber)
- Shrimp tempura
- Edamame
- Vegetable spring rolls with dipping sauce
- Chicken skewers with teriyaki glaze
- Cheese and fruit platter
- Chocolate fondue with marshmlets and strawberries

Instructions:
1. A huge platter Must have the various sushi rolls arranged on one side.
2. Emame and tempura shrimp Must be placed on the opposite side.
3. Place a center of vegetable spring rolls and dipping sauce.
4. Place the teriyaki-glazed chicken skewers on a different plate.
5. Serve various cheeses and seasonal fruits on a cheese and fruit tray.
6. Set up a strawberry and marshmlet dipping station with a chocolate fondue.

Nutrition (per serving):
Cals: 380, Protein: 18g, Carbs: 40g, Fat: 16g, Fiber: 6g

25. Birthday Celebration Platter:

Time: 30 mins
Servings: 8-10

Ingredients:
- Assorted mini cup ofcakes
- Split fresh fruits (strawberries, blueberries, kiwi, etc.)
- Colorful candy (gummy bears, jellybeans, etc.)
- Chocolate truffles
- Popcorn
- Pretzel sticks
- Assorted dips (chocolate sauce, caramel sauce)

Instructions:
1. Use a wooden board with bowls or arrange a sizable plate with divisions.
2. Put the little cup ofcakes in the platter's middle.
3. Sprinkle colorful candy and split fresh fruit all around the cup ofcakes.
4. Place a mini bowl on the platter and fill it with chocolate truffles.

5. Place it on the tray along with another mini bowl that has been filled with various dips.
6. Popcorn and pretzel sticks Must be placed in the remaining sections.
7. Enjoy the birthday party while serving!

Nutrition (per serving, approximate):
Cals: 250, Carbs: 40g, Protein: 4g, Fat: 8g, Fiber: 2g

26. Graduation Party Board:

Time: 45 mins
Servings: 12-15

Ingredients:
- Split baguette
- Assorted cheeses (cheddar, brie, gouda, etc.)
- Split salami and pepperoni
- Cherry tomatoes
- Assorted olives
- Split cucumber and bell peppers
- Hummus and pesto dip

Instructions:
1. Set up a big plate or board.
2. In the middle of the board, place the baguette slices.
3. Around the bread, arrange the various cheeses.
4. Between the cheeses, layer the salami and pepperoni slices.
5. Put cherry tomatoes in one portion of the board and various olives in another.
6. Bell peppers and cucumber slices Must be placed in the empty places.
7. Place mini bowls of pesto and hummus on the board.
8. Enjoy the graduation party while serving!

Nutrition (per serving, approximate):
Cals: 180, Carbs: 10g, Protein: 8g, Fat: 12g, Fiber: 2g

27. Anniversary Love Board:

Time: 30 mins
Servings: 2-4

Ingredients:
- Grilled shrimp skewers
- Lemon wedges
- Fresh dill and parsley
- Smoked salmon
- Split cucumbers
- Pickled onions
- Cream cheese
- Crackers or baguette slices

Instructions:
1. Set up a petite, charming board or dish.
2. Center the board with the cooked shrimp skewers.
3. For decoration, surround the shrimp with fresh dill and parsley.
4. Place lemon wedges and slices of smoked salmon on the board.
5. Split cucumbers and pickled onions can be added as a side dish.
6. Using a spreading knife, put a bowl of cream cheese on the board.
7. Around the board, scatter crackers or slices of bread.
8. Enjoy the anniversary celebration while serving!

Nutrition (per serving, approximate):
Cals: 250, Carbs: 10g, Protein: 18g, Fat: 15g, Fiber: 1g

28. Bridal Shower Elegance:

Time: 1 hr
Servings: 6-8

Ingredients:
- Combined greens salad
- Grilled chicken strips
- Cherry tomatoes
- Split avocado
- Split almonds
- Feta cheese cut ups
- Balsamic vinaigrette dressing
- Assorted crackers or breadsticks

Instructions:
1. Set up a sizable plate or board.
2. In the middle, place a bed of combined greens salad.
3. Top the salad with cooked chicken strips.
4. Around the chicken, strew cherry tomatoes and split avocado.
5. Overtop the salad with feta cheese cut ups and almond slices.
6. Balsamic vinaigrette dressing Must be served on the side.
7. Wrap the board in a variety of crackers or breadsticks.
8. Serve up some elegance at the bridal shower!

Nutrition (per serving, approximate):
Cals: 320, Carbs: 12g, Protein: 22g, Fat: 20g, Fiber: 4g

29. Baby Shower Delights:

Time: 1 hr

Servings: 8-10

Ingredients:

- Baby-shaped sugar cookies
- Baby-themed cake pops
- Mini fruit tarts
- Baby carrots and cucumber sticks
- Baby spinach dip
- Mini sandwiches (assorted fillings)

Instructions:

1. Set up a sizable plate or board.
2. Center the board with the baby-shaped sugar cookies.
3. Baby-themed cake pops and mini fruit tarts Must be placed all around the cookies.
4. Place cucumber sticks and tiny carrots on different regions of the board.
5. Baby spinach dip Must be poured into a mini bowl and set on the board.
6. For variation, scatter tiny sandwiches throughout the board.
7. Serve the baby shower treats and savor them!

Nutrition (per serving, approximate):
Cals: 280, Carbs: 30g, Protein: 5g, Fat: 15g, Fiber: 2g

30. Girls' Night In Fun:

Time: 45 mins

Servings: 4-6

Ingredients:

- Mini sliders (beef, chicken, or veggie)
- Sweet potato fries
- Mozzarella sticks
- Guacamole
- Salsa
- Tortilla chips
- Vegetable sticks (carrots, celery, bell peppers)

Instructions:

1. Set up a sizable plate or board.
2. The center of the board Must have the little sliders.
3. Add mozzarella sticks and sweet potato fries all around the sliders.
4. Place the guacamole and salsa in mini bowls on the board.
5. Around the bowls, scatter tortilla chips for dipping.
6. For a healthier option, arrange vegetable sticks on one side of the board.
7. Serve up some fun for the girls' night out!

Nutrition (per serving, approximate):
Cals: 350, Carbs: 30g, Protein: 15g, Fat: 20g, Fiber: 4g

31. Guys' Night Charsliceerie:

Time: 1 hr

Servings: 6-8

Ingredients:

- Assorted cured meats (salami, prosciutto, etc.)
- Cheese wedges (cheddar, pepper jack, etc.)
- Beer bread or artisan crackers
- Spicy mustard
- Dried fruits (apricots, figs, etc.)
- Combined nuts
- Pickles and olives

Instructions:

1. Set up a sizable plate or board.
2. The middle of the board Must be filled with various cured meats.
3. Cheese slices Must be placed around the meats.
4. You could also serve handmade crackers or beer bread.
5. On the board, place a mini bowl of spicy mustard.
6. On the board, strew assorted nuts and dried fruits.
7. Place pickles and olives on the board in different places.
8. The charsliceerie for the boys' night is ready; enjoy!

Nutrition (per serving, approximate):
Cals: 320, Carbs: 15g, Protein: 20g, Fat: 20g, Fiber: 2g

32. Kids' Party Adventure:

Time: 1 hr

Servings: 8-10

Ingredients:

- Mini pizza bites
- Chicken nuggets
- Mini corn dogs
- Veggie sticks (carrots, cucumber, bell peppers)
- Ranch dressing
- Ketchup
- Fruit skewers (grapes, strawberries, pineapple)

Instructions:
1. Set up a sizable plate or board.
2. Mini pizza bites Must be placed in the middle of the board.
3. Place mini corn dogs and chicken nuggets all around the pizza bites.
4. Place vegetable sticks in a different area of the board.
5. Place tiny bowls of ketchup and ranch dressing on the board.
6. Using grapes, strawberries, and pineapple, make fruit skewers and place them on the board.
7. Enjoy the children's party adventure while serving!

Nutrition (per serving, approximate):
Cals: 250, Carbs: 20g, Protein: 10g, Fat: 15g, Fiber: 2g

33. Movie Night Snack Board:

Time: 30 mins

Servings: 4-6

Ingredients:
- Popcorn (buttered and seasoned)
- Mini pretzels
- M&Ms or chocolate candies
- Cheese popcorn
- Caramel popcorn
- Combined nuts
- Soda or soft drinks

Instructions:
1. Set up a sizable plate or board.
2. Put the popcorn in the center of the board, seasoned and buttered.
3. Add chocolate candies or M&Ms and mini pretzels all over the popcorn.
4. Include distinct areas for caramel popcorn and cheese popcorn.
5. For more crunch, scatter combined nuts all over the board.
6. On the board, serve soda or other soft drinks in glasses.
7. The snack board for movie night is ready; enjoy!

Nutrition (per serving, approximate):
Cals: 280, Carbs: 35g, Protein: 5g, Fat: 15g, Fiber: 2g

34. Book Club Gathering:

Time: 45 mins

Servings: 6-8

Ingredients:
- Assorted finger sandwiches (cucumber, egg salad, etc.)
- Cheese and herb scones
- Fresh fruit platter
- Vegetable crudités (celery, carrot, bell peppers)
- Hummus and tzatziki dips
- Iced tea or lemonade

Instructions:
1. Set up a sizable plate or board.
2. Center a board with a variety of finger sandwiches.
3. On one side of the board, place some cheese and herb scones.
4. On a different side, set out a platter of fresh fruit.
5. Place vegetable crudités in mini bowls and arrange them on the board.
6. Dish out the tzatziki and hummus dips separately on the board.
7. Iced tea or lemonade Must be served in glasses on the board.
8. Enjoy the book club meeting while serving!

Nutrition (per serving, approximate):
Cals: 220, Carbs: 30g, Protein: 10g, Fat: 8g, Fiber: 4g

35. Wine Tasting Pairings

Time: 20 mins

Servings: 4

Ingredients:
- Assorted cheeses (such as Brie, Gouda, and Camembert)
- Assorted cured meats (such as prosciutto and salami)
- Grapes and split apples
- Assorted crackers and bread
- Nuts (almonds, walnuts)
- Honey or fig jam (for drizzling)

Instructions:
1. On a serving tray or board, arrange the cheeses, cured meats, grapes, slice apples, crackers, and bread.
2. Over the meat and cheese, strew the nuts.
3. For more sweetness, drizzle honey or fig jam over the cheeses.
4. Serve right away and savor with your preferred wines!

36. Craft Beer Tasting Board

Time: 15 mins
Servings: 4

Ingredients:

- Assorted craft beers (choose a variety of styles)
- Pretzels or pretzel bites
- Combined nuts
- Split sausages or bratwurst
- Cheese slices (cheddar, pepper jack)
- Mustard or beer cheese dip (store-bought or homemade)

Instructions:

1. Put the craft beers in a serving tray or on a board for beer flights.
2. Around the beers, arrange the pretzels, combined nuts, slice sausages, and cheese slices.
3. Serve with a beer cheese or mustard dip for dipping.
4. Invite visitors to sample and enjoy the various beers with the appetizers.

37. Whisky and Cigars Pairing

Time: 10 mins
Servings: 2

Ingredients:

- High-quality whisky or bourbon
- Assorted cigars (choose different strengths and flavors)

Instructions:

1. Two whisky glasses Must be filled with the whisky or bourbon.
2. For the paring, pick a range of cigars.
3. Cigars Must be lit, then the smoke Must grow.
4. Let the tastes to blend together as you sip the whisky and puff on the cigar.
5. Discuss and enjoy the distinct flavors of whisky and cigars.

38. Tropical Island Escape

Time: 25 mins
Servings: 2

Ingredients:

- 2 boneless, skinless chicken breasts, grilled and split
- 1 cup of cooked white rice
- Grilled pineapple slices
- Mango salsa (diced mango, red onion, cilantro, lime juice)
- Coconut shrimp
- Fresh green salad with passion fruit dressing

Instructions:

1. The chicken Must be prepared and slice into strips.
2. The white rice Must be prepared as directed on the box/pkg.
3. Diced mango, red onion, cilantro, and lime juice are combined in a bowl to make the mango salsa.
4. On a sizable serving tray, arrange the grilled pineapple pieces, coconut shrimp, green salad, chicken strips, and rice.
5. Enjoy the tropical delights by serving the Tropical Island Escape plate!

39. Coastal Sea Breeze Platter

Time: 20 mins
Servings: 4

Ingredients:

- Fresh oysters on the half shell
- Grilled shrimp skewers
- Crab cakes
- Seared scallops
- Lemon wedges
- Cocktail sauce and tartar sauce

Instructions:

1. Place the seared scallops, crab cakes, grilled shrimp skewers, and fresh oysters on a sizable tray.
2. On the platter, arrange lemon wedges for squeezing over the fish.
3. Cocktail sauce and tartar sauce Must be served on the side for dipping.
4. Enjoy the sea breeze's seaside flavors!

40. Hawaiian Luau Feast

Time: 30 mins
Servings: 6

Ingredients:

- Kalua pork (store-bought or homemade)
- Grilled teriyaki chicken
- Coconut shrimp
- Pineapple fried rice

- Hawaiian macaroni salad
- Fresh tropical fruit platter (mangoes, papayas, watermelon)

Instructions:
1. Kalua pork and grilled teriyaki chicken Must be prepared in advance.
2. The coconut shrimp Must be prepared as directed on the packaging.
3. Prepare the Hawaiian macaroni salad and pineapple fried rice.
4. Put the pineapple fried rice, macaroni salad, coconut shrimp, teriyaki chicken, pineapple, and Kalua pork on a sizable luau-themed tray.
5. Serve alongside a platter of seasonal fresh fruit.
6. Enjoy a Hawaiian Luau Feast's delights!

41. Southern Comfort Board

Time: 25 mins
Servings: 4

Ingredients:
- Buttermilk fried chicken tenders
- Biscuits with honey butter
- Macaroni and cheese
- Collard greens
- Cornbread muffins
- Sweet tea or lemonade

Instructions:
1. Prepare the collard greens, buttermilk fried chicken tenders, honey butter biscuits, macaroni and cheese, and cornbread muffins.
2. Place the dishes on a sizable platter or serving board.
3. For a cool Southern Comfort experience, serve with sweet tea or lemonade.
4. Take pleasure in the warm and soulful flavors of the South!

42. Tex-Mex Fiesta Fun

Time: 25 mins
Servings: 4

Ingredients:
- Beef or chicken fajitas with peppers and onions
- Cheese quesadillas
- Guacamole, salsa, and sour cream
- Mexican rice
- Refried beans
- Tortilla chips

Instructions:
1. Peppers, onions, and meat or chicken are used to prepare fajitas.
2. Shredded cheese is folded inside tortillas to create cheese quesadillas, which are then grilled up to dilute.
3. Prepare salsa, sour cream, and guacamole for dipping.
4. Warm up the refried beans while the Mexican rice is cooking.
5. On a sizable Tex-Mex-inspired platter, arrange the fajitas, quesadillas, guacamole, salsa, sour cream, Mexican rice, and refried beans.
6. Scoop and dip with tortilla chips on the side.
7. Enjoy the Tex-Mex cuisine's colorful and zesty flavors!

43. Indian Spice Extravaganza

Time: 40 mins
Servings: 6

Ingredients:
- Chicken Tikka Masala
- Vegetable Samosas
- Butter Naan bread
- Basmati rice
- Raita (yogurt cucumber sauce)
- Mango chutney

Instructions:
1. Prepare the vegetable samosas and chicken tikka masala.
2. Cook the Basmati rice while rewarming the Butter Naan bread.
3. Combine yogurt and lightly diced cucumber to make raita.
4. On a sizable dish with an Indian theme, arrange the Chicken Tikka Masala, Vegetable Samosas, Butter Naan bread, Basmati rice, Raita, and Mango Chutney.
5. An Indian Spice Extravaganza's fragrant and fiery sensations can be served and enjoyed!

44. Thai Street Food Adventure

Time: 30 mins
Servings: 4

Ingredients:
- Pad Thai (chicken or shrimp)

- Thai spring rolls
- Green papaya salad
- Thai fish cakes
- Sticky rice with mango

Instructions:
1. Use chicken or shrimp to make the Pad Thai.
2. Thai fish cakes and spring rolls Must be prepared as directed on the packaging.
3. Green papaya Must be shredded and combined with lime juice, fish sauce, sugar, and chile to make the green papaya salad.
4. Serve the cooked sticky rice with mango slices.
5. On a sizable platter with a Thai theme, arrange the Pad Thai, Thai spring rolls, Green Papaya Salad, Thai fish cakes, and Sticky rice with mango.
6. Enjoy this adventure in Thai street food, which is variety and wonderful!

Nutrition (per serving):
Cals: 400, Carbs: 65g, Protein: 20g, Fat: 8g

45. Chinese Dim Sum Delights:

Time: 1 hr
Servings: 6

Ingredients:
- Wonton wrappers
- Ground pork or shrimp
- Scallions, ginger, garlic
- Soy sauce, sesame oil

Instructions:
1. Chop the scallions and combine them with the soy sauce, sesame oil, ginger, and garlic in a bowl with the ground pork or shrimp.
2. Stack a wonton wrapper with a scoop of the contents inside.
3. To seal the filling, wet the wrapper's edges and fold.
4. The dumplings Must be cooked for ten mins in the steamer.
5. Serve with your preferred dipping sauce or soy sauce.

Nutrition (per serving):
Cals: 250, Carbs: 30g, Protein: 15g, Fat: 8g

46. Korean BBQ Party:

Time: 1.5 hrs
Servings: 5

Ingredients:
- Thinly split beef (e.g., ribeye or bulgogi)
- Marinade: soy sauce, garlic, sesame oil, sugar, pear juice
- Assorted Korean side dishes (banchan)

Instructions:
1. For at least one hr, marinate the beef in a Mixture of soy sauce, garlic, sesame oil, sugar, and pear juice.
2. Grill the steak to your preferred doneness.
3. Serve alongside a variety of banchan and steaming rice.

Nutrition (per serving):
Cals: 350, Carbs: 20g, Protein: 25g, Fat: 18g

47. Vietnamese Street Eats:

Time: 1 hr
Servings: 4

Ingredients:
- Rice noodles
- Grilled pork or shrimp
- Bean sprouts, lettuce, mint, cilantro
- Crushed peanuts, fried shallots
- Fish sauce dressing

Instructions:
1. Rice noodles Must be prepared as directed on the packaging.
2. Put the cooked noodles, shrimp or pork that has been barbecued, and vegetables on a platter.
3. Add fried shallots and crushed peanuts as garnish.
4. Before serving, drizzle with fish sauce dressing. Calorie intake (per serving): 300 cals, 40g of carbs, 15g of protein, and 8g of fat.
5. Moroccan flavor Journey: Two hrs. Ingredients: 6 servings
6. Moroccan spice Mixture (including cumin, coriander, paprika, cinnamon, etc.) for chicken or lamb
7. Rice or couscous
8. Almonds and dried fruit (such as apricots and raisins) Instructions:
9. The meat Must be marinated for at least an hr after being rubbed with a Moroccan spice Mixture.
10. Cook the meat completely on the grill or in the oven.

11. Rice or couscous Must be prepared as directed on the box/pkg.
12. Over couscous or rice, plate the seasoned meat and garnish with almonds and dried fruits.

Nutrition (per serving):
Cals: 400, Carbs: 30g, Protein: 30g, Fat: 15g

48. Greek Mythical Feast:

Time: 2.5 hrs
Servings: 8

Ingredients:
- Lamb chops or souvlaki (skewers)
- Greek salad (cucumbers, tomatoes, olives, feta cheese)
- Tzatziki sauce
- Pita bread

Instructions:
1. Grill the lamb chops or skewers according to your choice after seasoning them.
2. Combine cucumbers, tomatoes, olives, and feta cheese to make the Greek salad.
3. With warm pita bread, Greek salad, and tzatziki sauce, serve the grilled lamb.
4. Turkish kebabs, made with spiced ground meat
5. Flatbread
6. grilled vegetables (tomatoes, bell peppers, and eggplant)
7. Greek yogurt Instructions:
8. Kebabs made of ground beef Must be formed, then grilled till done.
9. Vegetables Must be grilled up to soft and slightly browned.
10. Along with flatbread and Turkish yogurt, serve the kebabs and grilled vegetables.

Nutrition (per serving):
Cals: 380, Carbs: 30g, Protein: 25g, Fat: 18g

49. Israeli Hummus and Pita:

Time: 1 hr
Servings: 4

Ingredients:
- Chickpeas
- Tahini (sesame paste)
- Lemon juice, garlic, cumin
- Olive oil, paprika
- Pita bread

Instructions:
1. To prepare hummus, combine the chickpeas, tahini, lemon juice, garlic, and cumin.
2. Before serving, drizzle some olive oil and add some paprika to the hummus.
3. Pita bread Must be served warm.

Nutrition (per serving):
Cals: 280, Carbs: 35g, Protein: 10g, Fat: 12g

50. Lebanese Mezze Medley:

Time: 1.5 hrs
Servings: 6

Ingredients:
- Falafel (chickpea fritters)
- Tabbouleh (parsley salad with bulgur)
- Baba ganoush (roasted eggplant dip)
- Lebanese bread

Instructions:
1. The falafel Must be deep-fried or baked up to brown and crispy.
2. Combine parsley, bulgur, tomatoes, mint, and lemon juice to make tabbouleh.
3. Blend roasted eggplant, tahini, lemon juice, and garlic to create baba ganoush.
4. Serve Lebanese bread alongside the falafel, tabbouleh, and baba ganoush.

Nutrition (per serving):
Cals: 320, Carbs: 35g, Protein: 15g, Fat: 15g

51. Egyptian Pharaoh's Platter:

Time: 2.5 hrs
Servings: 8

Ingredients:
1. Egyptian rice, lentil, and pasta dish known as koshari
2. Hawawshi (pita packed with spicy pork)
3. (Combined greens, tomatoes, cucumbers, and pita chips) Fattoush salad Instructions:
4. Rice, lentils, and pasta are cooked together to make koshari, which is then garnished with tomato sauce.
5. Fill the pita with spiced meat, then grill it up to it is cooked through and crispy.
6. Apply your preferred dressing to the fattoush salad and top with pita chips.

Nutrition (per serving):
Cals: 420, Carbs: 55g, Protein: 20g, Fat: 12g

52. South African Braai Board:

Time: 1 hr preparation, 20 mins cooking
Servings: 4-6

Ingredients:

- 1 kg combined meat (steak, boerewors, chicken)
- 4-6 corn cobs
- 1 Big onion, split
- 2 bell peppers, split
- 250g mushrooms, whole
- 4-6 pieces of garlic bread
- Olive oil
- Salt and pepper as needed

Instructions:

1. The braai (South African grill) Must be heated to medium-high.
2. Rub salt, pepper, and olive oil on the meats.
3. The meats Must be braaied up to they are cooked to your preference.
4. Corn cobs Must be grilled up to browned and soft.
5. Olive oil is used to cook the thinly split bell peppers and onions up to they are tender.
6. On the barbecue, grill the mushrooms up to they are done.
7. On the grill, toast the garlic bread.
8. Place everything that has been grilled on a big board before serving.

Nutrition (per serving):
Cals: 500, Protein: 40g, Carbs: 25g, Fat: 28g

53. Australian BBQ Bonanza:

Time: 1.5 hrs preparation, 30 mins cooking
Servings: 6-8

Ingredients:

- 1.5 kg beef ribs
- 1 kg prawns, peel off and deveined
- 1 kg lamb chops
- 1 kg chicken wings
- 2 Big sweet potatoes, split
- 2 zucchinis, split lengthwise
- BBQ sauce
- Olive oil
- Salt and pepper as needed

Instructions:

1. Set the temperature of the grill to medium-high.
2. Olive oil, salt, and pepper Must be brushed on the meats and veggies.
3. Cook the lamb chops, chicken wings, and beef ribs on the grill up to done.
4. Prawns Must be grilled up to opaque and rosy.
5. Grill the zucchini and sweet potatoes up to they are soft and have grill marks.
6. During the last few mins of grilling, baste the meats with barbecue sauce.
7. Place everything that has been grilled on a big dish and serve.

Nutrition (per serving):
Cals: 700, Protein: 50g, Carbs: 30g, Fat: 40g

54. Brazilian Churrasco Experience:

Time: 2 hrs preparation, 40 mins cooking
Servings: 6-8

Ingredients:

- 1.5 kg beef picanha (top sirloin cap)
- 1 kg chicken hearts
- 1 kg linguiça (Brazilian sausage)
- 1 kg pork ribs
- 1 Big pineapple, split
- Chimichurri sauce
- Farofa (toasted cassava flour Mixture)
- Salt and pepper as needed

Instructions:

1. Heat the churrasco grill to a moderately hot setting.
2. Salt and pepper the picanha and the pork ribs.
3. Alternate between placing every meat on a separate long metal skewer.
4. The skewered meats Must be cooked to your preference on the churrasco grill.
5. On different skewers, grill the linguiça and chicken hearts up to done.
6. Slices of pineapple Must be grilled up to caramelized.
7. Make the farofa and the chimichurri sauce according to the instructions on the packaging.
8. With chimichurri sauce, farofa, and any additional sides, serve the churrasco skewers.

Nutrition (per serving):
Cals: 650, Protein: 45g, Carbs: 15g, Fat: 45g

55. Argentinean Asado Grill:

Time: 2.5 hrs preparation, 1 hr cooking
Servings: 6-8

Ingredients:

- 2 kg beef short ribs
- 1 kg beef sweetbreads
- 1 kg blood sausage (morcilla)
- 1 kg provoleta cheese
- 2 Big red onions, slice into rings
- 2 bell peppers, slice into strips
- 1 bunch of chimichurri sauce
- Olive oil
- Salt and pepper as needed

Instructions:

1. Set the grill's temperature to medium-high.
2. Olive oil, salt, and pepper are used to season the short ribs and sweetbreads.
3. Short ribs and sweetbreads Must be cooked thoroughly and browned on the grill.
4. Cook the blood sausage over a grill up to it is thoroughly cooked and browned.
5. Provoleta cheese Must be grilled up to dilute and bubbling.
6. Olive oil is used to sauté the bell pepper strips and onion rings up to they are tender.
7. As directed in the recipe, make the chimichurri sauce.
8. Place everything that has been grilled on a big dish and top with chimichurri sauce to serve.

Nutrition (per serving):
Cals: 750,Protein: 55g,Carbs: 10g,Fat: 55g

56.Chilean BBQ Extravaganza:

Time: 2 hrs preparation, 40 mins cooking
Servings: 6-8

Ingredients:

- 1.5 kg beef tenderloin, split into steaks
- 1 kg boneless pork Muster, cubed
- 1 kg chicken thighs, boneless and skinless
- 1 kg Big shrimp, peel off and deveined
- 1 kg chorizo sausages
- 4 Big bell peppers, slice into chunks
- 4 ripe tomatoes, slice into wedges
- 1 bunch of green onions
- Olive oil
- Paprika, cumin, salt, and pepper as needed

Instructions:

1. Set the grill's temperature to medium-high.
2. The beef tenderloin steaks are seasoned with salt, pepper, paprika, cumin, and olive oil.
3. Cubes of pork Muster are seasoned with salt, pepper, paprika, cumin, and olive oil.
4. Salt, pepper, paprika, cumin, and olive oil are used to season the chicken thighs.
5. Salt, pepper, paprika, and olive oil are used to season the shrimp.
6. Cook the shrimp, chorizo sausages, chicken thighs, pork Muster, beef tenderloin, and pork on the grill up to done.
7. Grill the tomatoes, bell peppers, and green onions up to they are tender and just browned.
8. Place everything that has been grilled on a big dish and serve.

Nutrition (per serving):
Cals: 600,Protein: 45g,Carbs: 20g,Fat: 35g

57.Peruvian Ceviche Fiesta:

Time: 30 mins preparation, 0 mins cooking (since it's a cold dish)
Servings: 4-6

Ingredients:

- 800g fresh white fish fillets (sea bass or flounder), diced
- 1 cup of fresh lime juice
- 1 red onion, thinly split
- 1-2 hot chili peppers (aji amarillo or habanero), lightly chop-up
- 1 cup of cherry tomatoes, halved
- 1 bunch of cilantro, chop-up
- 2-3 cloves of garlic, chop-up
- 1 sweet potato, boiled and split
- 1 cup of cooked corn kernels
- Salt and pepper as needed

Instructions:

1. Make sure the fish is completely covered by the lime juice before adding it to a sizable glass bowl with the diced fish. Up to the fish turns opaque, marinate it in the refrigerator for 20 to 30 mins.
2. Add the split red onion, hot chili peppers, cherry tomatoes, cilantro, and chop-up garlic after draining the excess lime juice from the fish. Combine thoroughly.
3. As needed, add salt and pepper to the food.
4. With boiled sweet potatoes and prepared corn kernels, serve chilled ceviche.

Nutrition (per serving):
Cals: 300

Protein: 30g, Carbs: 40g, Fat: 3g,

58. Colombian Street Food:

Time: 1 hr preparation, 30 mins cooking

Servings: 4-6

Ingredients:

- 500g yuca (cassava), peel off and slice into fries
- 500g green plantains, peel off and slice into slices
- 500g chorizo sausages, split
- 500g carne asada (thinly split grilled beef)
- 1 cup of hogao sauce (tomato and onion sauce)
- 1 cup of guacamole
- 1 cup of aji salsa (spicy Colombian salsa)
- Vegetable oil for frying
- Salt as needed

Instructions:

1. For frying, warm up the vegetable oil in a sizable saucepan over a medium-high heat.
2. Fry the green plantains and yuca in batches up to crispy and golden. Use a slotted spoon to take out and drain on paper towels. Sprinkle salt on top.
3. The chorizo sausages and carne asada Must be grilled up to fully cooked and slightly browned.
4. As directed by the recipes, make the aji salsa, hogao sauce, and guacamole.
5. Serve the grilled chorizo, carne asada, hogao sauce, guacamole, and aji salsa alongside the fried yuca and green plantains.

Nutrition (per serving):
Cals: 700, Protein: 30g, Carbs: 70g, Fat: 35g

59. Canadian Maple Syrup Indulgence:

Time: 1 hr preparation, 20 mins cooking

Servings: 4-6

Ingredients:

- 1 kg bone-in pork chops
- 1 kg sweet potatoes, peel off and slice into chunks
- 1 bunch of asparagus
- 1 cup of pure Canadian maple syrup
- 1/4 cup of balsamic vinegar
- 2 tbsp Dijon mustard
- Salt and pepper as needed

Instructions:

1. Set the grill's temperature to medium-high.
2. Add salt and pepper to the pork chops before serving.
3. Using a Mixture of maple syrup, balsamic vinegar, and dijon mustard as a basting sauce, grill the pork chops up to they are cooked through and have grill marks.
4. The sweet potatoes Must be grilled up to they are soft and caramelized.
5. Asparagus Must be lightly browned while grilling.
6. Place the sweet potatoes, asparagus, and grilled pork chops on a serving plate. Drizzle with more maple syrup, if preferred.

Nutrition (per serving):
Cals: 600, Protein: 40g, Carbs: 60g, Fat: 20g

60. Mexican Street Corn Fiesta:

Time: 30 mins preparation, 15 mins cooking

Servings: 4-6

Ingredients:

- 6 Big ears of corn, husked
- 1/2 cup of mayonnaise
- 1 cup of cut up cotija cheese
- 1 tsp chili powder
- 1 lime, slice into wedges
- Fresh cilantro, chop-up (for garnish)
- Salt and pepper as needed

Instructions:

1. Set the grill's temperature to medium-high.
2. Turning the corn as it cooks through and gets a little sear on the grill.
3. Mayonnaise Must be brushed on every ear of corn before being coated with cut up cotija cheese.
4. Add salt and pepper as needed, then sprinkle the chili powder over the corn.
5. Fresh cilantro is added as a garnish and served with the corn.

Nutrition (per serving):
Cals: 300, Protein: 8g, Carbs: 35g, Fat: 15g

61. Italian Pizza and Pasta Board:

Time: 2 hrs preparation, 20 mins cooking

Servings: 4-6

Ingredients:

- 500g pizza dough (store-bought or homemade)

- 1 cup of pizza sauce
- 2 cups of shredded mozzarella cheese
- Assorted pizza toppings (pepperoni, bell peppers, mushrooms, olives, etc.)
- 500g cooked pasta (spaghetti, penne, etc.)
- 2 cups of marinara sauce
- Fresh basil leaves (for garnish)
- Finely grated Parmesan cheese (for garnish)
- Olive oil

Instructions:
1. Pre-heat the oven to its maximum setting (about 475°F/ 245°C).
2. Roll out every of the minier balls of pizza dough into a thin crust.
3. Pizza sauce, shredded mozzarella, and other toppings Must be sprinkled on top of the pizza crusts.
4. Pizzas Must be baked in a preheated oven up to the cheese is dilute and bubbling and the crust is crisp.
5. The cooked spaghetti Must be added to a Big skillet of simmering marinara sauce. Warm the pasta through by tossing it to evenly distribute the sauce.
6. Place the pizzas and pasta on a sizable dish or board.
7. Fresh basil leaves and finely grated Parmesan cheese go on the pizza and pasta, respectively.
8. To give the pizza and pasta more flavor, drizzle them with olive oil.

Nutrition (per serving):
Cals: 750 (pizza), 400 (pasta), Protein: 25g (pizza), 10g (pasta),Carbs: 40g (pizza), 60g (pasta), Fat: 30g (pizza), 5g (pasta)

62.French Crepes

Time: 30 mins
Servings: 4

Ingredients:
- 1 cup of all-purpose flour
- 2 Big eggs
- 1 1/4 cups of milk
- 2 tbsp dilute butter
- 1 tbsp sugar (non-compulsory)
- Pinch of salt
- Butter or oil for frying

Instructions:
1. To make a smooth, thin batter, combine the flour, eggs, milk, dilute butter, sugar (if using), and salt in a combining bowl.
2. Add a tiny quantity of butter or oil to a non-stick pan that is already hot over medium heat.
3. A mini amount of batter Must be poured into the pan, and it Must be swirled to form a thin coating.
4. Cook the crepe for about 1-2 mins, or when the edges lift and the bottom is just starting to brown.
5. The crepe Must cook for a further 1–2 mins after being flipped.
6. With the remaining batter, repeat the procedure.
7. Serve the crepes with your preferred toppings, such as jam, whipped cream, fresh fruit, or Nutella.

Nutrition (per serving):
Cals: 180 kcal, Protein: 6g, Fat: 8g, Carbs: 21g, Fiber: 1g

63.Croissants

Time: 3 hrs (including resting and rising time)
Servings: 12

Ingredients:
- 2 cups of all-purpose flour
- 1/4 cup of granulated sugar
- 1 tsp salt
- 1 packet (2 1/4 tsp) active dry yeast
- 3/4 cup of unsalted butter, cold and slice into mini pieces
- 1/2 cup of cold milk
- 1/4 cup of cold water

Instructions:
1. Combine together the flour, sugar, salt, and yeast in a sizable combining bowl.
2. Use a pastry sliceter or your fingers to slice the cold butter into the flour Mixture up to you have coarse crumbs. Add the cold butter to the flour Mixture.
3. Once the dough comes together, combine in the cold milk and cold water.
4. The dough Must be turned out onto a lightly dusted surface and smoothed out by kneading for about 5 mins.
5. Refrigerate for an hr after forming the dough into a rectangle and covering it in plastic wrap.
6. The cold dough Must be rolled out into a broad rectangle and folded like a letter into thirds.

7. Roll out the dough once more, rotate it 90 Ds, and then fold it in thirds.
8. Repeat rolling and folding two more times, then place the dough in the refrigerator for a further one to two hrs or overnight.
9. Turn on the oven to 400 °F (200 °C).
10. The cold dough Must be rolled out into a long rectangle and then slice into triangles.
11. To make croissants, tightly roll every triangle beginning at the wide end.
12. The croissants Must rise for about 30 mins after being placed on a baking pan lined with parchment paper.
13. For 15 to 20 mins, or up to golden brown, bake the croissants.

Nutrition (per serving):
Cals: 220 kcal, Protein: 4g, Fat: 14g, Carbs: 19g, Fiber: 1g

64. Spanish Paella Party

Time: 1 hr
Servings: 6

Ingredients:

- 1/4 cup of olive oil
- 1 onion, lightly chop-up
- 3 cloves garlic, chop-up
- 1 red bell pepper, diced
- 1 yellow bell pepper, diced
- 1 1/2 cups of Arborio rice
- 1 tsp saffron threads (non-compulsory)
- 1 tsp smoked paprika
- 1/2 tsp cayenne pepper (non-compulsory, for heat)
- 4 cups of chicken or vegetable broth
- 1 cup of white wine
- 1 lb Big shrimp, peel off and deveined
- 1 lb chicken thighs, slice into bite-sized pieces
- 1 cup of green peas (fresh or refrigerate)
- 1 lemon, slice into wedges
- Salt and pepper as needed

Instructions:
1. Heat the olive oil in a sizable shlet skillet or paella pan over medium heat.
2. Add the chop-up garlic and onion, and cook up to melted.
3. Cook for a couple more mins after adding the diced bell peppers.
4. Stir the Arborio rice with the oil and vegetables in the pan after adding it.
5. Add smoked paprika, cayenne pepper, and saffron, if used, to the pan after dissolving it in a few tbsp of warm broth.
6. White wine Must be added and simmered up to mostly absorbed.
7. One cup of at a time, gradually add the chicken or vegetable broth to the rice, stirring often and letting the liquid permeate before adding more.
8. Chicken chunks Must be seasoned with salt and pepper and cooked thoroughly in a separate pan while the rice is cooking. Place aside.
9. The shrimp are fried in the same pan up to they are pink and fully cooked after being seasoned with salt and pepper. Place aside.
10. Add the cooked chicken, shrimp, and green peas to the pan and spread them out evenly after the rice is almost creamy and tender.
11. Continue cooking the rice up to it is done and has a socarrat (slightly crispy bottom).
12. Lemon wedges Must be served alongside the paella.

Nutrition (per serving):
Cals: 470 kcal, Protein: 30g, Fat: 15g, Carbs: 50g, Fiber: 4g

65. Portuguese Tapas Bonanza

Time: 45 mins
Servings: 4-6

Ingredients:

- 1 lb Portuguese chorizo, split
- 1 lb Manchego cheese, cubed
- 1 cup of green olives
- 1 cup of black olives
- 1 cup of marinated artichoke hearts
- 1 cup of roasted red peppers, split
- 1 cup of cherry tomatoes
- 1 loaf Portuguese or rustic bread, split
- Olive oil, for drizzling

Instructions:
1. On a sizable serving platter or on individual tapas plates, arrange the split chorizo, cubed Manchego cheese, green and black olives, marinated artichoke hearts, roasted red peppers, and cherry tomatoes.
2. Slices of Portuguese or rustic bread Must be served alongside the tapas.
3. If you would want the tapas to have more taste, drizzle some olive oil over them.

Nutrition (per serving, assuming 4 servings):
Cals: 580 kcal, Protein: 25g, Fat: 41g, Carbs: 29g, Fiber: 7g

66. British Fish and Chips

Time: 45 mins

Servings: 4

Ingredients:

- 4 Big potatoes, peel off and slice into thick fries
- 4 cod fillets (or haddock), skinless and boneless
- 1 cup of all-purpose flour
- 1 tsp baking powder
- 1 cup of cold sparkling water
- Salt and pepper as needed
- Vegetable oil for frying

Instructions:

1. Set the oven's temperature to 200 C (400 F).
2. The slice potatoes Must be rinsed in cold water and dried with paper towels.
3. To 180°C (350°F), heat the vegetable oil in a deep fryer or a sizable pot.
4. Fry the potatoes in batches for 5-7 mins per batch, or up to brown and crispy. Take out, then dry off with paper towels.
5. Add salt and pepper to the fish fillets before serving.
6. To create the batter, combine the flour, baking soda, sparkling water, salt, and pepper in a Big bowl.
7. Fish fillets Must be dipped into the batter, letting any extra drip off.
8. The battered fish Must be fried in the hot oil for about 4–5 mins on every side, or up to golden and well cooked. On paper towels, drain.
9. With your favorite dipping sauces, such as tartar sauce or malt vinegar, serve the fish and chips.

Nutrition (per serving):
Cals: 600 kcal, Protein: 30g, Fat: 25g, Carbs: 65g, Fiber: 6g

67. German Oktoberfest Feast

Time: 2 hrs

Servings: 6

Ingredients:

- 1 (4-5 lb) pork roast or pork Muster
- Salt and pepper as needed
- 1 tbsp vegetable oil
- 1 Big onion, split
- 2 cloves garlic, chop-up
- 2 cups of beef broth
- 1 bottle (12 ozs) German beer
- 1 tbsp caraway seeds (non-compulsory)
- 1/4 cup of Dijon mustard
- 1/4 cup of brown sugar
- 1/4 cup of apple cider vinegar
- 6 Big pretzels
- German-style sauerkraut (for serving)

Instructions:

1. Set the oven's temperature to 325°F (160°C).
2. On all sides, season the pork roast with salt and pepper.
3. Heat the vegetable oil over medium-high heat in a sizable oven-safe saucepan or Dutch oven.
4. The pork roast Must be properly browned on all sides. The roast Must be taken out of the saucepan and placed aside.
5. Split onions Must be cooked up to soft in the same saucepan before adding chop-up garlic and cooking for an additional min.
6. Add the beer and beef broth, along with any caraway seeds you're using.
7. The pig roast Must be placed back in the pot, covered with a lid, and roasted in the oven.
8. About 1 1/2 to 2 hrs of roasting the pork is required to achieve tenderness and easy fork separation.
9. Make the glaze by blending the Dijon mustard, brown sugar, and apple cider vinegar in a mini bowl while the pig is roasting.
10. Take out the pot's lid during the final thirty mins of roasting, glaze the pork, and continue roasting uncovered.
11. When the pork is finished cooking, take out it from the saucepan and let it rest before slicing.
12. Pretzels and German-style sauerkraut Must be served alongside the split pork.

Nutrition (per serving):
Cals: 550 kcal, Protein: 40g, Fat: 30g, Carbs: 25g, Fiber: 2g

68. Austrian Schnitzel Delight

Time: 45 mins

Servings: 4

Ingredients:

- 4 veal or pork slicelets, lbed thin
- Salt and pepper as needed
- 1/2 cup of all-purpose flour
- 2 Big eggs, beaten
- 1 cup of breadcrumbs (preferably panko)
- Vegetable oil for frying

- Lemon wedges for serving

Instructions:
1. On both sides, season the veal or pork slicelets with salt and pepper.
2. Every slicelet Must be thoroughly floured before being dredged.
3. Following a little press to help the breadcrumbs stick, coat the floured slicelets with beaten eggs before serving.
4. Using a Big skillet over medium-high heat, warm the vegetable oil.
5. The breaded slicelets Must be cooked through and golden brown after 3 to 4 mins of frying in heated oil on every side.
6. The schnitzels Must be taken out of the skillet and dried on paper towels.
7. Lemon wedges Must be served alongside the schnitzels.

Nutrition (per serving):
Cals: 400 kcal, Protein: 25g, Fat: 18g, Carbs: 30g, Fiber: 1g

69. Hungarian Goulash Board

Time: 2 hrs
Servings: 6

Ingredients:
- 2 lbs beef stew meat, slice into chunks
- Salt and pepper as needed
- 2 tbsp vegetable oil
- 2 onions, chop-up
- 3 cloves garlic, chop-up
- 2 tbsp Hungarian sweet paprika
- 1 tsp caraway seeds
- 1 tsp marjoram
- 1 tbsp tomato paste
- 4 cups of beef broth
- 4 Big potatoes, peel off and slice into chunks
- 2 carrots, peel off and split
- 1 green bell pepper, chop-up
- 1 cup of sour cream
- Chop-up fresh parsley for garnish
- Cooked egg noodles or spaetzle (for serving)

Instructions:
1. Salt and pepper the meat for the beef stew.
2. Vegetable oil Must be heated over medium-high heat in a sizable pot or Dutch oven.
3. In the hot oil, the beef chunks are browned on both sides. They Must be taken out of the saucepan and put aside.
4. Cook the chop-up onions in the same saucepan up to they are transparent before adding the chop-up garlic and cooking for an additional min.
5. The flavors will release as you stir in the Hungarian sweet paprika, caraway seeds, marjoram, and tomato paste.
6. Add the beef stock and put the browned beef back in the pot. Bring to a boil, lower the heat to a simmer, cover the pot, and cook for 1 1/2 to 2 hrs, or up to the beef is cooked.
7. To the pot, add the diced potatoes, carrots, and green bell pepper. Keep the vegetables boiling up to they are fully cooked and the stew has thickened.
8. To give the goulash creaminess, stir in the sour cream.
9. With cooked egg noodles or spaetzle on the side and fresh parsley garnish, serve the Hungarian goulash.

Nutrition (per serving):
Cals: 450 kcal, Protein: 30g, Fat: 20g, Carbs: 35g, Fiber: 5g

70. Finnish Fisherman's Platter:

Time: 1 hr
Servings: 4

Ingredients:
- 500g combined Finnish fish fillets (salmon, trout, perch, etc.)
- 1 onion, thinly split
- 2 carrots, split
- 200g new potatoes, halved
- 200g green beans, trimmed
- 1 lemon, split
- Fresh dill, for garnish
- Salt and pepper as needed
- 50ml vegetable broth
- 50ml white wine
- 2 tbsp butter

Instructions:
1. Set the oven's temperature to 200 C (390 F).
2. On a baking sheet, arrange the fish, veggies, and lemon slices.
3. Add white wine and vegetable broth after seasoning with salt and pepper.
4. Spread the ingredients with the butter.
5. Bake the tray for 30 mins while it is covered with aluminum foil.
6. Once the fish is cooked through and the

vegetables are soft, take out the foil and bake for an additional 10-15 mins.
7. Before serving, garnish with fresh dill.

Nutrition (per serving):
Cals: 350, Protein: 25g, Fat: 12g, Carbs: 30g, Fiber: 6g

71. Danish Smørrebrød Spread:

Time: 30 mins

Servings: 6

Ingredients:
- 6 slices rye bread
- 200g smoked salmon
- 100g pickled herring
- 100g roast beef
- 1 cucumber, thinly split
- 1 red onion, thinly split
- 50g radishes, thinly split
- Fresh dill, for garnish
- 100g remoulade sauce (mayonnaise-based sauce with pickles and capers)
- 100g liver pate

Instructions:
1. Lay out the slices of rye bread.
2. Spread the remoulade sauce on the remaining two slices after spreading the liver pate on two of them.
3. Add different toppings to every slice, such as roast beef, pickled herring, cucumber, red onion, and radishes.
4. Add some fresh dill as garnish.
5. Serve as an enticing smörgsbord open-faced.

Nutrition (per serving):
Cals: 280, Protein: 18g, Fat: 14g, Carbs: 20g, Fiber: 6g

72. Norwegian Gravlax and Aquavit:

Time: 2 days (including curing time)

Servings: 8

Ingredients:
- 500g salmon fillet, skin-on
- 2 tbsp coarse sea salt
- 1 tbsp sugar
- 1 tbsp crushed black peppercorns
- 1 Big bunch fresh dill
- Aquavit (Scandinavian spirit)

Instructions:
1. Salmon Must be rinsed and dried with paper towels.
2. In a bowl, combine the sea salt, sugar, and black peppercorns.
3. On a sizable dish or tray, spread a layer of plastic wrap.
4. On the plastic wrap, distribute half of the salt Mixture.
5. The salmon fillet Must be placed skin-side down on the salt Mixture.
6. The fish Must be covered with the remaining salt Mixture.
7. Over the fish, place the dill.
8. Make sure the salmon is completely covered in aquavit.
9. Refrigerate the salmon for 48 hrs after carefully wrapping it in plastic wrap.
10. Gravlax Must be split thin and the salmon Must be unwrapped.
11. Serve with black toast and classic glasses of aquavit.

Nutrition (per serving):
Cals: 220, Protein: 22g, Fat: 12g, Carbs: 2g, Fiber: 0g

73. Irish Pub Grub Platter:

Time: 1 hr

Servings: 4

Ingredients:
- 500g Irish bangers (sausages)
- 500g mashed potatoes
- 1 Big onion, thinly split and caramelized
- 200g green peas, cooked
- 50g butter
- Salt and pepper as needed
- 200ml beef gravy
- Fresh parsley, for garnish

Instructions:
1. Irish bangers Must be cooked thoroughly and browned in a skillet over medium heat.
2. Using boiled potatoes, butter, salt, and pepper, make mashed potatoes.
3. In a different pan, caramelize the onion slices up to they are golden brown.
4. On a platter, arrange the bangers, mashed potatoes, caramelized onions, and boiled peas.
5. Cover the bangers with beef gravy.
6. Before serving, garnish with fresh parsley.

Nutrition (per serving):
Cals: 600, Protein: 25g, Fat: 35g, Carbs: 45g, Fiber: 8g

74. Scottish Haggis and Whisky:

Time: 1 hr

Servings: 6

Ingredients:

- 500g haggis (traditional Scottish dish made from sheep's heart, liver, and lungs)
- 6 potatoes, boiled and mashed
- 200g turnips, boiled and mashed
- 200g whisky sauce (whisky, cream, and stock)
- 50g butter
- Salt and pepper as needed

Instructions:

1. The haggis Must be prepared as directed on the packaging.
2. Separately cook the turnips and potatoes up to they are fork-tender, then mash them with butter, salt, and pepper.
3. whiskey, cream, and stock are simmered together to create the whiskey sauce.
4. Place the mashed potatoes, mashed turnips, and haggis on a plate.
5. Over the haggis, pour the whisky sauce.
6. Serving whisky on the side, savor the traditional Scottish dinner.

Nutrition (per serving):
Cals: 400, Protein: 15g, Fat: 15g, Carbs: 45g, Fiber: 6g

75. Welsh Rarebit and Ale:

Time: 30 mins

Servings: 4

Ingredients:

- 200g cheddar cheese, finely grated
- 2 tbsp butter
- 2 tbsp all-purpose flour
- 1 tsp mustard powder
- 120ml ale or beer
- 1 tbsp Worcestershire sauce
- 4 slices toasted bread
- Fresh parsley, for garnish

Instructions:

1. Melt the butter in a saucepan over medium heat.
2. To create a roux, whisk in the flour and mustard powder.
3. To prevent lumps, add the ale gradually while stirring continually.
4. The Mixture Must boil for a while to thicken before adding Worcestershire sauce.
5. After turning off the heat, add the shredded cheddar and whisk up to smooth.
6. The toasted bread Must be covered with the Welsh rarebit sauce.
7. Before serving, garnish with fresh parsley.

Nutrition (per serving):
Cals: 350, Protein: 15g, Fat: 20g, Carbs: 25g, Fiber: 2g

76. American Southern BBQ:

Time: 8 hrs (including marinating and cooking time)

Servings: 6

Ingredients:

- 1 whole chicken, slice into pieces
- 500g pork ribs
- 500g beef brisket
- 1 cup of BBQ sauce
- Dry rub (paprika, brown sugar, salt, pepper, garlic powder, onion powder)
- Coleslaw and cornbread, for serving

Instructions:

1. All over the chicken, pig ribs, and beef brisket, rub the dry rub Mixture. Let them to marinade for a minimum of two hrs and ideally overnight.
2. Set the grill or smoker to a low, indirect heat setting (between 225°F and 250°F).
3. The meats Must be smoked on the grill for a number of hrs to achieve the necessary level of tenderness and internal temperature.
4. During the final thirty mins of cooking, baste the meats with barbecue sauce.
5. Prior to serving, let the meats to rest for a short while.
6. Serve cornbread and slaw alongside the southern barbecue.

Nutrition (per serving):
Cals: 800, Protein: 60g, Fat: 40g, Carbs: 45g, Fiber: 3g

77. New Orleans Cajun Creole:

Time: 1 hr

Servings: 4

Ingredients:

- 500g shrimp, peel off and deveined
- 200g smoked sausage, split

- 1 onion, chop-up
- 1 green bell pepper, chop-up
- 2 stalks celery, chop-up
- 3 cloves garlic, chop-up
- 400g canned diced tomatoes
- 2 tbsp Cajun seasoning
- 1 tbsp hot sauce (non-compulsory for extra spice)
- 2 tbsp vegetable oil
- Cooked rice, for serving

Instructions:
1. All over the chicken, pig ribs, and beef brisket, rub the dry rub Mixture. Let them to marinade for a minimum of two hrs and ideally overnight.
2. Set the grill or smoker to a low, indirect heat setting (between 225°F and 250°F).
3. The meats Must be smoked on the grill for a number of hrs to achieve the necessary level of tenderness and internal temperature.
4. During the final thirty mins of cooking, baste the meats with barbecue sauce.
5. Prior to serving, let the meats to rest for a short while.
6. Serve cornbread and slaw alongside the southern barbecue.

Nutrition (per serving):
Cals: 400, Protein: 25g, Fat: 20g, Carbs: 30g, Fiber: 5g

78. Texan Steakhouse Board:

Time: 45 mins
Servings: 4

Ingredients:
- 4 beef steaks (e.g., ribeye, New York strip, or tenderloin)
- 1 tbsp olive oil
- Salt and pepper as needed
- 4 tbsp comlb butter (butter combined with chop-up herbs like parsley, thyme, and rosemary)
- Grilled vegetables (e.g., bell peppers, zucchini, asparagus)
- Baked sweet potatoes
- Texas-style BBQ sauce

Instructions:
1. Prepare your grill or grill pan on the stove.
2. Olive oil Must be applied to the steaks before adding salt and pepper.
3. The steaks Must be cooked to your preference.
4. Before serving, let the steaks rest for a few mins.
5. Put a dollop of comlb butter on top of the steaks before serving.
6. Place roasted sweet potatoes and grilled vegetables on the board.
7. Pour some Texas-style barbecue sauce over the potatoes and vegetables.

Nutrition (per serving):
Cals: 600, Protein: 40g, Fat: 40g, Carbs: 25g, Fiber: 4g

79. Californian Avocado Dream:

Time: 20 mins
Servings: 2

Ingredients:
- 2 Big ripe avocados, halved and pitted
- 200g cherry tomatoes, halved
- 1 mini red onion, thinly split
- 1 cucumber, diced
- 100g feta cheese, cut up
- 50g pine nuts, toasted
- Fresh basil and cilantro, chop-up
- 2 tbsp balsamic glaze
- 2 tbsp olive oil
- Salt and pepper as needed

Instructions:
1. Cherry tomatoes, red onion, cucumber, feta cheese, pine nuts, basil, and cilantro Must all be combined in a bowl.
2. Add salt and pepper, then drizzle olive oil over the Mixture. Gently blend by tossing.
3. The tomato-cucumber combination Must be placed inside every avocado half.
4. Balsamic glaze Must be drizzled over the stuffed avocados.
5. Serve the Californian Avocado Dream as a light entrée or refreshing appetizer.

Nutrition (per serving):
Cals: 450, Protein: 10g, Fat: 35g, Carbs: 25g, Fiber: 12g

80. Hawaiian Poke Paradise

Time: 20 mins
Servings: 4

Ingredients:

- 1 lb fresh sushi-grade ahi tuna, cubed
- 1/4 cup of soy sauce
- 1 tbsp sesame oil
- 1 tbsp rice vinegar
- 1 tsp finely grated fresh ginger
- 2 green onions, thinly split
- 1 avocado, diced
- 1/2 cucumber, diced
- 1 tbsp sesame seeds
- 2 tbsp chop-up fresh cilantro
- 1 tbsp furikake (Japanese rice seasoning)
- Cooked white or brown rice, for serving

Instructions:

1. To make the marinade, combine the soy sauce, sesame oil, rice vinegar, and shredded ginger in a sizable bowl.
2. Toss the diced tuna lightly in the marinade to coat. To let the flavors to mingle, cover the bowl and place it in the fridge for at least 10 mins.
3. Prepare the toppings while the tuna is marinating. Combine the diced avocado, cucumber, green onions, sesame seeds, and cilantro in a separate bowl.
4. Take the tuna out of the refrigerator when it has marinated, then put the poke bowls together. In every serving dish or plate, spoon a serving of cooked rice.
5. The avocado-cucumber Mixture Must be placed on top of the rice after the tuna that has been marinated.
6. For an additional taste boost, top the poke bowls with furikake.
7. The Hawaiian Poke Paradise Must be served right away.

NUTRITION INFO (per serving):
Cals: 320 kcal, Protein: 28g, Fat: 17g, Carbs: 15g, Fiber: 4g, Sugar: 2g, Sodium: 860mg

81. New England Clambake

Time: 1 hr 30 mins

Servings: 6

Ingredients:

- 6 live lobsters
- 24 littleneck clams, scrubbed
- 1 lb mussels, cleaned and debearded
- 8 ears of corn, husked and halved
- 1 lb smoked sausage, split
- 2 lbs mini red potatoes
- 1 cup of dilute butter
- Fresh lemon wedges
- Fresh parsley, chop-up, for garnish

Instructions:

1. Add a layer of seaweed or damp seaweed wrappings to the bottom of a big pot or clam bake pit.
2. In the pot, arrange the potatoes, corn, sausage, clams, and mussels in layers. Add salt and pepper to every layer.
3. Put a lid on the saucepan or a foil cover that fits snugly over it.
4. The shellfish Must be well cooked and the potatoes Must be fork-tender after about an hr of cooking the clambake over high heat.
5. Take out the pot carefully from the heat.
6. On a sizable platter, serve the New England clambake, drizzle with dilute butter, and top with fresh parsley. Lemon wedges Must be served separately.

82. New York Deli Board

Time: 20 mins

Servings: 6

Ingredients:

- 1 lb pastrami, thinly split
- 1 lb corned beef, thinly split
- 1/2 lb Swiss cheese, split
- 1/2 lb cheddar cheese, split
- 6 dill pickles
- 1/2 cup of Dijon mustard
- 1/2 cup of mayonnaise
- 12 slices rye bread

Instructions:

1. On a sizable platter or serving board, arrange the pastrami, corned beef, Swiss cheese, and cheddar cheese.
2. Place the split rye bread and dill pickles on the board.
3. Serve the sandwiches' condiments—Dijon mustard and mayonnaise—in mini dishes.
4. Let everyone use the ingredients to construct their own New York Deli sandwiches.

83. Chicago Deep-Dish Party

Time: 1 hr 30 mins

Servings: 8

Ingredients:

- 1 batch deep-dish pizza dough (store-bought or homemade)
- 1 lb Italian sausage, cooked and cut up
- 1 can (28 ozs) crushed tomatoes
- 1 tsp dried oregano
- 1/2 tsp garlic powder
- 1/4 tsp red pepper flakes (non-compulsory)
- 2 cups of shredded mozzarella cheese
- 1/2 cup of finely grated Parmesan cheese
- 1 green bell pepper, diced
- 1 mini onion, diced
- 1 cup of split pepperoni
- Olive oil

Instructions:

1. Turn on the oven to 425 °F (220 °C).
2. To fit a greased 9-inch deep-dish pizza pan or a springform pan, roll out the deep-dish pizza dough.
3. The dough Must be pressed into the pan's bottom and sides.
4. Crushed tomatoes, dried oregano, garlic powder, and red pepper flakes (if using) Must all be combined in a bowl.
5. On the bottom of the dough, evenly distribute half of the mozzarella cheese.
6. Over the cheese, arrange the cooked Italian sausage, diced green bell pepper, diced onion, and pepperoni slices.
7. Over the toppings, pour the tomato sauce Mixture.
8. Finely grated Parmesan cheese and the leftover mozzarella cheese Must be added on top.
9. Olive oil Must be used sparingly to the cheese.
10. The Chicago Deep-Dish Party pizza Must be baked in the preheated oven for 35 to 40 mins, or up to the cheese is bubbling and the dough is golden brown.
11. Before Cutting and serving, let it cool for a while.

84. Tex-Mex Nacho Fiesta

Time: 25 mins
Servings: 6

Ingredients:

- 1 bag (10-12 ozs) tortilla chips
- 2 cups of shredded cheddar cheese
- 1 can (15 ozs) black beans, drained and rinsed
- 1 cup of cooked and seasoned ground beef or shredded chicken
- 1 cup of diced tomatoes
- 1/2 cup of diced red onion
- 1/4 cup of split jalapenos (non-compulsory, for spice)
- 1/4 cup of chop-up fresh cilantro
- 1/2 cup of sour cream
- 1/4 cup of salsa
- Guacamole, for serving

Instructions:

1. Set your oven's temperature to 375°F (190°C).
2. On a sizable baking sheet, spread the tortilla chips out in a single layer.
3. Over the chips, evenly distribute the shredded cheddar cheese.
4. Over the cheese and chips, distribute the cooked ground beef or chicken, along with the black beans.
5. Bake for 10 to 15 mins in a preheated oven, or up to the cheese is dilute and bubbling.
6. After taking it out of the oven, garnish it with chop-up cilantro, red onion, jalapenos, and diced tomatoes.
7. Pour salsa and sour cream on top of the nachos.
8. Tex-Mex Nacho Fiesta Must be served right away with guacamole on the side.

85. Southwest Chili and Cornbread

Time: 1 hr 30 mins
Servings: 8

Ingredients for Chili:

- 2 lbs ground beef
- 1 Big onion, diced
- 3 cloves garlic, chop-up
- 1 can (15 ozs) kidney beans, drained and rinsed
- 1 can (15 ozs) black beans, drained and rinsed
- 1 can (15 ozs) diced tomatoes
- 1 can (6 ozs) tomato paste
- 2 cups of beef broth
- 2 tbsp chili powder
- 1 tbsp cumin
- 1 tsp paprika
- Salt and pepper as needed
- Olive oil

Ingredients for Cornbread:

1. Olive oil is heated in a big pot over medium heat.

2. When the onions and garlic are added, sauté them up to they are transparent.
3. With a spatula, split up the ground beef into minier pieces as you add it and sauté it up to it is browned.
4. Add the kidney beans, black beans, tomato paste, beef broth, cumin, chili powder, paprika, salt, and pepper after stirring in the beans.
5. Stirring occasionally, bring the chili to a simmer, then lower the heat and let it cook for at least an hr. If more beef broth is required to revery the appropriate consistency, do so.
6. How to make cornbread:
7. Prepare an 8-inch square baking dish with oil and preheat the oven to 375°F (190°C).
8. Combine the cornmeal, flour, sugar, baking soda, and salt in a combining dish.
9. The buttermilk, dilute butter, and egg Must all be thoroughly blended in a different bowl.
10. After adding the liquid components, combine the dry ingredients only up to they are barely blended.
11. Spread the cornbread batter evenly after pouring it into the prepared baking dish.
12. Bake for 20 to 25 mins in the preheated oven, or up to a toothpick inserted in the center comes out clean.
13. Before Cutting, let the cornbread cool for a few mins.
14. Pour the Southwest Chili into bowls and top every serving with a slice of cornbread.

86. Midwestern Hot Dog Party

Time: 20 mins
Servings: 8

Ingredients:

- 8 hot dog buns
- 8 all-beef hot dogs
- 1 cup of chop-up onions
- 1 cup of chop-up tomatoes
- 1 cup of pickle relish
- 1 cup of shredded cheddar cheese
- 1 cup of coleslaw
- Mustard, ketchup, and other condiments of choice

Instructions:

1. According to the directions on the box/pkg, grill or cook the hot dogs.
2. Put the buns with the hot dogs together on a serving plate.
3. As toppings, provide bowls of coleslaw, shredded cheddar cheese, pickle relish, split onions, and tomatoes.
4. Let everyone add their preferred toppings and condiments to their Midwestern hot dogs.

87. Pacific Northwest Salmon Soiree

Time: 30 mins
Servings: 4

Ingredients:

- 4 salmon fillets
- 2 tbsp olive oil
- 2 tbsp soy sauce
- 2 tbsp honey
- 1 tbsp Dijon mustard
- 2 cloves garlic, chop-up
- 1 tsp finely grated fresh ginger
- Lemon wedges, for serving

Instructions:

1. To create the marinade, combine the olive oil, soy sauce, honey, Dijon mustard, chop-up garlic, and ginger in a mini bowl.
2. Pour the marinade over the salmon fillets that have been placed in a shlet dish. Give them about 15 mins to marinate.
3. Your grill or grill pan Must be preheated over medium-high heat.
4. Salmon fillets Must be grilled for 4-5 mins on every side, or up to they are cooked through and have grill marks, after being take outd from the marinade.
5. Lemon wedges Must be served alongside the salmon feast from the Pacific Northwest.

88. Floridian Citrus Celebration

Time: 15 mins
Servings: 6

Ingredients:

- 4 cups of combined salad greens
- 2 oranges, peel off and segmented
- 1 grapefruit, peel off and segmented
- 1 avocado, split
- 1/2 cup of cut up feta cheese
- 1/4 cup of chop-up almonds
- 2 tbsp olive oil
- 1 tbsp fresh lemon juice
- 1 tsp honey

- Salt and pepper as needed

Instructions:
1. Combine the combined salad greens, grapefruit, orange, and avocado slices with the feta cheese cut ups and chop-up almonds in a Big salad bowl.
2. To prepare the dressing, combine the olive oil, fresh lemon juice, honey, salt, and pepper in a mini bowl.
3. Toss the salad carefully to evenly distribute the dressing over all of the ingredients.
4. Serve the salad from the Floridian Citrus Celebration right away.

89. Caribbean Rum Punch Party

Time: 10 mins
Servings: 6

Ingredients:
- 2 cups of pineapple juice
- 1 cup of orange juice
- 1 cup of dark rum
- 1/4 cup of coconut cream
- 1/4 cup of lime juice
- 2 tbsp grenadine syrup
- Pineapple slices, orange slices, and maraschino cherries for garnish
- Ice cubes

Instructions:
1. Combine the coconut cream, lime juice, dark rum, pineapple juice, orange juice, and grenadine syrup in a sizable pitcher.
2. The Mixture must be well blended after being stirred.
3. Ice cubes Must be placed in glasses before adding the Caribbean Rum Punch.
4. A pineapple slice, an orange slice, and a maraschino cherry Must be used to decorate every glass.
5. Serve the Caribbean Rum Punch Party and take care when you consume it!

Note:
Please remember that alcohol Must only be consumed by adults of legal drinking age.

90. Central American Tamales Board:

Time: 3 hrs
Servings: 6-8

Ingredients:
- 2 cups of masa harina (corn flour)
- 1 1/2 cups of chicken or vegetable broth
- 1/2 cup of lard or vegetable shortening
- 1 tsp baking powder
- 1/2 tsp salt
- 1 cup of cooked and shredded chicken or pork
- 1 cup of salsa or your favorite sauce
- Banana leaves (or parchment paper), slice into squares
- Various toppings: sour cream, diced tomatoes, chop-up cilantro, split avocado, and queso fresco

Instructions:
1. Masa harina, broth, lard, baking powder, and salt are combined in a sizable bowl up to a smooth dough comes together.
2. Spread a dollop of the masa dough on a square of banana leaf. Place some salsa and shreddable pork or chicken in the middle.
3. With a toothpick, fold the banana leaf over the filling and fasten.
4. In a sizable saucepan or steamer, steam the tamales for 1.5 to 2 hrs, or up to the masa is thoroughly cooked.
5. For a delicious experience, serve the tamales on a board with a variety of toppings and sauces.

NUTRITION INFO (per serving):
Cals: 350, Fat: 15g, Carbs: 45g, Protein: 12g

91. South American Empanada Fiesta:

Time: 1 hr
Servings: 4-6

Ingredients:
- 2 cups of all-purpose flour
- 1/2 tsp salt
- 1/2 cup of unsalted butter, cold and slice into mini pieces
- 1/2 cup of cold water
- 1 lb ground beef or chicken
- 1 onion, lightly chop-up
- 2 cloves garlic, chop-up
- 1 tsp cumin
- 1 tsp paprika
- Salt and pepper as needed
- Oil for frying

Instructions:

1. Combine salt and flour in a Big basin. Butter Must be incorporated into the Mixture up to it resembles coarse crumbs. The dough Must be moistened and worked into a smooth ball. 30 mins of refrigeration under cover.
2. Cook the ground meat in a skillet with the onions, garlic, cumin, paprika, salt, and pepper up to it is browned and thoroughly cooked.
3. Set the oven's temperature to 375°F (190°C).
4. On a floured board, roll out the dough and slice circles with a diameter of about 5 inches.
5. Every circle Must have a spoonful of the meat filling in the center. The dough Must then be folded over, and the sides Must be pressed with a fork to seal.
6. The empanadas Must be fried in hot oil up to golden brown on both sides. A different option is to bake them for 20 to 25 mins, or up to just barely browned.
7. Enjoy your fiesta while serving the empanadas with the chimichurri sauce!

NUTRITION INFO (per serving):
Cals: 380, Fat: 22g, Carbs: 25g, Protein: 20g

92. North African Spice Odyssey:

Time: 2.5 hrs
Servings: 4-6

Ingredients:

- 1 lb lamb, cubed
- 1 onion, lightly chop-up
- 2 cloves garlic, chop-up
- 2 tbsp olive oil
- 1 can (14 oz) diced tomatoes
- 1 cup of chicken broth
- 1 cup of dried apricots, chop-up
- 1/2 cup of raisins
- 1/4 cup of slivered almonds
- 2 tsp ground cumin
- 1 tsp ground coriander
- 1 tsp ground cinnamon
- 1/2 tsp ground ginger
- Salt and pepper as needed
- Cooked couscous for serving

Instructions:

1. Olive oil Must be heated over medium heat in a big saucepan or tagine. Add the onions and garlic and cook up to tender.
2. Brown the lamb cubes all over after adding them.
3. Add all the spices, dried apricots, raisins, chicken stock, and diced tomatoes. Add salt and pepper as needed.
4. The Mixture Must be brought to a boil, then simmer for about two hrs, covered, on low heat, up to the lamb is fork-tender and the flavors are well-balanced.
5. The slivered almonds Must be toasted up to golden brown in a separate pan.
6. Over cooked couscous, spoon the North African spice stew and top with toasted almonds.

NUTRITION INFO (per serving):
Cals: 480, Fat: 19g, Carbs: 43g, Protein: 35g

93. West African Jollof Joy:

Time: 1 hr
Servings: 6-8

Ingredients:

- 2 cups of long-grain parboiled rice
- 1 lb chicken or beef, slice into pieces
- 1 onion, chop-up
- 2-3 ripe tomatoes, chop-up
- 1 red bell pepper, chop-up
- 1 Scotch bonnet pepper (adjust to your spice preference)
- 3 cups of chicken broth
- 2 tbsp tomato paste
- 2 tbsp vegetable oil
- 1 tsp thyme
- 1 tsp curry powder
- 1 tsp paprika
- Salt and pepper as needed

Instructions:

1. Vegetable oil Must be heated over medium heat in a big pot. Translucent onions Must be sautéed.
2. Brown the beef or chicken pieces on all sides after adding them.
3. Add the diced red bell pepper, Scotch bonnet pepper, and tomatoes. Cook the tomatoes up to they are mushy.
4. Add the curry powder, paprika, thyme, tomato paste, salt, and pepper. additional 2 to 3 mins of cooking.
5. Chicken broth and parboiled rice Must be added. Bring to a boil, lower heat to a simmer, cover, and cook for 20 to 25 mins, or up to rice is tender and liquid has been absorbed.
6. Serve the West African Jollof with your preferred side dishes after fluffing the rice with a fork.

NUTRITION INFO (per serving):
Cals: 380, Fat: 12g, Carbs: 45, Protein: 25g

94. East African Safari Platter:

Time: 2 hrs
Servings: 4-6

Ingredients:

- 1 lb tender beef or lamb, cubed
- 1 Big onion, chop-up
- 2 cloves garlic, chop-up
- 2 tbsp vegetable oil
- 2 tomatoes, chop-up
- 1 cup of coconut milk
- 1 cup of beef or vegetable broth
- 2 tbsp curry powder
- 1 tsp turmeric
- 1 tsp cumin
- 1 tsp paprika
- Salt and pepper as needed
- Cooked white rice for serving

Instructions:

1. Vegetable oil Must be heated over medium heat in a big skillet or pot. Onions and garlic are sautéed up to aromatic.
2. Add the cubed lamb or beef, and brown it well.
3. Add the diced tomatoes, curry powder, turmeric, cumin, paprika, salt, and pepper along with the coconut milk, beef or vegetable broth.
4. The Mixture Must be brought to a boil, then simmer for 1.5 to 2 hrs, covered, up to the beef is fork-tender and the flavors are well-balanced.
5. Enjoy the delicious tastes of the East African Safari Platter with cooked white rice.

NUTRITION INFO (per serving):
Cals: 450, Fat: 25g, Carbs: 15g, Protein: 40g

95. South African Boerewors Braai:

Time: 1.5 hrs
Servings: 4-6

Ingredients:

- 1 lb beef sausages
- 1 lb pork sausages
- 2 tbsp ground coriander
- 1 tbsp ground cumin
- 1 tbsp paprika
- 1 tsp ground allspice
- 1 tsp black pepper
- 1/2 tsp ground nutmeg
- 1/2 tsp ground cloves
- 1/4 cup of vinegar
- 2 tbsp vegetable oil
- Rolls or bread for serving

Instructions:

1. Ground coriander, ground cumin, paprika, ground allspice, black pepper, ground nutmeg, and ground cloves Must all be combined in a bowl.
2. Vinegar and vegetable oil Must be combined in a different basin.
3. The sausages Must be placed in a big platter after being forked. Then, evenly sprinkle the spice Mixture over the sausages after pouring the vinegar-oil Mixture over them.
4. The meal Must be covered and marinated for at least an hr (or overnight for better flavor) in the refrigerator.
5. Heat the grill or barbecue to a moderately hot setting. Boerewors sausages Must be cooked through and well browned after grilling for 15 to 20 mins with occasional turning.
6. In rolls or with bread, serve the boerewors braai and savor a true South African treat.

NUTRITION INFO (per serving):
Cals: 580, Fat: 45g, Carbs: 8g, Protein: 35g

96. Arabian Nights Extravaganza:

Time: 2 hrs
Servings: 4-6

Ingredients:

- 1 lb boneless chicken thighs, slice into pieces
- 1 Big onion, lightly chop-up
- 3 cloves garlic, chop-up
- 1 cup of plain yogurt
- 1/4 cup of lemon juice
- 1/4 cup of olive oil
- 1 tsp ground cumin
- 1 tsp ground coriander
- 1/2 tsp ground cinnamon
- 1/4 tsp ground cardamom
- Salt and pepper as needed
- Skewers for grilling

Instructions:

1. Yogurt, lemon juice, olive oil, chop-up garlic, cumin, coriander, cinnamon, cardamom, salt, and pepper Must all be combined in a bowl.

2. Add the chicken pieces and thoroughly bathe them in the marinade. For better flavor, let the bowl covered in the refrigerator for at least an hr.
3. Heat the grill or barbecue to a moderately hot setting.
4. The chicken Must be cooked through and slightly browned after grilling for 15 to 20 mins with intermittent flipping of the skewers.
5. For a taste of Middle Eastern delicacy, serve the Arabian Nights Extravaganza with rice, pita bread, or a crisp salad.

NUTRITION INFO (per serving):
Cals: 380, Fat: 20g, Carbs: 10g, Protein: 35g

97. Middle Eastern Shawarma Feast:

Time: 3 hrs

Servings: 6-8

Ingredients:

- 2 lbs boneless chicken or beef, thinly split
- 1 Big onion, lightly chop-up
- 4 cloves garlic, chop-up
- 1/4 cup of lemon juice
- 1/4 cup of olive oil
- 1 tsp ground cumin
- 1 tsp ground coriander
- 1 tsp ground paprika
- 1/2 tsp ground turmeric
- 1/4 tsp ground cinnamon
- 1/4 tsp ground cardamom
- Salt and pepper as needed
- Pita bread and your favorite toppings for serving (split tomatoes, cucumbers, lettuce, tahini sauce, etc.)

Instructions:

1. Combine lemon juice, olive oil, chop-up garlic, chop-up onions, ground cumin, ground coriander, ground paprika, turmeric, ground cinnamon, ground cardamom, salt, and pepper in a Big bowl.
2. To the marinade, add the thinly split beef or chicken, and thoroughly coat. For better flavor, let the bowl covered in the fridge for at least two hrs.
3. Heat the grill or barbecue to a moderately hot setting.
4. The marinated meat Must be threaded onto skewers, then grilled for 15 to 20 mins, rotating once or twice, up to well cooked and beautifully browned.
5. Grilling the pita bread for a min on every side will preheat it.
6. By putting grilled meat and your preferred toppings inside pita bread, you may serve the Middle Eastern shawarma feast. Enjoy it rolled up!

NUTRITION INFO (per serving):
Cals: 420, Fat: 18g, Carbs: 20g, Protein: 45g

98. Persian Mezze Magic:

Time: 1 hr

Servings: 4-6

Ingredients:

- 1 cup of cooked basmati rice
- 1 cup of cooked chickpeas
- 1 cup of yogurt
- 1 cucumber, diced
- 1 tomato, diced
- 1/4 cup of chop-up fresh mint
- 1/4 cup of chop-up fresh parsley
- 1/4 cup of chop-up fresh dill
- 2 tbsp lemon juice
- 2 tbsp olive oil
- Salt and pepper as needed
- Pita bread or lavash for serving

Instructions:

1. Combine cooked basmati rice and cooked chickpeas in a sizable bowl.
2. Yogurt, diced cucumber, diced tomato, chop-up parsley, chop-up dill, lemon juice, olive oil, salt, and pepper Must all be combined in a separate bowl.
3. Rice and chickpeas Must be added along with the yogurt Mixture, and everything Must be thoroughly combined.
4. With pita bread or lavash, serve the Persian Mezze Magic for a delicious variety of tastes and textures.

NUTRITION INFO (per serving):
Cals: 320, Fat: 12g, Carbs: 42g, Protein: 12g

99. Indian Tandoori Bonanza:

Time: 2 hrs

Servings: 4-6

Ingredients:

- 2 lbs chicken (drumsticks, thighs, or boneless pieces)

- 1 cup of plain yogurt
- 2 tbsp lemon juice
- 2 tbsp tandoori masala
- 1 tbsp ground cumin
- 1 tbsp ground coriander
- 1 tbsp paprika
- 1/2 tsp ground turmeric
- 1/4 tsp cayenne pepper (adjust to your spice preference)
- 4 cloves garlic, chop-up
- 2-inch piece of ginger, finely grated
- Salt and pepper as needed
- Lemon wedges and cilantro for garnish

Instructions:
1. Combine yogurt, lemon juice, tandoori masala, cumin, coriander, paprika, turmeric, cayenne pepper, chop-up garlic, ginger, salt, and pepper in a sizable bowl.
2. Add the chicken pieces and thoroughly bathe them in the marinade. For better flavor, let the bowl covered in the refrigerator for at least an hr.
3. Heat the grill or barbecue to a moderately hot setting.
4. Grill the chicken with the marinade for 15 to 20 mins, rotating once or twice, or up to thoroughly cooked and attractively blackened.
5. For a burst of Indian flavors, serve the Indian Tandoori Bonanza with lemon wedges and cilantro.

NUTRITION INFO (per serving):
Cals: 350, Fat: 15g, Carbs: 10g, Protein: 40g

100. South Indian Dosa Delights:

Time: 30 mins
Servings: 4

Ingredients:
- 1 cup of rice (parboiled or regular)
- 1/4 cup of urad dal (black gram)
- 1/4 cup of chana dal (split chickpeas)
- 1/2 tsp fenugreek seeds
- Salt as needed
- Water (for soaking and grinding)
- Oil or ghee (clarified butter) for cooking

Instructions:
1. Wash the urad dal, chana dal, and rice. 4-6 hrs or overnight Must be spent soaking them in water with the fenugreek seeds.
2. Take out the soaking ingredients from the water, and then blend them into a homogeneous batter, adding water as necessary.
3. Combine the batter well after adding salt. Permit it to ferment for 8–10 hrs or over night.
4. A nonstick or cast-iron skillet Must be heated to medium. To make a thin dosa, pour a ladleful of batter and spread it out in a circular motion.
5. Cook the dosa till the edges are golden brown and crisp by drizzling oil or ghee around them.
6. Warm up and serve with chutney and sambar.

Nutrition (per serving):
Cals: 150 kcal, Carbs: 30g, Protein: 5g, Fat: 1g, Fiber: 2g

101. Southeast Asian Satay Soiree:

Time: 1 hr
Servings: 6

Ingredients:
- 1 lb chicken or beef, thinly split
- 1 cup of coconut milk
- 2 tbsp soy sauce
- 1 tbsp fish sauce
- 1 tbsp curry powder
- 1 tbsp brown sugar
- 1 tsp turmeric powder
- 2 cloves garlic, chop-up
- 1-inch piece of ginger, finely grated
- Wooden skewers (pre-soaked in water)

Instructions:
1. To create the marinade, combine the finely grated ginger, coconut milk, soy sauce, fish sauce, curry powder, brown sugar, and turmeric powder in a bowl.
2. Split beef or chicken Must be added to the marinade, covered, and chilled for at least 30 mins.
3. The pre-soaked wooden skewers are then threaded with the marinated meat.
4. Cook the skewers for 4-5 mins on every side, or up to thoroughly cooked, on a grill or barbeque set to medium-high heat.
5. Serve with sweet chili sauce or peanut sauce for dipping.

Nutrition (per serving - chicken satay):
Cals: 250 kcal, Carbs: 5g, Protein: 25g, Fat: 15g, Fiber: 1g

102. Thai Tom Yum and Pad Thai:

Time: 45 mins

Servings: 4

Ingredients for Tom Yum:

- 4 cups of chicken or vegetable broth
- 1 stalk lemongrass, bruised and slice into pieces
- 3-4 kaffir lime leaves
- 1 inch piece of galangal or ginger, split
- 2 cloves garlic, chop-up
- 2 red chilies, split (adjust to spice preference)
- 1 cup of button mushrooms, split
- 1 cup of cherry tomatoes, halved
- 1/2 cup of coconut milk
- 2 tbsp fish sauce
- 1 tbsp soy sauce
- 1 tbsp lime juice
- Fresh cilantro for garnish

Instructions for Tom Yum:

1. Bring the vegetable or chicken broth to a boil in a pot.
2. Add the following ingredients: chop-up garlic, red chiles, galangal or ginger, lemongrass, and kaffir lime leaves. Cook for ten mins.
3. Add cherry tomatoes and diced mushrooms. Simmer for a further five mins.
4. Add lime juice, fish sauce, soy sauce, and coconut milk after stirring. Continue to simmer for a few mins.
5. Serve hot and garnish with fresh cilantro.

Nutrition (per serving - Tom Yum):
Cals: 120 kcal, Carbs: 8g, Protein: 5g, Fat: 8g, Fiber: 2g

103. Japanese Ramen and Tempura:

Time: 1 hr

Servings: 4

Ingredients for Ramen:

- 8 oz ramen noodles
- 4 cups of chicken or vegetable broth
- 2 tbsp soy sauce
- 2 tbsp miso paste
- 1 tbsp sesame oil
- 1 cup of split mushrooms
- 2 cups of baby spinach
- 2 boiled eggs, halved
- Split green onions and nori seaweed for garnish

Instructions for Ramen:

1. Ramen noodles Must be prepared as directed on the packaging. Drain, then set apart.
2. Bring the vegetable or chicken broth to a simmer in a pot. Miso paste, soy sauce, and sesame oil Must all be added. Stir up to the miso is dissolved.
3. Add baby spinach and chop-up mushrooms to the broth. Up to the vegetables are soft, simmer for a short while.
4. The cooked ramen noodles Must be slice up among serving dishes. Over the noodles, pour the heated broth and vegetables.
5. Add boiled eggs slice in half, green onions slice into slices, and torn nori seaweed on top.

Nutrition (per serving - Ramen):
Cals: 350 kcal, Carbs: 45g, Protein: 15g, Fat: 12g, Fiber: 5g

104. Chinese Hot Pot Adventure:

Time: 1 hr

Servings: 4

Ingredients:

- 6 cups of chicken or vegetable broth
- 2 tbsp soy sauce
- 2 tbsp oyster sauce
- 1 tbsp hoisin sauce
- 1 tbsp sesame oil
- Assorted thinly split meats (e.g., beef, chicken, lamb)
- Assorted seafood (e.g., shrimp, fish balls, squid)
- Assorted vegetables (e.g., bok choy, Napa cabbage, mushrooms)
- Tofu, cubed
- Udon or rice noodles
- Dipping sauces (e.g., sesame sauce, soy sauce with garlic)

1. Instructions:
2. Bring the chicken or vegetable broth to a boil in a big pot. Stir well before adding the hoisin sauce, sesame oil, soy sauce, and oyster sauce.
3. Around the hot pot, place the tofu, noodles, veggies, and shellfish that have been thinly split.
4. Everyone can add their favorite items to the simmering broth to cook when the hot pot is placed in the middle of the table.
5. After they've been cooked, the components can be dipped into the dipping sauces and eaten.

Nutrition (per serving - Hot Pot, estimated):
Cals: Varies depending on ingredients and portion size.

105. Korean Kimchi and BBQ:

Time: 2 hrs (including marinating time)
Servings: 4

Ingredients for Kimchi:

- 1 medium Napa cabbage
- 1/4 cup of sea salt
- 1 tbsp finely grated ginger
- 3 cloves garlic, chop-up
- 2 tbsp fish sauce
- 1 tbsp soy sauce
- 1 tbsp Korean red pepper flakes (gochugaru)
- 1 tbsp sugar
- 4 green onions, split

Instructions for Kimchi:

1. The Napa cabbage Must be slice into bite-sized pieces after being quartered lengthwise.
2. Dissolve sea salt in water in a big basin. For approximately an hr, add the chop-up cabbage and let it sit for it to wilt.
3. Drain the cabbage well after giving it a thorough rinse to eliminate any extra salt.
4. To make the kimchi paste, combine the sugar, fish sauce, soy sauce, Korean red pepper flakes, ginger, and garlic in a separate bowl.
5. Slice the green onions, then stir them into the paste.
6. Make sure the cabbage is evenly coated with the kimchi paste before combining it with the cabbage.
7. In a fresh glass jar, pack the kimchi firmly, pushing it down to take out any air bubbles.
8. Before putting the kimchi in the refrigerator, let it ferment at room temperature for a couple of days with the jar covered.

Nutrition (per serving - Kimchi):
Cals: 30 kcal, Carbs: 7g, Protein: 2g, Fat: 0g, Fiber: 3g

106. Vietnamese Pho and Spring Rolls:

Time: 2 hrs (including broth preparation)
Servings: 4

Ingredients for Pho:

- 8 cups of beef or vegetable broth
- 8 oz rice noodles
- 1 lb thinly split beef (eye round or sirloin)
- 1 onion, split
- 2-inch piece of ginger, split
- 3-4 star anise pods
- 4-5 whole cloves
- 1 cinnamon stick
- 2 tbsp fish sauce
- 1 tbsp sugar
- Fresh bean sprouts, Thai basil, lime wedges, and split chilies for garnish

Instructions for Pho:

1. Split onion and ginger Must be charred in a pot over an open flame or in a dry pan up to they are just beginning to turn black.
2. Add star anise, cloves, and a cinnamon stick to the pot along with beef or veggie stock. Bring to a boil, then reduce the heat and simmer for 30 to 60 mins to let the flavors blend.
3. Return the broth to the pot after straining the solids out. As needed-test the seasoning, add sugar and fish sauce.
4. Rice noodles Must be prepared in accordance with the directions on the box/pkg, then slice up among serving bowls.
5. Place the noodles on top of the thinly split beef.
6. The meat will cook as the hot broth is poured over the noodles and steak after bringing the soup to a boil.
7. Add lime wedges, Thai basil, fresh bean sprouts, and thinly split chilies as garnish. Serve warm.

Nutrition (per serving - Pho, estimated):
Cals: 350 kcal (may vary depending on ingredients and portion size)

107. Mexican Churros and Horchata:

Time: 1 hr
Servings: 4

Ingredients for Churros:

- 1 cup of water
- 2 tbsp sugar
- 1/2 tsp salt
- 2 tbsp vegetable oil
- 1 cup of all-purpose flour
- 2 quarts vegetable oil (for frying)
- 1/4 cup of sugar combined with 1 tsp ground cinnamon (for coating)

Instructions for Churros:

1. Combine water, sugar, salt, and vegetable oil in a pot. Over medium heat, bring to a boil.
2. All-purpose flour is added after the saucepan has been taken off the heat. Up up to a smooth dough forms, stir briskly.
3. 350–375°F (175–190°C) vegetable oil Must be heated in a deep pot or pan.

4. Fill a piping bag with a star-shaped nozzle with the churro dough.
5. Pipe 4-6 inch long churros carefully into the heated oil. Fry them till crispy and golden brown.
6. After removing the churros from the oil, blot any leftover oil on paper towels.
7. Warm churros Must be coated by rolling them in the cinnamon-sugar Mixture.

Nutrition (per serving - Churros, estimated):
Cals: 300 kcal (may vary depending on the size and amount of oil absorbed)

108. Spanish Churros and Chocolate

Time: 45 mins
Servings: 4

Ingredients:
- 1 cup of water
- 2 tbsp sugar
- 1/2 tsp salt
- 2 tbsp vegetable oil
- 1 cup of all-purpose flour
- Vegetable oil for frying
- 1/4 cup of sugar (for coating)
- 1 tsp ground cinnamon (for coating)
- 1 cup of dark chocolate, chop-up
- 1/2 cup of heavy cream

Instructions:
1. Combine water, sugar, salt, and vegetable oil in a pot. up to a boil.
2. Add the flour after removing from the heat. Stir everything up up to a smooth dough forms.
3. For frying, warm up some vegetable oil in a Big pan.
4. The dough Must be put into a piping bag before being piped into the boiling oil.
5. Cook up to golden and crispy, then take from the oil and pat dry with paper towels.
6. To coat the churros, combine sugar and cinnamon in a shlet plate.
7. Warm churros Must be coated by rolling them in the sugar-cinnamon Mixture.
8. Pour the cream over the chop-up chocolate after heating it to almost boiling for the chocolate dip. up to smooth, stir.
9. Serve the chocolate dip alongside the churros.

Nutrition (per serving):
Cals: 380kcal Carbs: 51g Protein: 5g Fat: 18g Saturated Fat: 8g Cholesterol: 30mg Sodium: 240mg Fiber: 2g Sugar: 23g

109. German Black Forest Feast

Time: 1 hr 30 mins
Servings: 8

Ingredients:
- 2 cups of all-purpose flour
- 2 cups of sugar
- 3/4 cup of unsweetened cocoa powder
- 1 1/2 tsp baking powder
- 1 1/2 tsp baking soda
- 1 tsp salt
- 2 Big eggs
- 1 cup of milk
- 1/2 cup of vegetable oil
- 2 tsp vanilla extract
- 1 cup of boiling water
- 2 cups of heavy cream
- 1/4 cup of powdered sugar
- 1 tsp vanilla extract
- 2 cups of cherries, pitted
- 1/2 cup of cherry liqueur (non-compulsory)
- Chocolate shavings for garnish

Instructions:
1. Oven Must be heated to 350°F (175°C). Prepare two 9-inch round cake pans with oil and flour.
2. Combine the flour, sugar, baking soda, salt, baking powder, and cocoa powder in a big bowl.
3. Then, combine the dry ingredients with the milk, oil, eggs, and vanilla essence.
4. Slowly stir in the hot water. It will be a thin batter.
5. A toothpick inserted in the center Must come out clean after baking for 30-35 mins after equally pouring the Mixture into the prepared pans.
6. Whip the heavy cream, sugar, and vanilla extract up to stiff peaks form while the cakes cool.
7. Soak the pitted cherries in cherry liqueur, if preferred.
8. Spread whipped cream over one layer of the cakes after they have completely cooled, then top it with a layer of cherries.
9. After adding the second cake layer, finish off the dessert with whipped cream.
10. Add more cherries and chocolate shavings as a garnish.
11. Before serving, chill.

Nutrition (per serving):
Cals: 580kcal Carbs: 78g Protein: 7g Fat: 29g Saturated Fat:

15g Cholesterol: 120mg Sodium: 500mg Fiber: 4g Sugar: 53g

110. Swiss Chocolate Heaven

Time: 1 hr 30 mins
Servings: 12

Ingredients:

- 1 3/4 cups of all-purpose flour
- 1 1/2 cups of sugar
- 3/4 cup of unsweetened cocoa powder
- 1 1/2 tsp baking powder
- 1 1/2 tsp baking soda
- 1 tsp salt
- 2 Big eggs
- 1 cup of whole milk
- 1/2 cup of vegetable oil
- 2 tsp vanilla extract
- 1 cup of boiling water
- 1 cup of heavy cream
- 1/4 cup of powdered sugar
- 1 tsp vanilla extract
- 1/2 cup of hazelnuts, toasted and chop-up
- Chocolate curls for garnish

Instructions:

1. Oven Must be heated to 350°F (175°C). Prepare two 9-inch round cake pans with oil and flour.
2. Combine the flour, sugar, baking soda, salt, baking powder, and cocoa powder in a big bowl.
3. Then, combine the dry ingredients with the milk, oil, eggs, and vanilla essence.
4. Slowly stir in the hot water. It will be a thin batter.
5. A toothpick inserted in the center Must come out clean after baking for 30-35 mins after equally pouring the Mixture into the prepared pans.
6. Whip the heavy cream, sugar, and vanilla extract up to stiff peaks form while the cakes cool.
7. Spread whipped cream over one layer of the cakes after they have completely cooled, then top with chop-up hazelnuts.
8. After adding the second cake layer, finish off the dessert with whipped cream.
9. Add more hazelnuts and chocolate curls as a garnish.

Nutrition (per serving):
Cals: 420kcal Carbs: 58g Protein: 6g Fat: 20g Saturated Fat: 6g Cholesterol: 55mg Sodium: 350mg Fiber: 4g Sugar: 36g

111. British Sticky Toffee Pudding

Time: 1 hr 15 mins
Servings: 6

Ingredients:

- 1 cup of dates, pitted and chop-up
- 1 tsp baking soda
- 1 cup of boiling water
- 1/4 cup of unsalted butter, melted
- 3/4 cup of granulated sugar
- 2 Big eggs
- 1 1/2 cups of all-purpose flour
- 1 tsp baking powder
- 1/4 tsp salt
- 1 tsp vanilla extract
- 1/2 cup of heavy cream
- 1/2 cup of brown sugar
- 1/4 cup of unsalted butter
- 1/4 cup of heavy cream (for sauce)
- 1 tsp vanilla extract (for sauce)

Instructions:

1. Set the oven's temperature to 350°F (175°C). Grease a baking pan that is 8 inches square.
2. Baking soda and split dates are combined in a bowl. After covering them with hot water, let them stand for ten mins.
3. Melted butter and granulated sugar Must be creamed up to light and fluffy in a separate basin.
4. Add the vanilla essence after adding every egg one at a time.
5. Combine the salt, baking powder, and flour in a separate bowl.
6. Alternate adding the dry ingredients and the date Mixture to the butter-sugar Mixture gradually.
7. When the toothpick is inserted cleanly, bake the batter for 35–40 mins in the preheated baking dish.
8. Brown sugar, butter, and heavy cream Must be warmed in a pot over medium heat while the pudding bakes.
9. Stirring continuously, bring to a boil, then simmer for two mins.
10. After taking the saucepan from the heat, thoroughly whisk in the vanilla essence.
11. When the pudding is done, use a skewer to make holes in it and drizzle some toffee sauce on top. To serve, keep some sauce aside.
12. Serve every slice warm with more toffee sauce sprinkled on top.

Nutrition (per serving):
Cals: 550kcal Carbs: 85g Protein: 6g Fat: 22g Saturated Fat: 14g Cholesterol: 130mg Sodium: 470mg Fiber: 3g Sugar: 59g

112. American Apple Pie Delight

Time: 1 hr 30 mins

Servings: 8

Ingredients:

- 2 pie crusts (store-bought or homemade)
- 6 cups of peel off and split apples (Granny Smith or your choice)
- 3/4 cup of granulated sugar
- 2 tbsp all-purpose flour
- 1 tsp ground cinnamon
- 1/4 tsp ground nutmeg
- 1 tbsp lemon juice
- 2 tbsp unsalted butter, slice into mini pieces
- 1 egg, beaten (for egg wash)
- 1 tbsp granulated sugar (for sprinkling)

Instructions:

1. Set the oven's temperature to 375°F (190°C). In a 9-inch pie plate, put one pie crust.
2. Split apples, sugar, flour, cinnamon, nutmeg, and lemon juice Must all be combined in a big basin.
3. Fill the pie crust in the dish with the apple Mixture, and then sprinkle some butter on top.
4. The second pie crust Must be used to cover the pie, closing the edges and creating ventilation slots in the top.
5. Sprinkle sugar over the top crust after brushing it with the beaten egg.
6. Bake for roughly 50 mins, or up to the apples are soft and the crust is brown.
7. Before serving, let the pie cool for at least 30 mins.

Nutrition (per serving):
Cals: 380kcal Carbs: 58g Protein: 4g Fat: 15g Saturated Fat: 6g Cholesterol: 40mg Sodium: 230mg Fiber: 3g Sugar: 34g

113. Canadian Maple Pecan Pleasure

Time: 1 hr

Servings: 12

Ingredients:

- 1 9-inch pie crust (store-bought or homemade)
- 1 1/2 cups of pecans, chop-up
- 3/4 cup of pure maple syrup
- 1/2 cup of packed brown sugar
- 1/4 cup of unsalted butter, dilute
- 3 Big eggs, lightly beaten
- 1 tsp vanilla extract
- 1/4 tsp salt

Instructions:

1. Set the oven's temperature to 350°F (175°C). In a 9-inch pie plate, put the pie crust.
2. Over the entire bottom of the pie crust, distribute the chop-up pecans evenly.
3. Maple syrup, brown sugar, dilute butter, eggs, vanilla extract, and salt Must all be thoroughly blended in a bowl.
4. Over the pecans in the pie shell, pour the Mixture.
5. Bake the filling for 45 to 50 mins, or up to it has set.
6. Before serving, let the pie cool fully.

Nutrition (per serving):
Cals: 350kcal Carbs: 39g Protein: 4g Fat: 21g Saturated Fat: 6g Cholesterol: 70mg Sodium: 180mg Fiber: 2g Sugar: 29g

114. Australian Lamington Love

Time: 1 hr

Servings: 12

Ingredients:

- 1 3/4 cups of all-purpose flour
- 2 tsp baking powder
- 1/2 tsp salt
- 1/2 cup of unsalted butter, melted
- 3/4 cup of granulated sugar
- 2 Big eggs
- 1 tsp vanilla extract
- 1/2 cup of whole milk
- 3 cups of desiccated coconut
- 2 cups of powdered sugar
- 1/3 cup of unsweetened cocoa powder
- 1/2 cup of boiling water
- 2 tbsp unsalted butter, dilute

Instructions:

1. Set the oven's temperature to 350°F (175°C). A 9x13-inch baking dish Must be greased and floured.
2. Combine the salt, baking powder, and flour in a bowl.
3. Melted butter and granulated sugar Must be creamed up to light and fluffy in a separate basin.
4. Add the vanilla essence after adding every egg one at a time.

5. Alternate adding milk and dry ingredients to the butter-sugar Mixture gradually.
6. A toothpick inserted Must come out clean after baking for 25 to 30 mins after uniformly spreading the batter into the prepared baking dish.
7. Slice the cake into squares after leting it to cool fully.
8. Place the desiccated coconut in a mini bowl.
9. Powdered sugar, unsweetened cocoa powder, hot water, and dilute butter Must all be combined in a different basin and whisked up to smooth.
10. Coat all sides of every cake square by dipping it into the chocolate Mixture.
11. Desiccated coconut Must be completely rolled over the chocolate-covered cake.
12. To let the coated Lamingtons set, place them on a wire rack.

Nutrition (per serving):
Cals: 310kcal Carbs: 45g Protein: 3g Fat: 15g Saturated Fat: 11g Cholesterol: 55mg Sodium: 180mg Fiber: 2g Sugar: 31g

115. Brazilian Brigadeiro Bliss

Time: 30 mins
Servings: 20

Ingredients:

- 1 can (14 oz) sweetened condensed milk
- 2 tbsp unsweetened cocoa powder
- 2 tbsp unsalted butter
- Chocolate sprinkles

Instructions:

1. Butter, sweetened condensed milk, and cocoa powder are combined in a non-stick pan.
2. Cook the Mixture, stirring often with a wooden spoon over low heat, up to it thickens and begins to peel away from the pan's bottom (approximately 10 to 15 mins).
3. The Mixture Must be taken off the fire and leted to cool to room temperature.
4. To avoid sticking, grease your hands with butter or oil. Take mini amounts of the Mixture and form them into balls with a diameter of about 1 inch.
5. Every ball Must be completely covered in chocolate sprinkles.
6. Put the Brigadeiros on a platter or in tiny paper cups of.

Nutrition (per serving, one Brigadeiro):
Cals: 90kcal Carbs: 12g Protein: 1g Fat: 4g Saturated Fat: 3g Cholesterol: 10mg Sodium: 30mg Fiber: 0g Sugar: 11g

116. Argentinean Alfajores Amor

Time: 1 hr 30 mins
Servings: 20

Ingredients:

- 1 3/4 cups of all-purpose flour
- 1 cup of cornstarch
- 1/2 tsp baking powder
- 1/4 tsp baking soda
- 1/2 tsp salt
- 3/4 cup of unsalted butter, melted
- 1 cup of powdered sugar
- 3 Big egg yolks
- 1 tsp vanilla extract
- Dulce de leche (caramel spread)
- Shredded coconut, for rolling

Instructions:

1. Combine the flour, cornstarch, salt, baking soda, and baking powder in a bowl.
2. Cream melted butter and powdered sugar in a another bowl up to frothy.
3. Add the vanilla extract after adding every egg yolk one at a time.
4. Combine up to just combined after gradually incorporating the dry ingredients into the butter-sugar Mixture.
5. Refrigerate the dough for at least 30 mins after forming it into a disc, covering it with plastic wrap.
6. A baking sheet Must be lined with parchment paper and the oven Must be preheated to 350°F (175°C).
7. On a floured surface, roll out the cold dough to a thickness of roughly 1/4 inch.
8. Using a cookie sliceter, make mini circles and arrange them on the baking sheet that has been prepared.
9. Up to the edges are just beginning to turn golden, bake for 10 to 12 mins.
10. The Alfajores Must be put together after the cookies have totally cooled.
11. Sandwich a cookie with another cookie after generously spreading dulce de leche on the bottom side of one of the cookies.
12. To coat the edges of the sandwiched cookies, roll them in coconut shreds.
13. The remaining cookies Must be repeated.

Nutrition (per serving, one Alfajor):
Cals: 150kcal Carbs: 20g Protein: 2g Fat: 7g Saturated Fat: 4g Cholesterol: 40mg Sodium: 60mg Fiber: 0g Sugar: 10g

117. Turkish Baklava and Tea

Time: 2 hrs

Servings: 16 pieces

Ingredients:

- 1 box/pkg (16 oz) phyllo dough
- 1 cup of unsalted butter, dilute
- 2 cups of chop-up walnuts or pistachios
- 1 tsp ground cinnamon
- 1 cup of granulated sugar
- 1 cup of water
- 1/2 cup of honey
- 1 tsp lemon juice
- Turkish tea leaves
- Water
- Sugar

Instructions:

1. Set the oven's temperature to 350°F (175°C).
2. Combine the ground cinnamon and chop-up nuts in a basin. Place aside.
3. A baking dish Must be butter-greased.
4. Brush dilute butter over a sheet of phyllo dough before placing it in the baking dish.
5. As you stack and butter every sheet, repeat the process up to you have 8 to 10 layers.
6. The nut Mixture Must be spread thinly over the phyllo dough.
7. Once all the nuts have been utilized, layer phyllo dough and nuts one more time, finishing with a top layer of phyllo dough (approximately 8–10 layers total).
8. Slice the baklava into diamond or square shapes using a sharp knife.
9. Baklava Must be baked in the preheated oven for 45 to 50 mins, or up to golden brown.
10. Make the syrup while the baklava is baking. Lemon juice, water, honey, and sugar are all combined in a pan. Bring to a boil, then reduce the heat and simmer for 10 mins, or up to it slightly thickens.
11. After taking the baklava out of the oven, immediately drizzle the hot syrup on top.
12. Before serving, let the baklava totally cool.
13. Turkish tea is made by heating water in a teapot, adding Turkish tea leaves, and leting the Mixture to steep for several mins. Serve sweetened.

NUTRITION INFO *(per serving):*
Cals: 320 kcal, Fat: 19g, Carbs: 35g, Protein: 5g

118. Greek Baklava and Ouzo

Time: 2 hrs

Servings: 16 pieces

Ingredients:

- 1 box/pkg (16 oz) phyllo dough
- 1 cup of unsalted butter, dilute
- 2 cups of chop-up walnuts or almonds
- 1 tsp ground cinnamon
- 1 cup of granulated sugar
- 1 cup of water
- 1/2 cup of honey
- 1 tsp lemon juice
- Ouzo (Greek anise-flavored liqueur)

Instructions:

1. Follow the same directions (steps 1–8) as for the Turkish Baklava and Tea recipe.
2. Pour Ouzo over the baklava after it has finished baking and while it is still hot to give it a Greek flair.
3. The syrup is made in the same manner as in the Turkish Baklava recipe, except that Ouzo is used in place of water for flavor.

NUTRITION INFO *(per serving):*
Cals: 330 kcal, Fat: 20g, Carbs: 35g, Protein: 5g

119. Moroccan Mint Tea Magic

Time: 15 mins

Servings: 4

Ingredients:

- 4 cups of water
- 4 tsp loose green tea leaves
- 4 tbsp fresh mint leaves
- 4 tsp sugar (adjust as needed)

Instructions:

1. Bring water to a boil in a teapot.
2. Add some green tea leaves and brew for two to three mins.
3. Add sugar and new mint leaves. Stir thoroughly.
4. Tea Must be strained and served hot in glasses.

NUTRITION INFO *(per serving):*
Cals: 15 kcal, Fat: 0g, Carbs: 4g, Protein: 0g

120. Japanese Matcha and Mochi

Time: 1 hr

Servings: 6

Ingredients:

- 2 tsp matcha powder
- 2 cups of hot water (not boiling)
- 1 cup of glutinous rice flour (mochiko)
- 1/4 cup of sugar
- Cornstarch (for dusting)
- Red bean paste (anko) or ice cream (non-compulsory, for filling)

Instructions:

1. Matcha powder and hot water Must be blended together in a bowl.
2. Combine sugar and glutinous rice flour in a different bowl.
3. Pour the matcha Mixture into the flour Mixture gradually while stirring; continue up to a dough forms.
4. The dough must be smooth and no longer sticky after being kneaded.
5. The dough Must be rolled out to a thickness of about 1/4 inch on a clean surface dusted with cornstarch.
6. If using, fill every mini square of dough that has been slice into squares with a dab of red bean paste or ice cream.
7. To seal the filling inside the mochi, pinch the edges.
8. Serve right away or chill for a firmer texture.

NUTRITION INFO (per serving):
Cals: 160 kcal, Fat: 0g, Carbs: 39g, Protein: 2g

121. Indian Mango Lassi Love

Time: 10 mins

Servings: 2

Ingredients:

- 1 Big ripe mango, peel off and pitted
- 1 cup of plain yogurt
- 1/2 cup of milk
- 2 tbsp sugar (adjust as needed)
- 1/4 tsp ground cardamom (non-compulsory)
- Ice cubes

Instructions:

1. Mango, yogurt, milk, sugar, and cardamom (if using) Must all be combined in a blender.
2. Blend till creamy and smooth.
3. Once you've added ice cubes, blend the lassi again up to it's cooled and foamy.
4. Pour into glasses and start serving right away.

NUTRITION INFO (per serving):
Cals: 220 kcal, Fat: 3g, Carbs: 42g, Protein: 7g

122. Thai Mango Sticky Rice

Time: 1 hr

Servings: 4

Ingredients:

- 1 cup of glutinous rice
- 1 1/2 cups of coconut milk
- 1/4 cup of sugar
- 1/2 tsp salt
- 2 ripe mangoes, split
- Sesame seeds (non-compulsory, for garnish)

Instructions:

1. Glutinous rice Must be rinsed in clean water.
2. Combine the rice, coconut milk, sugar, and salt in a saucepan.
3. Stirring occasionally, cook the rice over low heat up to it absorbs the coconut milk and becomes sticky and cooked through.
4. Take it off the fire and give it a min to cool.
5. Serve the sticky rice with the mango slices on top, and if wanted, add sesame seeds as a garnish.

NUTRITION INFO (per serving):
Cals: 370 kcal, Fat: 17g, Carbs: 57g, Protein: 3g

123. Caribbean Rum Cake Delight

Time: 1 hr 30 mins

Servings: 10

Ingredients:

- 1 1/2 cups of all-purpose flour
- 2 tsp baking powder
- 1/2 tsp salt
- 1 cup of unsalted butter, melted
- 1 cup of granulated sugar
- 4 Big eggs
- 1/4 cup of dark rum
- 1 tsp vanilla extract
- 1/2 cup of milk
- 1/2 cup of chop-up nuts (pecans or walnuts)
- 1/2 cup of raisins
- 1/4 cup of powdered sugar (for dusting)

Instructions:
1. Set the oven's temperature to 350°F (175°C). Clean, flour, and grease a bundt pan.
2. Combine the salt, baking powder, and flour in a bowl. Place aside.
3. Butter and sugar Must be creamed till light and fluffy in a separate basin.
4. One at a time, beat well after every addition of an egg.
5. Add the vanilla and rum after that.
6. Alternately add milk while gradually incorporating the dry components into the wet ingredients. Just combine after combining.
7. Combine in the raisins and chop-up nuts.
8. Spread the batter evenly after adding it to the bundt pan that has been prepared.
9. 50 to 60 mins of baking time, or up to a toothpick inserted in the center of the cake comes out clean.
10. The cake Must cool in the pan for ten mins before being moved to a wire rack to finish cooling.
11. Before serving, sprinkle powdered sugar over the cooled cake.

NUTRITION INFO (per serving):
Cals: 440 kcal, Fat: 22g, Carbs: 54g, Protein: 6g

124. Hawaiian Pineapple Paradise

Time: 20 mins
Servings: 4

Ingredients:
- 1 ripe pineapple, peel off, cored, and slice into chunks
- 1 cup of coconut milk
- 1 tbsp honey (adjust as needed)
- Ice cubes
- Maraschino cherries and pineapple wedges (for garnish)

Instructions:
1. Pineapple chunks, coconut milk, and honey Must all be blended together.
2. Blend till creamy and smooth.
3. one you've added the ice cubes, combine the liquid one more to chill it.
4. Pour into cups of and top with pineapple wedges and maraschino cherries as decoration.

NUTRITION INFO (per serving):
Cals: 180 kcal, Fat: 9g, Carbs: 27g, Protein: 2g

125. Swiss Rösti and Rosti

Time: 30 mins
Servings: 4

Ingredients:
- 4 Big potatoes, peel off and finely grated
- 2 tbsp butter
- Salt and pepper as needed

Instructions:
1. Finely grated potatoes Must be placed in a clean kitchen towel and dried completely.
2. Butter Must be dilute over medium heat in a nonstick pan.
3. Spread the shredded potatoes out equally in the pan before adding them.
4. Add salt and pepper as needed.
5. Cook the rösti for 15 to 20 mins, sometimes flipping, or up to both sides are crispy and golden.
6. Serve hot with a variety of toppings, such as cheese, eggs, or smoked salmon, or as a side dish.

NUTRITION INFO (per serving):
Cals: 220 kcal, Fat: 8g, Carbs: 32g, Protein: 4g

126. Italian Panettone Perfection

Time: 3 hrs
Servings: 12

Ingredients:
- 4 cups of all-purpose flour
- 1/2 cup of sugar
- 1 packet active dry yeast (about 2 1/4 tsp)
- 1/2 cup of warm milk
- 4 Big eggs
- 1/2 cup of unsalted butter, melted
- 1 tsp vanilla extract
- 1/2 cup of candied fruit (citron, orange peel, lemon peel)
- 1/4 cup of raisins
- 1/4 cup of chop-up almonds
- Zest of 1 lemon
- Zest of 1 orange
- Pinch of salt

Instructions:
1. Dissolve the yeast in the warm milk in a mini bowl, and then wait up to it foams up, about 5 mins.
2. Combine the flour, sugar, and a mini amount of salt in a sizable combining basin.

3. The yeast Mixture, eggs, melted butter, and vanilla extract Must all be added to the center well.
4. The ingredients Must be combined to form a smooth dough.
5. Orange and lemon zests, raisins, candied fruit, and chop-up almonds can all be added. Knead the dough up to every ingredient is distributed equally.
6. The dough Must rise in a warm location for around 2 hrs, or up to it doubles in size. Cover the bowl with a clean cloth.
7. Set the oven's temperature to 350°F (175°C).
8. After punching down the dough, place it in a panettone mold or a tall, round cake pan that has been lined with parchment paper.
9. Let the dough to rise once more for 30 mins.
10. When the top of the panettone is golden brown and a toothpick put in the center of the cake comes out clean, bake it in the preheated oven for 40 to 45 mins.
11. Before serving, let the panettone cool fully.

NUTRITION INFO (per serving):
Cals: 330 kcal, Fat: 13g, Carbs: 47g, Protein: 7g

127. French Croissant:

Time: 12-14 hrs (including resting and proofing time)
Servings: 12 croissants

Ingredients:
- 500g all-purpose flour
- 10g salt
- 80g granulated sugar
- 10g instant yeast
- 300ml cold milk
- 100ml cold water
- 250g unsalted butter, cold but pliable
- 1 egg (for egg wash)

Instructions:
1. Combine the flour, salt, sugar, yeast, cold milk, and cold water in a Big combining basin. A smooth dough Must develop after combining.
2. The dough Must rest in the refrigerator for about an hr, covered with plastic wrap.
3. Making sure the butter is neither too soft nor too hard, roll out the cold but malleable butter into a square.
4. On a lightly dusted surface, roll out the dough into a sizable square.
5. Put the rolled butter in the middle of the dough and seal it fully by folding the dough's corners over the butter.
6. The dough-butter combination Must be rolled out into a Big rectangle and folded into thirds like a letter.
7. Refrigerate the dough for an hr after wrapping it in plastic wrap.
8. Step 6 of the folding procedure Must be repeated twice more, with the dough being chilled in between folds.
9. Triangles can be made from the dough by rolling it out to a thickness of about 1/4 inch.
10. To create the croissant shape, tightly roll every triangle, working your way up from the base to the tip.
11. Placing the formed croissants on a parchment-lined baking sheet.
12. They Must double in size after 2-3 hrs of proofing at room temperature under a moist cloth.
13. Set the oven to 200 °C (or 390 °F).
14. Egg wash, made by combining 1 beaten egg with a little water, Must be applied to the croissants.
15. Bake for 15 to 20 mins, or up to golden brown, in a preheated oven.
16. Warm up the dish and serve with café au lait.

128. Café au Lait:

Time: 5 mins
Servings: 1 serving

Ingredients:
- 1 cup of freshly brewed strong coffee
- 1 cup of hot milk
- Sugar (non-compulsory)

Instructions:
1. Make a pot of robust coffee using your favourite technique.
2. In a microwave or saucepan, heat the milk up to it is warm but not boiling.
3. Use a milk frother or whisk to whip up a creamy, fluffy foam from the boiling milk.
4. Coffee Must be poured hot into a big cup of or bowl.
5. Over the coffee, pour the frothed milk.
6. Taste and add sugar if desired.
7. Your Café au Lait is ready to be served with the French Croissants after a little stir.
8. Sangria and flan from Spain

129. Spanish Flan:

Time: 1 hr 30 mins (including baking and cooling time)
Servings: 6-8

Ingredients:

- 1 cup of granulated sugar
- 5 Big eggs
- 1 can (14 oz) sweetened condensed milk
- 1 can (12 oz) evaporated milk
- 1 tsp vanilla extract

Instructions:

1. Set your oven's temperature to 180 °C (350 °F).
2. Granulated sugar Must be dilute in a mini pot over medium heat, stirring occasionally, up to it turns golden caramel.
3. Pour the caramel evenly on the bottom of a flan mold or a 9-inch circular baking dish.
4. Whisk the eggs in a sizable combining bowl up to they are well-beaten.
5. The eggs Must be thoroughly combined with the evaporated milk, sweetened condensed milk, and vanilla essence.
6. Over the caramel in the flan form, pour the Mixture.
7. In order to create a water bath for even baking, place the flan mold inside a bigger baking dish or roasting pan.
8. Transfer the arrangement carefully to the preheated oven, and bake for 45–50 mins, or up to the flan is set but the center is still slightly jiggly.
9. The flan mold Must be taken out of the water bath and let to cool to room temperature.
10. When the flan has cooled, place it in the refrigerator for at least two hrs or overnight for best results.
11. To take out the flan from the mold and serve, carefully run a knife over the flan's edges. The caramel sauce will flow over the flan when you invert the form onto a serving plate.

130. Sangria:

Time: 10 mins (+ chilling time)
Servings: 4-6

Ingredients:

- 1 bottle (750 ml) red wine (Spanish Rioja or any fruity red wine)
- 1/4 cup of brandy
- 1/4 cup of orange liqueur (such as Cointreau or Triple Sec)
- 1 cup of orange juice
- 1/2 cup of apple or pear juice
- 1 orange, split
- 1 apple, split
- 1 lemon, split
- 1 lime, split
- 1 cinnamon stick
- 1-2 tbsp sugar (adjust as needed)
- Ice cubes
- Soda water or lemon-lime soda (non-compulsory)

Instructions:

1. Red wine, brandy, orange liqueur, orange juice, and apple or pear juice Must all be combined in a sizable pitcher.
2. The cinnamon stick is next added, along with the split fruits.
3. As desired, add sugar to the sangria.
4. Let the flavors to merge together by chilling the sangria in the refrigerator for at least two hrs.
5. Include ice cubes in the pitcher when you're ready to serve.
6. Just before serving, top it off with soda water or lemon-lime soda if you want a lighter, effervescent sangria.
7. Pour the fruity Spanish Flan and Sangria into glasses, making sure that every serving includes some fruit slices, and sip on them to cool up.

131. Portuguese Pastel de Nata:

Time: 2 hrs (including chilling time)
Servings: 12 pastéis de nata

Ingredients:

- 1 sheet puff pastry (store-bought or homemade)
- 2 cups of whole milk
- 1 cinnamon stick
- Zest of 1 lemon or orange
- 6 Big egg yolks
- 1/2 cup of granulated sugar
- 2 tbsp all-purpose flour
- 1 tsp vanilla extract
- Powdered sugar and ground cinnamon for dusting

Instructions:

1. Roll out the puff pastry into a thin sheet on a board dusted with flour.
2. The sheet Must be slice up into 12 equal squares. Gently press every square into a muffin tin cup of to form little pastry cups of. Make sure every cup of's base and sides are completely covered with

pastry. While you make the filling, chill the muffin tray in the refrigerator.
3. The milk, cinnamon stick, and lemon or orange zest Must all be heated in a saucepan over medium heat up to the milk begins to simmer. After removing from the heat, steep for 10 mins.
4. Egg yolks, sugar, flour, and vanilla extract Must be thoroughly blended and creamy in a combining dish.
5. After removing the cinnamon stick and citrus zest, slowly add the milk into the egg Mixture while whisking constantly to prevent curdling.
6. Return the Mixture to the pan and simmer it over low heat, continually stirring, up to it thickens and takes on the consistency of custard.
7. Once the custard has reveryed room temperature, take out the saucepan from the heat.
8. Turn on the oven to 220 °C (425 °F).
9. The cooled custard Must be poured into every cold pastry cup of up to it is about 3/4 filled.
10. The pastéis de nata Must be baked for 15 to 20 mins in a preheated oven, or up to the pastry is golden brown and the custard has black patches on top.
11. Once the pastéis de nata have cooled slightly, take out the muffin pan from the oven.
12. They Must be carefully taken out of the muffin pan and put on a wire rack to cool entirely.
13. Before serving, sprinkle some powdered sugar and ground cinnamon over the pastéis de nata.
14. Eton Mess Melody in Britain

132. Eton Mess Melody:

Time: 20 mins
Servings: 4

Ingredients:
- 4 meringue nests (store-bought or homemade)
- 2 cups of fresh strawberries, hulled and chop-up
- 1 cup of heavy cream
- 1 tbsp powdered sugar
- 1 tsp vanilla extract
- Fresh mint leaves for garnish (non-compulsory)

Instructions:
1. Slice the meringue nests into minier pieces and place them in a combining bowl.
2. Avoid overly crushing the strawberries as you delicately fold in the slice strawberries together with the broken meringue bits.
3. Whip the heavy cream, sugar, and vanilla extract in a separate dish up to stiff peaks form.
4. To achieve a light and fluffy texture, carefully incorporate the whipped cream into the meringue and strawberry Mixture.
5. Pour the Eton Mess Melody into bowls or serving glasses.
6. If preferred, add a few fresh mint leaves as a garnish.
7. Enjoy the delicious British Eton Mess Melody right away.

133. Mexican Tres Leches Treat:

Time: 1 hr 30 mins (including chilling time)
Servings: 12

Ingredients:
- 1 cup of all-purpose flour
- 1 1/2 tsp baking powder
- 1/4 tsp salt
- 5 Big eggs, separated
- 1 cup of granulated sugar, slice up
- 1/3 cup of whole milk
- 1 tsp vanilla extract
- 1 can (12 oz) evaporated milk
- 1 can (14 oz) sweetened condensed milk
- 1 cup of heavy cream
- Ground cinnamon or cocoa powder for garnish (non-compulsory)

Instructions:
1. Set your oven's temperature to 180 °C (350 °F). A 9x13-inch baking pan Must be greased.
2. Combine the flour, baking soda, and salt in a combining basin.
3. Beat the egg yolks with 3/4 cup of granulated sugar in a another bowl up to they are light and fluffy.
4. Combine well after adding the milk and vanilla essence to the egg yolk Mixture.
5. Combine just till combined after gradually incorporating the dry ingredients into the wet ones.
6. The egg whites Must be beaten up to soft peaks form in a different clean basin. Add the last 1/4 cup of granulated sugar gradually while combining the Mixture up to stiff peaks form.
7. Till they are completely combined, gently fold the whipped egg whites into the batter.
8. Spread the batter evenly after adding it to the baking dish that has been prepared.

9. Bake for about 25 to 30 mins in the preheated oven, or up to a toothpick inserted in the center comes out clean.
10. Pierce the cake all over with a fork or skewer while it's still warm.
11. Combine the evaporated milk, sweetened condensed milk, and heavy cream in a another bowl.
12. Make sure the milk Mixture gets within the cake's holes by evenly pouring it over the warm cake.
13. To help the cake absorb the milk Mixture, place the Tres Leches Treat in the refrigerator for at least an hr (or overnight).
14. Dust the top, if preferred, with cocoa powder or ground cinnamon before serving.
15. Enjoy this decadent Mexican Tres Leches Treat while it's still moist!

134. Israeli Malabi Marvel:

Time: 20 mins (+ chilling time)
Servings: 4-6

Ingredients:
- 1/2 cup of cornstarch
- 1/2 cup of water
- 4 cups of whole milk
- 1/2 cup of granulated sugar
- 1 tsp rosewater or orange blossom water (non-compulsory)
- Ground pistachios, shredded coconut, or rose petals for garnish (non-compulsory)

Instructions:
1. To make a smooth paste, combine the cornstarch and water in a mini basin. Leave it alone.
2. Whole milk and sugar Must be heated in a pot over medium heat while being regularly stirred up to it simmers.
3. Pour the cornstarch Mixture into the milk that is simmering while continuously stirring.
4. Stir continuously up to the Mixture thickens and bubbles.
5. If using, blend the Mixture with the rosewater or orange blossom water before adding it.
6. The Malabi Must gradually cool after the saucepan has been taken from the heat.
7. Pour the Malabi into mini bowls or serving glasses.
8. To set, wrap the glasses in plastic wrap and place them in the refrigerator for at least two hrs.
9. If you like, decorate the Malabi before serving with lightly chop-up pistachios, shredded coconut, or rose petals.
10. Enjoy some creamy, flavorful Israeli Malabi Marvel!

135. South African Milk Tart:

Time: 1 hr 30 mins (including chilling time)
Servings: 8

Ingredients: For the crust:
- 1 1/2 cups of all-purpose flour
- 1/2 cup of unsalted butter, cold and cubed
- 1/4 cup of granulated sugar
- 1 Big egg yolk
- 1 tbsp ice water (if needed)
- For the filling:
- 4 cups of whole milk
- 1 cinnamon stick
- 1 tsp vanilla extract
- 1/2 cup of granulated sugar
- 4 Big eggs
- 1/4 cup of cornstarch
- Ground cinnamon for dusting

Instructions: For the crust:
1. Pulse the flour, cold cubed butter, and sugar in a mixer up to the Mixture resembles breadcrumbs.
2. When the dough begins to come together, add the egg yolk and pulse once more. One tbsp at a time, if necessary, add ice water up to the dough comes together into a ball.
3. The dough Must be formed into a disk, covered with plastic wrap, and chilled for at least 30 mins.
4. Set your oven's temperature to 180 °C (350 °F).
5. Roll out the cold dough to fit a 9-inch tart pan on a surface dusted with flour.
6. Trim any extra dough from the edges before gently pressing the pastry into the tart pan.
7. Once the oven is warmed, prick the bottom of the crust with a fork and bake for about 15-20 mins, or up to golden brown. Set apart for cooling.
8. For the filling, warm the whole milk and cinnamon stick in a skillet over medium heat up to the Mixture just begins to simmer. After removing from the heat, steep for 10 mins. Next, take the cinnamon stick out.
9. Stir the sugar, eggs, and cornstarch together thoroughly in a combining bowl.
10. Pour the warm milk into the egg Mixture

gradually while whisking constantly to avoid curdling.
11. Reintroduce the Mixture to the pan, and cook it over low heat, continually stirring, up to it takes on the consistency of custard.
12. Add the vanilla extract after turning off the heat in the saucepan.
13. Spread the custard contents evenly throughout the cooled tart crust.
14. For decoration, sprinkling ground cinnamon over the tart's top.
15. The Milk Tart needs to be chilled for at least an hr (or overnight) to set.
16. For a delicious treat, slice and serve the South African Milk Tart!

136. Indian Kulfi:

Time: 40 mins (+ freezing time)
Servings: 6-8

Ingredients:

- 4 cups of whole milk
- 1/2 cup of sweetened condensed milk
- 1/4 cup of powdered milk (milk powder)
- 1/4 cup of chop-up nuts (almonds, pistachios, cashews)
- 1/4 tsp cardamom powder
- A pinch of saffron strands (non-compulsory)
- Kulfi molds or popsicle molds

Instructions:

1. Bring the whole milk to a boil in a big, heavy-bottomed pot over medium heat. To keep the milk from sticking to the pan's bottom, stir the Mixture occasionally.
2. Reduce the heat, stir regularly, and let the milk simmer up to it is roughly half its original volume. This could take 20 to 25 mins.
3. The simmering milk Must now have the sweetened condensed milk and powdered milk added. After thoroughly combining, cook for a further 5 mins.
4. To the Mixture, add the chop-up almonds, cardamom, and saffron threads (if using). Combine thoroughly.
5. Turn off the heat and let the Mixture to cool to room temperature.
6. Pour the kulfi Mixture into popsicle or kulfi molds after it has cooled.
7. Popsicle sticks Must be placed inside every kulfi before covering the molds with foil or plastic wrap.

8. Let the kulfi set for at least six hrs, ideally overnight, with the molds in the freezer.
9. On a hot day, indulge in some creamy, luscious Indian kulfi!

137. Indian Falooda:

Time: 20 mins (+ chilling time)
Servings: 2

Ingredients:

- 1/4 cup of falooda sev or vermicelli noodles
- 2 cups of whole milk
- 2 tbsp rose syrup
- 1 tbsp sweet basil seeds (sabja seeds)
- 1/4 cup of chop-up combined fruits (strawberries, bananas, mangoes)
- 1 scoop of vanilla ice cream (non-compulsory)
- Chop-up nuts (pistachios, almonds) for garnish
- Rose petals for garnish (non-compulsory)

Instructions:

1. Follow the directions on the box/pkg while preparing the falooda sev or vermicelli noodles.
2. After being cooked, run cold water over the noodles and set them aside.
3. The sweet basil seeds Must be soaked in water in a mini basin for about 10 mins to cause swelling.
4. A tbsp of rose syrup, a spoonful of soaked basil seeds, a layer of cooked falooda sev, and a few pieces of chop-up combined fruits Must be layered in the order listed above in a glass or dish.
5. To fill the glass or bowl, pour cool milk over the layered ingredients.
6. If preferred, add a dollop of vanilla ice cream on top.
7. Rose petals and chop-up nuts make a lovely garnish.
8. Enjoy the delicious and refreshing Indian Falooda!

138. Korean Bingsu Bliss:

Time: 20 mins (+ chilling time)
Servings: 2

Ingredients:

- 2 cups of shaved ice (you can use an ice shaver or a mixer)
- 1/4 cup of sweetened condensed milk

- Assorted toppings (split fresh fruits, red bean paste, rice cakes, cereal, or anything you like)
- 1 scoop of vanilla ice cream (non-compulsory)

Instructions:
1. Use a mixer or an ice shaver to make the shaved ice. Ice Must resemble snow in texture.
2. Shaved ice Must be slice up among serving glasses or bowls.
3. Pour sweetened condensed milk on top of the ice shavings.
4. Add your preferred assortment of toppings, such as cereal, rice cakes, red bean paste, or slices of fresh fruit.
5. If you'd like, add a dollop of vanilla ice cream to the bingsu for more creaminess and taste.
6. Enjoy the delicious and refreshing Korean Bingsu Bliss!

139. Turkish Dondurma Delight:

Time: 30 mins (+ chilling time)
Servings: 4

Ingredients:
- 2 cups of whole milk
- 1 cup of heavy cream
- 3/4 cup of granulated sugar
- 2 tbsp cornstarch
- 1 tbsp salep powder (or substitute with cornstarch)
- 1/4 tsp mastic gum (non-compulsory, for a traditional flavor)
- 1 tsp rosewater or orange blossom water (non-compulsory)
- Chop-up pistachios or hazelnuts for garnish

Instructions:
1. Over medium heat, stir the whole milk, heavy cream, and granulated sugar together in a saucepan. Stir the sugar up to it melts.
2. To make a smooth paste, combine the cornstarch, salep powder, and/or a suitable replacement in a mini bowl with a little water.
3. When the Mixture starts to thicken, add the cornstarch Mixture to the pan and stir continuously over medium heat.
4. If used, add the mastic gum and stir up to it melts and is thoroughly incorporated.
5. Turn off the heat and let the dondurma Mixture to cool slightly.
6. If using, blend the Mixture with rosewater or orange blossom water.
7. Fill a shlet, freezer-safe container with the dondurma Mixture.
8. Once the dondurma has set, at least four hrs Must pass in the freezer with the container covered.
9. Let the dondurma to soften a little bit before serving by leting it to sit at room temperature for a while.
10. Turkish Dondurma Delight Must be served in bowls or cones with chop-up pistachios or hazelnuts on top.

140. Greek Loukoumades Love

Time: 1 hr
Servings: 4-6

Ingredients:
- 1 cup of all-purpose flour
- 1 tsp dry yeast
- 1/4 tsp salt
- 1 cup of warm water
- Vegetable oil for frying
- Honey, chop-up nuts, and cinnamon for topping

Instructions:
1. Combine flour, yeast, and salt in a combining basin. As you whisk, gradually add warm water up to the batter is smooth. For 30 mins, the bowl Must be covered to let for rising.
2. Vegetable oil Must be heated over medium heat in a Big saucepan. Into the hot oil, drop spoonfuls of the batter, and cook up to golden and puffy. Take out, then dry off with paper towels.
3. Sprinkle cinnamon and chop-up nuts on top of the loukoumades after drizzling honey over them. Serve hot.

Nutrition (per serving): Note:
Nutritional values may vary based on specific ingredients used.

141. Vietnamese Egg Coffee Euphoria

Time: 15 mins
Servings: 1

Ingredients:
- 2 tbsp sweetened condensed milk
- 1 tbsp robusta coffee powder
- 1 egg yolk
- 1 tsp sugar
- 1/4 cup of boiling water

Instructions:
1. Add the sweetened condensed milk to a glass.
2. The egg yolk and sugar Must be combined in a another bowl and whisked up to fluffy and creamy.
3. Pour the condensed milk over the brewed robusta coffee.
4. Spread the coffee with a light spoonful of the whipped egg yolk Mixture.
5. Enjoy the creamy texture by giving it a good stir before sipping.

Nutrition (per serving): Note:
Nutritional values may vary based on specific ingredients used.

142. Japanese Wagashi Wonderland

Time: 1.5 hrs

Servings: 12-16

Ingredients:
- 1 cup of sweet rice flour
- 1/4 cup of sugar
- 3/4 cup of water
- Food coloring (non-compulsory)
- Anko (sweet red bean paste) or fruit preserves for filling
- Kinako (soybean flour) or matcha powder for dusting

Instructions:
1. Sweet rice flour, sugar, and water Must be thoroughly combined in a pot. Cook over low heat, constantly stirring, up to it thickens to the consistency of dough.
2. After the dough has finished cooking, split it into minier pieces. Every piece can be colored differently by adding food coloring.
3. Flatten a mini amount of anko or fruit preserve in the center of a piece of dough. Roll the filling into a ball after wrapping it.
4. Apply the same procedure to the remaining dough and filling.
5. For coating, roll the wagashi with kinako or matcha powder.
6. Serve and pleasure in these delicious Japanese sweets!

Nutrition (per serving): Note:
Nutritional values may vary based on specific ingredients used.

143. Scandinavian Cinnamon Bun Joy

Time: 2 hrs

Servings: 12 buns

Ingredients:
- 4 cups of all-purpose flour
- 1/4 cup of granulated sugar
- 1 packet active dry yeast
- 1 cup of warm milk
- 1/4 cup of unsalted butter, dilute
- 1 Big egg
- 1/2 tsp salt
- 1/2 cup of brown sugar
- 2 tbsp ground cinnamon
- 1/4 cup of unsalted butter, melted
- Powdered sugar glaze (non-compulsory)

Instructions:
1. Combine the flour, salt, and granulated sugar in a sizable bowl. Warm milk and yeast Must be combined in a different basin. Give it five mins to get foamy.
2. The yeast Mixture Must be combined with dilute butter and an egg.
3. As you knead the dough, gradually incorporate the wet components into the dry ones.
4. In a warm location, cover the dough and let it to rise for an hr.
5. On a floured surface, roll out the dough into a broad rectangle.
6. Sprinkle cinnamon and brown sugar evenly over the dough after spreading melted butter over it.
7. To construct a log, tightly roll the dough starting at one end. Make 12 equally spaced slices.
8. The slices Must rise for a further 30 mins after being placed on a prepared baking pan.
9. Set the oven's temperature to 350°F (175°C). Golden brown buns Must have been baked for 20 to 25 mins.
10. You might coat the food with powdered sugar before serving.

Nutrition (per serving): Note:
Nutritional values may vary based on specific ingredients used.

144. Mexican Aguas Frescas Fiesta

Time: 15 mins

Servings: 4

Ingredients:

- 4 cups of fresh fruit (e.g., watermelon, cucumber, mango, pineapple), chop-up
- 4 cups of water
- 1/4 cup of fresh lime juice
- 1/4 cup of granulated sugar (adjust as needed)

Instructions:

1. The diced fruit, water, lime juice, and sugar Must all be blended together.
2. Blend up to sugar is dissolved and the Mixture is smooth.
3. Taste, and if necessary, add more sugar to balance sweetness.
4. Take out any pulp or seeds by straining the Mixture through a fine mesh strainer.
5. Serve the agua fresca over ice or chill it in the refrigerator.
6. If desired, add fresh fruit slices as a garnish before sipping this cool Mexican beverage.

Nutrition (per serving): Note:
Nutritional values may vary based on specific ingredients used.

145. Italian Affogato and Amaro

Time: 5 mins

Servings: 1

Ingredients:

- 1 scoop vanilla ice cream
- 1 shot espresso coffee
- 1 oz amaro liqueur (e.g., Amaretto or Averna)

Instructions:

1. Put a scoop of vanilla ice cream in a glass or coffee cup of.
2. Pour a shot of freshly made espresso over the ice cream.
3. To the cup of, add the amaro liquor.
4. Serve right away and savor the flavorful mingling of sweet ice cream, robust coffee, and amaro's herbal undertones.

Nutrition (per serving): Note:
Nutritional values may vary based on specific ingredients used.

146. Spanish Crema Catalana Dream

Time: 1.5 hrs

Servings: 4-6

Ingredients:

- 4 cups of whole milk
- 1 cinnamon stick
- Zest of 1 lemon
- 6 Big egg yolks
- 1 cup of granulated sugar
- 1/4 cup of cornstarch
- Caster sugar for caramelizing

Instructions:

1. The milk, cinnamon stick, and lemon zest are heated in a saucepan up to the milk begins to simmer. Take it off the heat and let it steep for 10 mins. Then take out the lemon zest and cinnamon stick.
2. Whisk egg yolks and sugar up to they are creamy and pale in a another bowl.
3. Combine the cornstarch into the egg Mixture up to it is well-combined.
4. While continuously whisking, slowly add the infused milk into the egg Mixture.
5. Reintroduce the Mixture to the pan, and cook it over low heat, continually stirring, up to it takes on the consistency of custard.
6. Individual ramekins Must be filled with crema Catalana and leted to cool to room temperature. After that, chill for at least an hr.
7. Before serving, top every crema Catalana with a thin layer of caster sugar and caramelize it with a kitchen torch or under the broiler.
8. Before serving, give the sugar a min to solidify.

Nutrition (per serving): Note:
Nutritional values may vary based on specific ingredients used.

147. Brazilian Caipirinha Carnival

Time: 10 mins

Servings: 1

Ingredients:

- 2 ozs cachaça (Brazilian rum)
- 1 lime, slice into wedges
- 2 tbsp granulated sugar
- Crushed ice

Instructions:

1. To extract the lime juice, combine the lime wedges and sugar in a strong glass.
2. Crushed ice Must be put in the drink.
3. Cachaça Must be poured over the ice and thoroughly combined.

4. If desired, garnish with a lime wheel or more lime wedges.
5. Enjoy a refreshing sip of this traditional Brazilian cocktail!

Nutrition (per serving): Note:
Nutritional values may vary based on specific ingredients used.

148. Turkish Turkish Delight Delight

Time: 2 hrs
Servings: 36 pieces

Ingredients:

- 2 cups of granulated sugar
- 2 cups of water
- Juice of 1 lemon
- 3/4 cup of cornstarch
- 1 tsp rosewater or orange blossom water
- Food coloring (non-compulsory)
- 1/2 cup of powdered sugar
- 1/2 cup of cornstarch

Instructions:

1. Over low heat, add sugar and water in a pot. Stir the sugar up to it melts.
2. The Mixture will begin to boil once you add lemon juice. Simmer for roughly 10 mins or up to it starts to thicken.
3. Combine cornstarch and water thoroughly in a bowl. As the syrup simmers, gradually stir in the cornstarch Mixture.
4. 15-20 mins of continuous simmering and stirring Must be enough for the Mixture to thicken and gelatinize.
5. Add the food coloring and rosewater or orange blossom water, if using.
6. Pour the Mixture onto a shlet dish that has been greased. The surface Must be even, and it Must sit at room temperature for at least an hr.
7. Combine cornstarch and powdered sugar in a separate dish. Turkish delight that has been set Must be slice into squares and covered with the sugar-cornstarch Mixture.
8. Placing layers of parchment paper between them will help keep the container sealed.

Nutrition (per serving): Note:
Nutritional values may vary based on specific ingredients used.

149. Greek Ouzo and Meze Melody

Time: 15 mins
Servings: Variable

Ingredients:

- Ouzo (anise-flavored liqueur)
- Assorted meze (mini appetizers) such as olives, feta cheese, tzatziki, grilled vegetables, dolmades, etc.

Instructions:

1. Put a little bit of Ouzo in every glass.
2. Put different meze dishes on a platter or individual plates.
3. Serve the Ouzo alongside the meze and take pleasure in the classic Greek aperitif and snacks.

Nutrition (per serving): Note:
Nutritional values may vary based on specific ingredients used.

150. Russian Vodka and Zakuski:

Time: 10 mins
Servings: 2

Ingredients:

- 2 ozs vodka
- Assorted Zakuski (traditional Russian appetizers like pickles, cured fish, cheese, etc.)

Instructions:

1. Vodka Must be briefly chilled with ice cubes or in a freezer.
2. On a platter or on individual plates, arrange the zakuski.
3. In shot glasses, pour the chilled vodka.
4. Serve the vodka and Zakuski together and savor this classic Russian combination.

NUTRITION INFO: (Vodka has no significant nutritional value)

151. Irish Irish Coffee Craze:

Time: 10 mins
Servings: 1

Ingredients:

- 1 ½ ozs Irish whiskey
- 1 cup of hot brewed coffee
- 1 tbsp brown sugar
- 2 tbsp heavy cream

Instructions:
1. Combine the hot coffee, Irish whiskey, and brown sugar in a heat-resistant glass or cup of.
2. up to the sugar melts, vigorously stir.
3. Pour the heavy cream over the back of a spoon to gently float it on top.
4. Enjoy this traditional Irish coffee right now.

NUTRITION INFO: (Approximate values per serving)
Cals: 185 kcal, Carbs: 8g, Fat: 12g, Protein: 0g, Fiber: 0g

152. Scottish Whisky and Shortbread:

Time: 5 mins
Servings: 1

Ingredients:
- 2 ozs Scotch whisky
- Shortbread cookies (store-bought or homemade)

Instructions:
1. Scotch whisky Must be poured into a glass.
2. Shortbread cookies Must be served alongside it.

NUTRITION INFO: (Whisky has no significant nutritional value)

153. American Mint Julep Madness:

Time: 5 mins
Servings: 1

Ingredients:
- 2 ½ ozs bourbon
- 4-6 fresh mint leaves
- ½ oz simple syrup (1:1 ratio of sugar and water)
- Crushed ice

Instructions:
1. Mint leaves Must be carefully muddled to release flavor in a julep cup of or tumbler.
2. Bourbon and simple syrup Must be added.
3. Crushed ice Must be added to the cup of, and everything Must be thoroughly combined.
4. Insert a mint sprig as garnish.
5. Enjoy this traditional American cocktail with a straw.

NUTRITION INFO: (Approximate values per serving)
Cals: 220 kcal, Carbs: 12g, Fat: 0g, Protein: 0g
Fiber: 0g

154. Italian Limoncello Love:

Time: 10 mins (+2 weeks for steeping)
Servings: 12-16 (as aperitifs)

Ingredients:
1. 10 organic lemons
2. 750 ml vodka
3. 2 cups of granulated sugar
4. 2 cups of water

Instructions:
1. After giving the lemons a thorough wash, use a vegetable peeler to take the zest only, leaving the white pith behind.
2. Put the lemon zest in a Big jar or glass container.
3. Lemon zest Must be covered with vodka, which Must then be snugly closed.
4. Let it to steep for about two weeks in a cold, dark spot, gently stirring the jar every few days.
5. The syrup is made by combining sugar and water in a skillet over medium heat after steeping. Let it cool after stirring up to the sugar has dissolved.
6. After removing the lemon zest using a strainer, combine the vodka with the syrup.
7. Before serving, place the refrigerate Limoncello in bottles and keep them there for at least 4 hrs.
8. As a cooling beverage for after dinner, serve chilled.

NUTRITION INFO: (Approximate values per serving)
Cals: 150 kcal, Carbs: 17g, Fat: 0g, Protein: 0g, Fiber: 0g,

155. French Kir Royale EXTRAVAGANZA:

Time: 5 mins
Servings: 1

Ingredients:
- 5 ozs chilled sparkling wine (Champagne or Prosecco)
- 1/2 oz crème de cassis (blackcurrant liqueur)

Instructions:
1. Insert a Champagne flute with the crème de cassis.
2. Add a glass of chilled sparkling wine on top.
3. Gently blend by stirring.
4. Garnish with a fresh blackberry or raspberry, if desired.
5. Cheers to this classy French cocktail.

NUTRITION INFO: (Approximate values per serving)
Cals: 110 kcal, Carbs: 4g, Fat: 0g, Protein: 0g, Fiber: 0g

156. Spanish Sangria and Tapas:

Time: 10 mins (+chilling time)
Servings: 4-6

Ingredients:

- 1 bottle red wine (750 ml)
- 1/4 cup of brandy
- 2 tbsp orange liqueur (e.g., Triple Sec)
- 1 cup of orange juice
- 1 cup of split combined fruits (oranges, apples, lemons, berries, etc.)
- 1/2 cup of split peveryes or nectarines
- 1-2 tbsp sugar (adjust as needed)
- Sparkling water or lemon-lime soda (non-compulsory, for added fizz)
- Ice cubes
- For Tapas: Assorted Spanish olives, cheese, cured meats, bread, etc.

Instructions:
1. Red wine, brandy, orange juice, orange liqueur, sugar, and split fruits Must all be combined in a sizable pitcher. up to the sugar melts, vigorously stir.
2. To enable the flavors to mingle, chill the sangria in the refrigerator for at least two hrs.
3. You can give it some zing before serving by adding sparkling water or lemon-lime soda (non-compulsory).
4. If preferred, decorate the glasses with additional fruit slices and serve the sangria over ice.
5. Serve a variety of appetizers with the sangria for a delicious taste of Spain.

NUTRITION INFO: (Approximate values per serving)
Cals: 180 kcal, Carbs: 17g, Fat: 0g, Protein: 1g, Fiber: 1g

157. Mexican Margarita Fiesta:

Time: 10 mins
Servings: 1

Ingredients:

- 2 ozs tequila
- 1 oz triple sec
- 1 oz freshly squeezed lime juice
- 1/2 oz simple syrup (1:1 ratio of sugar and water)
- Lime wedge and salt, for garnish
- Ice cubes

Instructions:
1. The rim of a glass Must be salted after being rimmed with a lime slice.
2. Ice cubes Must be put in the glass.
3. Combine the tequila, triple sec, lime juice, and simple syrup with ice in a shaker.
4. Pour the contents into the ready glass after giving the Mixture a good shake up to cooled.
5. Serve right away after adding a lime wedge as a garnish.

NUTRITION INFO: (Approximate values per serving)
Cals: 200 kcal, Carbs: 15g, Fat: 0g, Protein: 0g, Fiber: 0g

158. Caribbean Rum Punch Paradise:

Time: 10 mins
Servings: 4

Ingredients:

- 1 cup of dark rum
- 1 cup of pineapple juice
- 1/2 cup of orange juice
- 1/4 cup of lime juice
- 2 tbsp grenadine syrup
- 1 tbsp simple syrup (non-compulsory, for added sweetness)
- Pineapple slices, orange slices, and maraschino cherries for garnish
- Ice cubes

Instructions:
1. Combine the dark rum, pineapple, orange, lime, grenadine syrup, and simple syrup (if using) in a pitcher.
2. All the components Must be thoroughly combined.
3. Pour the rum punch into glasses over the ice after filling them with ice cubes.
4. Slices of pineapple, orange, and maraschino cherries can be used as garnish.
5. Serve while escaping to the Caribbean's tropical splendor.

NUTRITION INFO: (Approximate values per serving)
Cals: 190 kcal, Carbs: 23g, Fat: 0g, Protein: 0g, Fiber: 0g

159. Brazilian Caipirinha Carnival:

Time: 5 mins

Servings: 1

Ingredients:

- 2 ozs cachaça (Brazilian sugarcane spirit)
- 1 lime, slice into mini wedges
- 2 tbsp granulated sugar
- Crushed ice

Instructions:

1. To liberate the lime juice and oils, combine the lime wedges and sugar in a strong glass.
2. Crushed ice Must be put in the drink.
3. Cachaça Must be poured over the ice and thoroughly combined.
4. Enjoy this colorful Brazilian cocktail while being served with a straw.

NUTRITION INFO: (Approximate values per serving)
Cals: 170 kcal, Carbs: 22g, Fat: 0g, Protein: 0g, Fiber: 0g

160. Argentinean Mate:

Time: 10 mins

Servings: 1

Ingredients:

- 1 tbsp yerba mate leaves
- 1 cup of hot water (not boiling)
- Sugar or sweetener (non-compulsory)

Instructions:

1. Approximately two thirds of a mate gourd (or other heat-resistant cup of) Must be filled with yerba mate leaves.
2. Pour warm water into the gourd rather than boiling water since the latter could burn the leaves.
3. Give the yerba mate leaves some time to soak.
4. Put a metal bombilla (straw) into the gourd so that it touches the bottom.
5. Sip the traditional mate of Argentina through the bombilla.

161. Alfajores:

Time: 1 hr 30 mins

Servings: 12-15 cookies

Ingredients:

- 1 cup of all-purpose flour
- 1/2 cup of cornstarch
- 1/4 tsp baking soda
- 1 tsp baking powder
- 1/2 cup of unsalted butter, melted
- 1/3 cup of granulated sugar
- 2 egg yolks
- 1 tsp vanilla extract
- Dulce de leche (caramel spread)
- Shredded coconut (non-compulsory, for coating)

Instructions:

1. Set a baking sheet on your oven's 350°F (175°C) rack and preheat the oven.
2. Combine the flour, cornstarch, baking soda, and baking powder in a bowl.
3. Cream the butter and sugar in a another dish up to it is light and creamy.
4. Combine thoroughly before adding the egg yolks and vanilla essence to the butter Mixture.
5. As you gradually combine the dry and liquid ingredients, the dough will begin to come together.
6. On a floured surface, roll out the dough to a thickness of about 1/4 inch (6 mm), then slice out circles.
7. The cookies Must be baked for 10 to 12 mins, or up to just barely golden, on the preheated baking sheet.
8. Spread dulce de leche on one cookie and sandwich it with another after the cookies have cooled.
9. You could optionally roll the alfajores' sides with coconut shreds.

162. Turkish Ayran:

Time: 5 mins

Servings: 2

Ingredients:

- 1 cup of plain yogurt
- 1 cup of cold water
- A pinch of salt
- Fresh mint leaves (non-compulsory, for garnish)

Instructions:

1. Whisk the plain yogurt, cold water, and a dash of salt together up to thoroughly blended in a bowl.
2. If desired, add fresh mint leaves as a garnish after pouring the Mixture into glasses.
3. Turkish drinks are best served chilled.

163. Turkish Kebabs:

Time: 30 mins (marinating time included)

Servings: 4

Ingredients:

- 1 lb lamb or beef, slice into cubes
- 1 Big onion, finely grated
- 3 tbsp olive oil
- 2 tbsp plain yogurt
- 2 cloves garlic, chop-up
- 1 tsp ground cumin
- 1 tsp paprika
- Salt and pepper as needed

Instructions:

1. Finely grated onion, olive oil, plain yogurt, chop-up garlic, cumin, paprika, salt, and pepper Must all be combined in a bowl.
2. Make sure the meat is properly coated before adding the cubed meat to the marinade. To marinate, cover and place in the refrigerator for at least one hr (or better yet, overnight).
3. Get the grill or the broiler ready. Onto skewers, thread the marinated meat.
4. The kebabs Must be grilled or broiled for 10 to 15 mins, turning them once or twice, or up to they are cooked to your preferred doneness.
5. Turkish kebabs can be served with rice, salad, or pita bread.

164. Greek Frappé:

Time: 5 mins

Servings: 1

Ingredients:

- 2 tsp instant coffee
- 2 tsp sugar
- 2 tbsp water
- Cold water
- Milk (non-compulsory)
- Ice cubes

Instructions:

1. Combine the instant coffee, sugar, and 2 tbsp of water in a shaker or jar.
2. When the liquid starts to foam, securely close the lid and shake it for about 30 seconds.
3. Pour the foamy coffee Mixture over the ice in a glass that has been filled with ice cubes.
4. To achieve the strength and flavor you choose, add cold water (and milk, if desired).
5. Stir thoroughly, then savor the cooling Greek Frappé.

165. Greek Baklava:

Time: 1 hr 30 mins

Servings: 24 pieces

Ingredients:

- 1 box/pkg phyllo dough (16 oz), thawed
- 1 cup of unsalted butter, dilute
- 2 cups of chop-up walnuts or pistachios
- 1 tsp ground cinnamon
- 1 cup of granulated sugar
- 1 cup of water
- 1/2 cup of honey
- 1 tsp vanilla extract

Instructions:

1. Grease a baking dish and preheat the oven to 350°F (175°C).
2. The ground cinnamon and chop-up nuts Must be combined in a bowl.
3. In the baking dish, place a layer of phyllo dough and brush it with dilute butter. Repeat this process, buttering and piling the sheets one at a time.
4. Over the phyllo dough, scatter some of the nut Mixture.
5. Phyllo sheets and nuts Must be layered up to you run out of both, with a final phyllo dough layer on top.
6. Slice the baklava into diamond or square shapes using a sharp knife.
7. Baklava Must be baked in the preheated oven for 50 to 60 mins, or up to golden brown.
8. Make the syrup by blending sugar, water, honey, and vanilla essence in a saucepan while the baklava bakes. Once it has boiled, turn down the heat, and let it simmer for about five mins.
9. Pour the hot syrup over the baklava as soon as it's finished baking, making sure to cover every piece.
10. Before serving, let the baklava totally cool.

166. Russian Kvass:

Time: 2 days

Servings: 6

Ingredients:

- 8 cups of water
- 1 cup of rye bread crumbs or stale rye bread
- 1/2 cup of sugar
- 1/4 tsp active dry yeast

Instructions:
1. Rye breadcrumbs or stale rye bread Must be added to boiling water in a big kettle.
2. After about 15 mins of simmering at a lower heat, turn off the heat and let the pot cool to room temperature.
3. Discard the bread crumbs and strain the liquid into a fresh container.
4. Add the yeast to the Mixture after the sugar has been dissolved.
5. It Must mature for 1-2 days at room temperature under a clean cloth cover before tasting slightly tart.
6. Before serving, let the kvass cool in the fridge. Make it into a cool beverage to enjoy.

167. ussian Blini:

Time: 30 mins
Servings: 4-6

Ingredients:

- 1 cup of all-purpose flour
- 1 cup of milk
- 2 Big eggs
- 1 tbsp vegetable oil
- Pinch of salt
- Butter (for cooking)

Instructions:
1. Combine the milk and flour in a bowl up to combined well.
2. Once the batter is thoroughly blended and lump-free, add the eggs, vegetable oil, and salt.
3. Melt a tiny quantity of butter in a non-stick skillet over medium heat.
4. Pour about 1/4 cup of the batter into the skillet, then spread it thinly by swirling it around.
5. The blini Must be cooked for 1-2 mins on every side, or up to golden brown.
6. With the remaining batter, repeat the procedure.
7. You can top the blini with anything you like, including sour cream, jam, smoked salmon, caviar, or caviar.

168. Indian Masala Chai Charm:

Time: 15 mins
Servings: 2

Ingredients:

- 2 cups of water
- 2 cups of whole milk
- 2 tbsp loose black tea leaves or 2 tea bags
- 2-3 tbsp sugar (adjust as needed)
- 3-4 green cardamom pods, lightly crushed
- 1-inch piece of fresh ginger, split
- 1 cinnamon stick
- 2-3 whole cloves

Instructions:
1. Tea leaves or tea bags, crushed cardamom pods, split ginger, cinnamon stick, and cloves Must all be added to boiling water in a pot.
2. To enable the flavors to meld, turn the heat down and simmer the food for about 5 mins.
3. The spiced tea combination is next given the addition of milk and sugar, and it is gently simmered.
4. Let it to boil for a further five mins, stirring now and then.
5. Serve hot masala chai in mugs after straining. Take pleasure in the delicious Indian Masala Chai Charm!

169. Thai Iced Tea:

Time: 15 mins
Servings: 2

Ingredients:

- 2 cups of water
- 2 tbsp Thai tea leaves
- 2 tbsp sweetened condensed milk
- 2 tbsp evaporated milk
- 2 tbsp sugar (adjust as needed)
- Ice cubes

Instructions:
1. Thai tea leaves Must be added to boiling water in a saucepan.
2. After taking the pan off the heat, let the tea steep for approximately five mins.
3. While the tea is still hot, strain it into a pitcher and whisk in the sugar up to it dissolves.
4. Let the tea to cool to room temperature before chilling it in the refrigerator.
5. Pour the chilled Thai tea over the ice in cups of that have been filled with ice cubes.
6. Stir together evaporated milk and sweetened condensed milk in every glass.
7. Enjoy the distinctive flavors of Thai iced tea!

170. Thai Mango Sticky Rice:

Time: 30 mins

Servings: 4

Ingredients:

- 1 cup of glutinous rice (sticky rice)
- 1 ½ cups of coconut milk
- ½ cup of sugar
- ¼ tsp salt
- 2 ripe mangoes, split
- Sesame seeds (non-compulsory, for garnish)

Instructions:

1. Glutinous rice Must be thoroughly rinsed in cold water up to the water is clear. Rice Must be submerged in water for at least 30 mins and possibly all night.
2. Rice Must be drained and put in a cheesecloth-lined steamer. The rice Must be steamed for 20 to 25 mins, or up to soft.
3. Coconut milk, sugar, and salt Must be heated in a pot over medium heat. Stirring is necessary to smooth out the Mixture and dissolve the sugar.
4. Half of the coconut milk Mixture Must be poured over the cooked sticky rice after turning off the stove. Let the rice to soak in the coconut milk by letting it sit for a short while.
5. Slices of ripe mango Must be placed on top of the sticky rice that has been infused with coconut before drizzling the remaining coconut milk Mixture over everything.
6. The mango sticky rice can optionally have sesame seeds added for taste and texture.

171. Japanese Iced Matcha Melody:

Time: 10 mins

Servings: 2

Ingredients:

- 2 tsp matcha green tea powder
- 2 cups of cold water
- 1 cup of milk (dairy or plant-based)
- 2 tbsp honey or sweetener of your choice (adjust as needed)
- Ice cubes

Instructions:

1. Matcha green tea powder and a little water are whisked together in a bowl to create a smooth paste.
2. Add the remaining water little by little while whisking, then wait up to the matcha is completely dissolved.
3. When adding honey or another sweetener, whisk the matcha Mixture thoroughly.
4. Place ice cubes in a different glass and add your preferred milk to it.
5. Pour the matcha Mixture over the milk gradually and stir it just enough to incorporate it.
6. Enjoy the delicious flavor and brilliant green color of the ice-cold Japanese Matcha Melody.

172. Chinese Bubble Tea Bonanza:

Time: 15 mins

Servings: 2

Ingredients:

- 1/2 cup of black tapioca pearls (boba)
- 2 cups of water
- 2 tbsp black tea leaves or 2 tea bags
- 1/4 cup of sweetened condensed milk
- 1/4 cup of sugar syrup (combine equal parts sugar and water, then heat up to sugar dissolves)
- 1 cup of milk (dairy or plant-based)
- Ice cubes

Instructions:

1. The tapioca pearls Must be prepared in a saucepan per the directions on the box/pkg. Usually, they need to be boiled in water for 10 mins or so to become soft and chewy.
2. The cooked tapioca pearls Must be rinsed with cold water before being placed in a bowl with sugar syrup to maintain their sweetness and moisture.
3. Add the black tea leaves or tea bags to the boiling 2 cups of water in a separate pot. Before filtering the tea, let it steep for a few mins.
4. Stir the tea with the sweetened condensed milk up to thoroughly blended.
5. Tapioca pearls are slice up between two glasses with ice cubes already in them.
6. After adding the milk to the pearls, combine the black tea.
7. If you'd like, you can optionally change the sweetness by introducing more sugar syrup.
8. Before savoring the delicious Chinese Bubble Tea Bonanza with its amusing tapioca pearls, stir it thoroughly.

173. Korean Iced Coffee Delight:

Time: 10 mins

Servings: 2

Ingredients:

- 2 cups of freshly brewed coffee, cooled
- 1 cup of milk (dairy or plant-based)
- 2 tbsp sweetened condensed milk
- 2 tbsp chocolate syrup or cocoa powder (non-compulsory, for a mocha twist)
- Ice cubes

Instructions:

1. Freshly brewed coffee, milk, and sweetened condensed milk Must all be combined in a pitcher.
2. When combining the ingredients, add cocoa powder or chocolate syrup for a mocha-inspired touch.
3. Pour the iced coffee Mixture over the ice in two glasses filled with ice cubes.
4. Enjoy the delicious and creamy Korean Iced Coffee Delight after a thorough stirring.

174. Vietnamese Iced Coffee Euphoria:

Time: 10 mins

Servings: 2

Ingredients:

- 2 tbsp coarsely ground coffee (dark roast recommended)
- 1/4 cup of sweetened condensed milk
- 1 cup of hot water
- Ice cubes

Instructions:

1. Use boiling water and a French press or a traditional Vietnamese drip filter to brew the coarsely ground coffee.
2. Pour the coffee over two glasses of ice cubes while it is still hot, distributing it evenly across the glasses.
3. Every glass Must get 2 tbsp of sweetened condensed milk, which Must be thoroughly combined in.
4. Before sipping and enjoying the exquisite Vietnamese Iced Coffee Euphoria, let the iced coffee chill down even more.

175. Moroccan Mint Tea Marvel

Time: 10 mins

Servings: 2

Ingredients:

- 2 cups of water
- 2 tsp green tea leaves
- 1/4 cup of fresh mint leaves
- 2 tbsp sugar or honey (adjust as needed)

Instructions:

1. Bring the water to a boil in a teapot.
2. Fill the teapot with the mint and green tea leaves.
3. Depending on the desired strength, let it steep for 3 to 5 mins.
4. Add honey or sugar and stir up to combined.
5. Serve the tea hot after pouring it into mugs.

176. Hawaiian Pina Colada Paradise

Time: 5 mins

Servings: 1

Ingredients:

- 1 cup of pineapple chunks (fresh or canned)
- 1/2 cup of coconut milk
- 1/4 cup of rum (non-compulsory for alcoholic version)
- Ice cubes

Instructions:

1. The pineapple chunks, coconut milk, and rum (if using) Must all be combined in a blender.
2. Ice cubes can be put in the blender.
3. Blend till creamy and smooth.
4. Pour into a glass, then top with a cherry or pineapple slice as a garnish.

177. Swiss Iced Chocolate Dream

Time: 10 mins

Servings: 2

Ingredients:

- 2 cups of milk
- 1/4 cup of chocolate syrup
- 1 tsp vanilla extract
- Whipped cream (non-compulsory, for garnish)
- Chocolate shavings (non-compulsory, for garnish)

Instructions:

1. Milk, chocolate syrup, and vanilla extract Must all be put in a blender.
2. Blend everything thoroughly.
3. Ice cubes Must be put in two glasses.
4. Over the ice, pour the chocolate Mixture.

5. If desired, garnish with whipped cream and chocolate shavings.

178. Italian Aperol Spritz Sensation

Time: 5 mins
Servings: 1

Ingredients:

- 3 parts Aperol liqueur
- 2 parts prosecco (or any sparkling wine)
- 1 splash of soda water
- Ice cubes
- Orange slice, for garnish

Instructions:

1. Add ice cubes to a wine glass.
2. Prosecco and Aperol liquor are added.
3. Add a little soda water on top.
4. Gently blend by stirring.
5. Add an orange slice as a garnish.

179. French Champagne Soiree

Time: 5 mins
Servings: 1

Ingredients:

- 4 oz champagne
- 1 oz cognac
- 1 sugar cube
- Angostura bitters (non-compulsory)
- Lemon twist, for garnish

Instructions:

1. In a champagne glass, put the sugar cube.
2. (Non-compulsory) Add a few dashes of Angostura bitters.
3. Cognac Must be poured over the sugar cube.
4. Add chilled champagne on the top.
5. Add a lemon twist as a garnish.

180. Spanish Gin and Tonic Extravaganza

Time: 5 mins
Servings: 1

Ingredients:

- 2 oz gin
- 4 oz tonic water
- Juniper berries
- Lemon or lime slices
- Ice cubes

Instructions:

1. Ice cubes Must be added to a gin balloon glass.
2. Add the tonic water and gin.
3. To blend, gently stir.
4. Lemon or lime slices and juniper berries can be used as garnish.

181. Mexican Paloma and Tacos

Time: 20 mins
Servings: 2

Paloma Ingredients:

- 2 cups of grapefruit soda (or substitute with fresh grapefruit juice and club soda)
- 1/4 cup of tequila
- 1 tbsp lime juice
- Salt, for rimming the glasses
- Lime wedges, for garnish

Instructions:

1. Paloma: Use a lime wedge to rub the salt onto the rims of two glasses.
2. Ice cubes Must be put in every glass.
3. Tequila, lime juice, grapefruit soda, and ice Must all be put in a shaker.
4. Stir thoroughly before straining into the prepared glasses.
5. slices of lime for garnish.
6. Taco: Stuff taco shells with your preferred cooked and shredded meat.
7. Add salsa, sour cream, shredded lettuce, chop-up tomatoes, and shredded cheese as toppings.

182. Caribbean Piña Colada Party

Time: 5 mins
Servings: 1

Ingredients:

- 1 cup of pineapple juice
- 1/2 cup of coconut cream
- 1/4 cup of white rum
- Pineapple slice and maraschino cherry, for garnish
- Ice cubes

Instructions:

1. White rum, coconut cream, and pineapple juice Must all be combined in a blender.

2. Ice cubes can be put in the blender.
3. Blend till creamy and smooth.
4. Pour into a glass, top with a maraschino cherry and a pineapple slice, and serve.

183. Turkish Raki and Meze Melody

Time: 15 mins

Servings: 2

Raki Ingredients:

- 2 oz raki (anise-flavored spirit)
- 4 oz water
- Ice cubes

Instructions:

1. Raki: Add ice cubes to two glasses.
2. Over the ice in every glass, pour raki.
3. To make the raki the desired strength, add water.
4. Enjoy with the meze selection after a gentle stir.
5. Meze: Arrange pita bread, hummus, cucumber slices, cherry tomatoes, feta cheese, olives, and olive oil on a tray. Serve raki at the same time.

184. Greek Ouzo and Tzatziki

Time: 10 mins

Servings: 2

Ouzo Ingredients:

- 2 oz ouzo (anise-flavored spirit)
- 4 oz water
- Ice cubes
- Tzatziki Ingredients:
- 1 cup of Greek yogurt
- 1/2 cucumber, finely grated and squeezed to take out excess moisture
- 2 cloves garlic, chop-up
- 1 tbsp olive oil
- 1 tbsp fresh dill, chop-up
- Salt and pepper, as needed

Instructions:

1. Vegetable oil Must be heated over medium-high heat in a sizable pot or Dutch oven. Cook the stew meat well all over.
2. Add the chop-up garlic and onion to the saucepan. Cook the onion up to it turns translucent.
3. Add the diced potatoes, thyme, salt, pepper, tomato paste, beef stock, and Guinness stout.
4. The stew Must be brought to a boil, then simmer for 1.5 to 2 hrs, covered, or up to the meat is cooked.
5. If necessary, adjust the seasoning. Serve warm alongside crusty bread.

NUTRITION INFO (per serving):
Cals: 380 kcal Protein: 28g Carbs: 26g Fat: 15g Fiber: 4g

185. American Craft Beer

Tasting Time:

N/A Servings: N/A

Ingredients:

- Assorted American craft beers of your choice

Instructions:

1. Choose a range of American craft beers from various breweries and varieties.
2. Depending on the style, chill the beers to the proper serving temperature, which is often between 40 and 55 °F (4 and 12 °C).
3. Set up a tasting flight so every beer is in a mini glass.
4. Before moving on to the stronger, more robust beers, start with the lighter, softer beers.
5. To evaluate and appreciate the variety of American craft beer, make notes on the flavors, smells, and qualities of every beer.

NUTRITION INFO: N/A (As beer is alcoholic, it contains cals but limited nutritional value.)

186. Canadian Caesar and Poutine

Time: 20 mins

Servings: 2

Ingredients:

- For Canadian Caesar:
- 2 oz vodka
- 4 oz Clamato juice (or tomato juice)
- 1/2 tsp hot sauce
- 1 tsp Worcestershire sauce
- Pinch of salt and pepper
- Ice
- Celery stalk and lime wedge for garnish
- For Poutine:
- 1 lb (450g) russet potatoes, slice into fries
- 1 cup of cheese curds
- 1 cup of beef gravy

Instructions:
1. Celery salt and lime juice are used to rim the glasses.
2. Add ice to the cups of.
3. Vodka, Clamato juice, spicy sauce, Worcestershire sauce, salt, and pepper Must all be combined in a shaker.
4. Stir thoroughly before straining into the prepared glasses.
5. A lime wedge and celery stem Must be used to garnish every glass.
6. To make poutine:
7. Bake the fries as directed on the box/pkg or using your preferred method after preheating the oven.
8. The beef gravy Must be heated and boiling in a saucepan.
9. When ready to serve, arrange the heated fries on a serving platter, top with cheese curds, and then ladle hot gravy over everything.

NUTRITION INFO (per serving for Poutine):
Cals: 550 kcal Protein: 15g Carbs: 65g Fat: 26g Fiber: 4g

(Note: The NUTRITION INFO for the Canadian Caesar is not included as it may vary based on the ingredients and proportions used.)

187. Australian Vegemite and Tim Tams

Time: 5 mins
Servings: 1

Ingredients:
- 2 slices of bread
- Butter or margarine
- Vegemite spread
- Tim Tams (Australian chocolate biscuits)

Instructions:
1. Toasted bread Must be as crisp as you like it to be.
2. On the toast that is still hot, spread butter or margarine.
3. Spread a thin layer of Vegemite over the toast with butter. Vegemite is powerful and salty, so use caution.
4. For a sweet treat, serve alongside a serving of Tim Tams.

NUTRITION INFO (per serving):
Cals: 380 kcal Protein: 8g Carbs: 46g Fat: 18g Fiber: 4g

188. Brazilian Caipiroska and Coxinha

Time: 1 hr
Servings: 4

Ingredients:
- 2 limes, slice into wedges
- 2 tbsp granulated sugar
- Ice cubes
- 6 oz vodka
- Soda water (non-compulsory)
- For Coxinha:
- 1 lb (450g) chicken breast, cooked and shredded
- 1 tbsp olive oil
- 1 mini onion, lightly chop-up
- 2 cloves garlic, chop-up
- 1 cup of chicken broth
- 1 cup of all-purpose flour
- 1 cup of milk
- Salt and pepper as needed
- Vegetable oil (for frying)

Instructions:
1. To extract the juice from the lime wedges, muddle them with sugar in a strong glass.
2. Add vodka after adding ice cubes to the glass. Stir thoroughly.
3. If you'd like a lighter beverage, top off with soda water.
4. To Coxinha:
5. The chop-up onion and garlic Must be sautéed in olive oil in a skillet up to transparent.
6. After a few mins of cooking, add the chicken shreds and season with salt and pepper.
7. Bring the chicken broth to a boil in a different pot. To prevent lumps, add the flour gradually while stirring continuously.
8. As the Mixture thickens and resembles mashed potatoes, turn the heat down and stir in the milk.
9. Let the dough to cool before taking a tiny piece, flattening it, and placing a dollop of the chicken filling in the middle.
10. Shape the dough into little drumstick-like cones and mold it around the filling.
11. In a Big, deep pan, heat vegetable oil. Fry the coxinhas till crispy and golden.

NUTRITION INFO (per serving for Coxinha):
Cals: 300 kcal Protein: 18g Carbs: 28g Fat: 12g Fiber: 1g

189. Argentinean Malbec and Asado

Time: 2.5 to 3 hrs
Servings: 6

Ingredients:

- 2 lbs (900g) beef ribs or skirt steak
- 2 lbs (900g) pork ribs
- Salt and pepper as needed
- Chimichurri sauce (for serving)

Instructions:

1. Set the grill up for direct heat at a medium-high level.
2. Add salt and pepper to the beef and pork ribs.
3. Place the ribs on the grill and cook for 20 to 30 mins on every side, depending on how done you like your ribs.
4. Use your preferred marinade or sauce to baste the ribs from time to time while grilling.
5. With the chimichurri sauce on the side, serve the barbecued ribs.

NUTRITION INFO (per serving for Asado):
Cals: 500 kcal Protein: 30g Carbs: 0g Fat: 40g Fiber: 0g

190. Thai Singha Beer and Pad Thai

Time: 30 mins

Servings: 4

Ingredients:

- 8 oz rice noodles
- 2 tbsp vegetable oil
- 1 lb (450g) chicken or shrimp, peel off and deveined (or tofu for a vegetarian option)
- 3 cloves garlic, chop-up
- 2 eggs, beaten
- 1 cup of bean sprouts
- 3 green onions, chop-up
- 1/4 cup of chop-up peanuts
- Lime wedges for serving
- For Pad Thai Sauce:
- 3 tbsp fish sauce (or soy sauce for a vegetarian option)
- 1 tbsp tamarind paste
- 1 tbsp brown sugar
- 1 tsp chili flakes (adjust to your spice preference)

Instructions:

1. Rice noodles Must be prepared as directed on the box/pkg, drained, and then set aside.
2. To create the Pad Thai sauce, combine the fish sauce (or soy sauce), tamarind paste, brown sugar, and chili flakes in a mini bowl. Place aside.
3. In a wok or sizable pan, heat the vegetable oil over medium-high heat. Stir-fry for a min after adding the garlic, chop-up.
4. Cook the chicken, shrimp, or tofu in the pan up to almost finished.
5. Pour the beaten eggs into the other side of the pan while pushing the ingredients to one side. Cook the eggs by scrambling them.
6. Pour the Pad Thai sauce over the cooked rice noodles after adding them to the pan. Stir everything together up to the noodles are thoroughly heated and covered in sauce.
7. Toss for another min after adding the bean sprouts and chop-up green onions to the pan.
8. Serve the Pad Thai hot with lime wedges and chop-up peanuts as garnishes.

NUTRITION INFO (per serving for Pad Thai):
Cals: 420 kcal Protein: 22g Carbs: 55g Fat: 12g Fiber: 3g

191. Japanese Sake and Sashimi

Time: 15 mins

Servings: 2

Ingredients:

- Assorted sashimi (salmon, tuna, yellowtail, etc.)
- Soy sauce, for dipping
- Wasabi and pickled ginger, for serving
- Japanese sake

Instructions:

1. Slices of various sashimi Must be arranged on a serving platter.
2. Mini bowls of soy sauce Must be provided for dipping.
3. On the side, add wasabi and pickled ginger for flavor.
4. Japanese sake Must be served cold with the sashimi in tiny cups of.

NUTRITION INFO (per serving for sashimi):
Cals: Varies depending on the types of fish and portion sizes. Protein: Varies depending on the types of fish. Carbs: Varies (usually minimal in sashimi) Fat: Varies depending on the types of fish. Fiber: Varies (usually minimal in sashimi)

192. Chinese Baijiu and Dumplings

Time: 1 hr

Servings: 4

Ingredients:

- 1 lb (450g) ground pork

- 1 cup of lightly chop-up Napa cabbage
- 1/2 cup of chop-up green onions
- 2 tbsp soy sauce
- 1 tbsp sesame oil
- 1 tbsp finely grated ginger
- 1 clove garlic, chop-up
- 1 box/pkg round dumpling wrappers
- Water (for sealing dumplings)
- For Dipping Sauce:
- 2 tbsp soy sauce
- 1 tbsp rice vinegar
- 1 tsp sesame oil
- 1 tsp chili oil (non-compulsory)
- Chop-up green onions (for garnish)

Instructions:

1. Combine the ground pork with the Napa cabbage, green onions, soy sauce, sesame oil, finely grated ginger, and chop-up garlic in a sizable bowl.
2. A tiny spoonful of the filling Must be placed in the center of one dumpling wrapper before the edges are lightly moistened with water.
3. The wrapper Must be folded in half to create a half-circle. Press the corners together firmly to seal.
4. Continue up to all of the filling has been used.
5. The dumplings Must be cooked for 3–4 mins, or up to they float to the top, in a big saucepan of boiling water.
6. With a slotted spoon, take out the dumplings and serve them hot.
7. To use as dipping sauce:
8. Combine soy sauce, rice vinegar, sesame oil, and chile oil (if using) in a mini bowl.
9. Add chop-up green onions as a garnish to the sauce.

NUTRITION INFO (per serving for Dumplings):
Cals: 400 kcal Protein: 24g Carbs: 38g Fat: 16g Fiber: 2g

193. Korean Soju and Kimbap

Time: 45 mins

Servings: 4

Ingredients:

- 4 cups of cooked sushi rice
- 4 sheets of roasted seaweed (nori)
- 8-12 strips of cooked and seasoned bulgogi beef or ham
- 1 cucumber, slice into thin strips
- 2 carrots, slice into thin strips and blanched
- 4 eggs, beaten and made into thin omelets
- 1 tbsp sesame oil
- 1 tbsp sesame seeds
- Kimbap sauce (combine 2 tbsp soy sauce, 1 tbsp rice vinegar, and 1/2 tbsp sesame oil)
- For Soju:
- Korean Soju (usually consumed straight or with ice)

Instructions:

1. For simple rolling, place a bamboo sushi rolling mat on a spotless surface and cover it with plastic wrap.
2. A sheet of roasted seaweed Must be placed shiny side down on the mat.
3. Over the seaweed, uniformly distribute a thin layer of sushi rice, leaving about 1 inch at the top border.
4. Along the rice, arrange the cooked bulgogi beef or ham, cucumber, carrots, and omelet slices.
5. Sprinkle sesame seeds and sesame oil over the stuffing.
6. Wrap the kimbap tightly in the bamboo mat before carefully rolling it away from you.
7. To seal the roll, wet the top edge of the seaweed with water.
8. Use a sharp knife to slice the kimbap into bite-sized pieces.
9. Kimbap sauce Must be served alongside the dish.
10. For soju, serve cold Korean soju in miniature shot glasses or over ice.

NUTRITION INFO (per serving for Kimbap):
Cals: 320 kcal Protein: 12g Carbs: 50g Fat: 8g Fiber: 3g

194. Vietnamese Bia Hoi

Time: 10 mins

Servings: 2

Ingredients:

- 330ml Bia Hoi beer (or any light lager beer)

Instructions:

1. Beer Bia Hoi Must be chilled in the fridge.
2. In two glasses, pour the cold beer.
3. Serve right away and savor the flavor of refreshment!

195. Vietnamese Banh Mi

Time: 30 mins

Servings: 2

Ingredients:

- 2 mini baguettes
- 200g thinly split grilled pork (or any protein of your choice)
- Pickled vegetables (carrots, daikon)
- Fresh cilantro leaves
- Fresh cucumber slices
- Mayonnaise
- Soy sauce
- Maggi seasoning sauce (non-compulsory)

Instructions:

1. The baguettes Must be split in half and lightly toasted.
2. On one side of the baguette, spread mayonnaise, and on the other, soy sauce.
3. On the baguette, arrange the grilled pork, pickled veggies, cucumber slices, and cilantro.
4. If using, drizzle with Maggi seasoning sauce.
5. Sandwich is then sealed, lightly pressed, and served.

196. Moroccan Mint Tea

Time: 15 mins
Servings: 4

Ingredients:

- 4 cups of water
- 4 tsp loose green tea
- 1 bunch fresh mint leaves
- Sugar (as needed)

Instructions:

1. In a teapot, bring water to a boil.
2. Clean the teapot, then put fresh mint leaves and loose green tea in it.
3. Over the tea and mint, pour the boiling water.
4. Steep it for three to five mins.
5. As desired, add sugar.
6. Serve the tea hot after pouring it into glasses.

197. Moroccan Couscous

Time: 25 mins
Servings: 4

Ingredients:

- 1 cup of couscous
- 1 ½ cups of vegetable or chicken broth
- 1 tbsp olive oil
- 1 mini onion, lightly chop-up
- 2 cloves garlic, chop-up
- 1 tsp ground cumin
- 1/2 tsp ground cinnamon
- Salt and pepper as needed
- 1/4 cup of chop-up fresh cilantro or parsley
- 1/4 cup of raisins or chop-up dried apricots (non-compulsory)

Instructions:

1. Over medium heat, warm the olive oil in a big pot.
2. Add the chop-up onion and cook up to transparent and tender.
3. Salt, pepper, ground cinnamon, ground cumin, and chop-up garlic Must all be added. one more min of cooking.
4. Add the chicken or vegetable broth, then bring to a boil.
5. Add the non-compulsory raisins or chop-up dried apricots along with the couscous.
6. After turning off the heat and covering the pot, wait five mins.

Fluff the couscous with a fork, stir in the fresh cilantro or parsley, and serve.

198. Hawaiian Blue Hawaiian Bliss (Cocktail)

Time: 5 mins
Servings: 1

Ingredients:

- 1 1/2 oz rum
- 1 oz blue curaçao liqueur
- 2 oz pineapple juice
- 1 oz cream of coconut
- Pineapple slice and maraschino cherry for garnish

Instructions:

1. Ice Must be put in a shaker.
2. In the shaker, combine the rum, blue curaçao, pineapple juice, and cream of coconut.
3. Thoroughly shake up to cooled.
4. Pour the strained contents into an ice-filled, chilled glass.
5. Add a pineapple slice and a maraschino cherry as garnish.
6. Enjoy your Blue Hawaiian Bliss tropical beverage!

199. Swiss Absinthe

Time: 5 mins

Servings: 1

Ingredients:

- 1 part absinthe
- 3-5 parts cold water
- Sugar cube (non-compulsory)

Instructions:

1. Fill the glass with the absinthe.
2. Put the sugar cube on top of the glass with an absinthe spoon (or a regular spoon, if you want).
3. To dilute the absinthe, drizzle a slow stream of cold water over the sugar cube.
4. Mixture Must be stirred up to the sugar is dissolved and the beverage becomes murky.
5. Embrace the traditional Swiss Absinthe.

200. Swiss Fondue

Time: 30 mins

Servings: 4

Ingredients:

- 1 clove garlic, halved
- 1 1/2 cups of white wine (dry)
- 1 tbsp lemon juice
- 2 cups of shredded Emmental cheese
- 2 cups of shredded Gruyere cheese
- 1 tbsp cornstarch (non-compulsory, for thickness)
- A pinch of nutmeg
- Cubed French bread, steamed vegetables, apples (for dipping)

Instructions:

1. The garlic clove Must be slice in half and rubbed inside a fondue pot.
2. White wine and lemon juice Must be added to the fondue pot and heated over low heat.
3. Add the finely grated Gruyere and Emmental cheeses gradually while swirling continuously in a figure-eight motion up to dilute and smooth.
4. If you want a thicker fondue, combine a little wine with the cornstarch and stir it into the cheese Mixture.
5. Add nutmeg to season with a pinch.
6. With cubed French bread, steamed vegetables, and apple slices for dipping, place the fondue pot on a fondue stand.

201. Italian Negroni (Cocktail)

Time: 5 mins

Servings: 1

Ingredients:

- 1 oz gin
- 1 oz Campari
- 1 oz sweet vermouth
- Orange slice or twist for garnish

Instructions:

1. Add ice to a combining glass.
2. To the combining glass, add gin, Campari, and sweet vermouth.
3. Combine thoroughly up to cold.
4. Pour the Mixture through a strainer into an ice-filled rocks glass.
5. Add an orange slice or twist as a garnish.
6. Drink and enjoy a traditional Italian Negroni.

202. Italian Antipasti Platter

Time: 20 mins

Servings: 4

Ingredients:

- Split prosciutto
- Split salami or soppressata
- Marinated olives
- Marinated artichoke hearts
- Roasted red peppers
- Fresh mozzarella balls
- Cherry tomatoes
- Grissini (breadsticks)
- Crostini or split baguette

Instructions:

1. On a big platter, arrange the cherry tomatoes, mozzarella balls, prosciutto, salami, olives, artichoke hearts, roasted red peppers, and so on.
2. Serve alongside split baguette, grissini, and crostini.
3. Enjoy a delicious antipasti dish from Italy.

203. French Kir Breton Bonanza (Cocktail)

Time: 5 mins

Servings: 1

Ingredients:

- 4 oz dry sparkling apple cider (or apple champagne)
- 1 oz crème de cassis (blackcurrant liqueur)

- Fresh blackberries or a lemon twist for garnish

Instructions:
1. Insert a champagne flute with the crème de cassis.
2. Add dry sparkling apple cider to finish.
3. Add a lemon twist or fresh blackberries as a garnish.
4. The French Kir Breton Bonanza is fun.

204. Spanish Tinto de Verano Love

Time: 5 mins

Servings: 1

Ingredients:
- 2 oz red wine
- 2 oz lemon-lime soda (or sparkling water)
- Lemon or lime slices for garnish
- Ice cubes

Instructions:
1. Ice cubes Must be added to a glass.
2. Over the ice, pour red wine.
3. Add sparkling water or lemon-lime soda.
4. Gently blend by stirring.
5. Slices of lime or lemon may be garnished.
6. Take pleasure in the cooling Tinto de Verano Love.

205. Mexican Michelada

Time: 5 mins

Servings: 1

Ingredients:
- 1 chilled Mexican lager beer (e.g., Corona)
- 2 oz tomato juice or Clamato
- 1/2 oz fresh lime juice
- Hot sauce (e.g., Tabasco) as needed
- Worcestershire sauce as needed
- Tajín or salt for rimming the glass
- Ice cubes
- Lime wedge and celery stalk for garnish

Instructions:
1. Use a lime slice to run Tajn or salt around the rim of a glass before dipping it in the seasoning.
2. Ice cubes Must be put in the glass.
3. Include Clamato or tomato juice, lime juice from fresh limes, spicy sauce, and Worcestershire sauce.
4. Add some cold Mexican lager beer to the combine.
5. Gently stir the flavors together.
6. Add a lime wedge and a celery stem as garnish.
7. Enjoy the spicy Michelada from Mexico.

206. Mexican Guacamole

Time: 15 mins

Servings: 4

Ingredients:
- 3 ripe avocados
- 1 mini onion, lightly chop-up
- 1-2 ripe tomatoes, diced
- 1 jalapeño or serrano chili, seeded and lightly chop-up
- 1/4 cup of chop-up fresh cilantro
- 2 tbsp fresh lime juice
- Salt and pepper as needed
- Tortilla chips (for serving)

Instructions:
1. Take out the pits from the avocados, then scoop out the meat into a basin.
2. Use a fork or potato masher to mash the avocados up to they have the consistency you like.
3. Add the lime juice, chop-up cilantro, diced tomatoes, diced chile, and chop-up onion to the Mixture.
4. As needed, add salt and pepper to the food.
5. Enjoy the guacamole with some tortilla chips!

207. Caribbean Rum Runner Parade (Cocktail)

Time: 5 mins

Servings: 1

Ingredients:
- 1 oz light rum
- 1 oz dark rum
- 1 oz banana liqueur
- 1 oz blackberry liqueur
- 2 oz orange juice
- 2 oz pineapple juice
- Splash of grenadine
- Pineapple slice and maraschino cherry for garnish
- Ice cubes

Instructions:
1. Ice Must be put in a shaker.
2. Orange juice, pineapple juice, blackberry liqueur, banana liqueur, dark rum, light rum, and a dash of grenadine can all be added.
3. Thoroughly shake up to cooled.
4. Pour the strained Mixture into an ice-filled glass.
5. Add a pineapple slice and a maraschino cherry as garnish.
6. Drink while picturing the Caribbean Rum Runner Parade.

208. Turkish Sahlep

Time: 15 mins
Servings: 2

Ingredients:
- 2 cups of milk
- 2 tbsp sahlep powder (if unavailable, use cornstarch)
- 2 tbsp sugar (adjust as needed)
- A pinch of ground cinnamon or ground nutmeg for garnish

Instructions:
1. Whisk the milk and sahlep powder together thoroughly in a saucepan.
2. The milk Mixture Must be heated over medium heat while being regularly stirred up to it thickens and gently boils.
3. Take from the heat, then pour into mugs or cups of.
4. Add some ground nutmeg or cinnamon on top.
5. Serve the warming Turkish Sahlep warm and savor it.

209. Turkish Baklava

Time: 1 hr
Servings: 12-16

Ingredients:
- 1 box/pkg phyllo dough (16 oz), thawed
- 1 1/2 cups of unsalted butter, dilute
- 1 1/2 cups of chop-up walnuts or pistachios
- 1/2 cup of granulated sugar
- 1/2 tsp ground cinnamon
- 1 cup of water
- 1 cup of granulated sugar
- 1/2 cup of honey
- 1 tsp lemon juice

Instructions:
1. Turn on the oven to 350 °F (175 °C).
2. Chop-up walnuts or pistachios, 1/2 cup of sugar, and ground cinnamon Must be combined in a bowl.
3. Dilute butter Must be used to brush a baking dish.
4. Brush dilute butter over a layer of phyllo dough before placing it in the dish.
5. Up till there are around 8 layers, repeat the process, layering and buttering every sheet.
6. Over the phyllo layers, evenly distribute the nut Mixture.
7. The remaining phyllo sheets (approximately 8 additional layers) Must be buttered and layered on top of the nuts.
8. Slice the baklava into diamond or square shapes using a sharp knife.
9. Bake for about 45 mins, or up to crisp and golden brown, in a preheated oven.
10. Make the syrup by blending water, 1 cup of sugar, honey, and lemon juice in a saucepan while the baklava is baking. After bringing to a boil, simmer for 10 mins.
11. The hot syrup Must be poured over the baklava as soon as it is taken out of the oven, making sure to go into all the slices.
12. Before serving and enjoying the delectable Turkish dessert, let the baklava cool fully.

210. Greek Metaxa and Koulourakia

Time: 1 hr
Servings: Makes about 30 cookies

Ingredients:
- 1 cup of unsalted butter, melted
- 1 cup of sugar
- 2 Big eggs
- 1/2 cup of Metaxa (Greek brandy)
- 1 tsp vanilla extract
- 4 cups of all-purpose flour
- 1 tsp baking powder
- 1/4 tsp salt
- Sesame seeds (for topping)

Instructions:
1. Cream the butter and sugar in a big bowl up to they are light and creamy. One at a time, add the eggs, beating thoroughly after every addition.
2. Add the Metaxa and vanilla extract and combine thoroughly.

3. Combine the salt, baking soda, and flour in a separate basin. When a soft dough forms, gradually add this dry combination to the wet Mixture and stir.
4. Turn on the oven to 350 °F (175 °C). Use parchment paper to cover a baking sheet.
5. A mini bit of dough Must be rolled into a rope. Create a figure-eight shape with the rope known as a "koulourakia."
6. Sesame seeds Must be sprinkled on top of the cookies before baking for 15-20 mins, or up to gently golden.
7. Before serving, let the Koulourakia cool on a wire rack.

211. Indian Kingfisher Beer and Samosas

Time: 1 hr
Servings: 4-6

Ingredients:

- 2 cups of all-purpose flour
- 1/4 cup of vegetable oil
- 1/2 tsp salt
- Water (for dough)
- 1 cup of boiled and mashed potatoes
- 1/2 cup of green peas (cooked or refrigerate)
- 1/2 tsp cumin seeds
- 1/2 tsp turmeric
- 1/2 tsp garam masala
- 1/2 tsp chili powder
- Salt as needed
- Vegetable oil (for frying)
- For Serving:
- Kingfisher Beer (or any other Indian beer)

Instructions:

1. Make the samosa dough first. Combine the flour, salt, and vegetable oil in a bowl. Work in the water gradually while kneading the dough up to it is firm. After giving it a damp cloth to cover, give it 30 mins to rest.
2. Warm up a few tsp of vegetable oil in a pan for the filling. Sizzle the cumin seeds after adding them. After that, incorporate the mashed potatoes, green peas, salt, turmeric, garam masala, and chili powder. Combine thoroughly and heat the filling through for a few mins. Observe cooling.
3. The dough Must be slice up into mini balls, and every Must be rolled into an oval form. The oval Must now be slice up into two semicircles.
4. One semicircle at a time, moisten the straight edge with water, shape into a cone, and seal the edges.
5. Put the potato Mixture into the cone and push the edges together to close the top.
6. For frying, warm up some vegetable oil in a Big pan. Samosas Must be crisp and golden brown after frying.
7. Serve a cool Kingfisher Beer alongside the hot samosas.

212. Thai Leo Beer and Satay

Time: 1 hr (Marinating time included)
Servings: 4-6

Ingredients:

- 1 lb chicken or beef, thinly split
- 1/4 cup of soy sauce
- 2 tbsp fish sauce
- 2 tbsp vegetable oil
- 1 tbsp curry powder
- 1 tbsp turmeric powder
- 1 tbsp honey
- Wooden skewers (pre-soaked in water)
- Thai Leo Beer (or any other Thai beer) for serving

Instructions:

1. To prepare the marinade, combine the soy sauce, fish sauce, vegetable oil, curry powder, turmeric powder, and honey in a bowl.
2. Split beef or chicken Must be added to the marinade, thoroughly coated, and let to marinate for at least 30 mins (or longer for optimum flavor).
3. A grill or grill pan Must be preheated to high heat.
4. Put the soaked wooden skewers in the meat that has been marinated.
5. The satay skewers Must be cooked through and slightly browned after grilling them for two to three mins on every side.
6. Serve the satay with a chilled Thai Leo Beer and a side of peanut sauce.

213. Japanese Whisky Highball Frenzy

Time: 5 mins
Servings: 1

Ingredients:

- 2 oz Japanese whisky (e.g., Yamazaki, Hibiki, or Nikka)

73

- Ice cubes
- Chilled soda water
- Lemon or lime twist (for garnish)

Instructions:
1. Ice cubes are placed in a tall glass.
2. Over the ice, pour the Japanese whisky.
3. Pour a fresh glass of soda water on top.
4. Stir the ingredients together gently.
5. Add a lemon or lime twist as garnish.
6. Take pleasure in the cool Japanese Whisky Highball Frenzy!

214. Korean Hite Beer and Bibimbap

Time: 45 mins
Servings: 4

Ingredients:
- 4 cups of cooked short-grain rice
- 1 cup of cooked and seasoned ground beef (or chicken/tofu for vegetarian)
- 2 cups of assorted vegetables (carrots, spinach, mushrooms, zucchini, bean sprouts, etc.)
- 4 eggs
- Sesame oil
- Sesame seeds
- Bibimbap sauce (gochujang-based sauce)
- Hite Beer (or any other Korean beer) for serving

Instructions:
1. The different veggies Must be prepared by blanching or sautéing them individually, then adding sesame oil and a little salt as needed. When putting the bibimbap together afterwards, keep every veggie separate.
2. With a little soy sauce, sesame oil, and sesame seeds, cook the ground beef in a pan. If you're using tofu or poultry, season it appropriately.
3. Fry four eggs over-easy or with the sunny side up.
4. Put a portion of rice in a bowl and start putting the bibimbap together. Separately arrange the seasoned meat and cooked vegetables on top of the rice.
5. Fry an egg and place it in the middle of the bibimbap.
6. Add some bibimbap sauce and more sesame seeds for decoration.
7. Before eating, properly combine everything.
8. Serve a chilled Hite Beer alongside the bibimbap.

215. Vietnamese Bia Hoi and Pho

Time: 2 hrs
Servings: 4-6

Ingredients:
- For the Pho:
- 8 cups of beef broth
- 8 oz flat rice noodles
- 1/2 lb thinly split beef (eye round or flank steak)
- 1 medium onion, thinly split
- 2-3 green onions, split
- 2 tbsp fresh cilantro, chop-up
- 2 tbsp Thai basil leaves (or regular basil), chop-up
- Bean sprouts, lime wedges, and jalapeno slices for serving
- For the Bia Hoi:
- Bia Hoi (Vietnamese draft beer)

Instructions:
1. The beef stock Must be simmering in a big pot.
2. The broth will soften when you add the thinly split onions and let it cook for a few mins.
3. Following the directions on the box/pkg, prepare the rice noodles, drain, and set aside.
4. Slice the steak into thin slices and save it.
5. Put some cooked rice noodles in a bowl and start assembling the pho. Add a few slices of raw meat on top.
6. The steak and noodles Must be covered with the hot beef broth. The slices of beef will cook in the boiling liquid.
7. As a garnish, place some bean sprouts, lime wedges, jalapeño slices, chop-up green onions, cilantro, and basil on a platter and serve the pho. These garnishes can be added by diners as they please.
8. Sip a cool glass of Bia Hoi while enjoying the pho.

216. Moroccan Mint Tea and Harira

Time: 1 hr
Servings: 6-8

Ingredients:
- 1 tbsp olive oil
- 1 onion, lightly chop-up
- 2 cloves garlic, chop-up
- 1/2 cup of dried chickpeas, soaked overnight (or canned)
- 1/2 cup of red lentils
- 1/2 cup of diced tomatoes
- 1/4 cup of chop-up fresh cilantro
- 1/4 cup of chop-up fresh parsley

- 1/4 cup of vermicelli or broken spaghetti
- 1 tsp ground ginger
- 1 tsp ground cumin
- 1/2 tsp ground cinnamon
- 1/2 tsp ground turmeric
- 4 cups of vegetable or chicken broth
- Salt and pepper as needed
- For the Moroccan Mint Tea:
- 4 cups of water
- 3-4 tsp gunpowder green tea (or any green tea)
- 1/2 cup of fresh mint leaves
- Sugar or honey as needed

Instructions:
1. In a big pot over medium heat, warm the olive oil for the harira. Add the chop-up onions and garlic, and cook up to they are soft and just starting to brown.
2. Red lentils and soaked chickpeas Must be added to the saucepan (or canned). Add the chop-up cilantro, parsley, vermicelli or broken spaghetti, as well as the ground ginger, cumin, cinnamon, and turmeric.
3. Add the chicken or vegetable broth and season with salt and pepper. When the chickpeas and lentils are cooked, about 40 mins after bringing the stew to a boil, lower the heat, cover it, and let it simmer.
4. Boil 4 cups of water to make the Moroccan Mint Tea in the meantime. Add fresh mint leaves and gunpowder green tea after removing from the heat. Give it some time to steep. Tea can be tastefully sweetened with sugar or honey.
5. When the Harira is prepared, make any necessary seasoning adjustments. Serve it hot with a side of Moroccan Mint Tea.

217. Hawaiian Mai Tai Luau

Time: 5 mins
Servings: 1

Ingredients:
- 2 oz light rum
- 1 oz dark rum
- 1 oz orange curaçao or triple sec
- 2 oz freshly squeezed lime juice
- 1/2 oz orgeat syrup (almond syrup)
- Ice cubes
- Pineapple slice and maraschino cherry (for garnish)

Instructions:
1. Ice cubes Must be put in a shaker.
2. The shaker Must be filled with the light rum, dark rum, orange curaçao, lime juice, and orgeat syrup.
3. Stir the ingredients thoroughly.
4. Pour the strained Mixture into an ice-filled glass.
5. Add a cherry maraschino and a pineapple slice as garnish.
6. Enjoy a tropical Mai Tai Luau while sipping.

218. Swiss Glacier Martini Magic:

Time: 5 mins
Servings: 1

Ingredients:
- 2 oz vodka
- 1 oz melon liqueur
- 1 oz blue curaçao
- Ice cubes
- Lemon twist (for garnish)

Instructions:
1. Vodka, blue curaçao, and melon liqueur Must all be added to a cocktail shaker.
2. Shake the shaker vigorously after adding ice cubes.
3. Pour the Mixture through a strainer into a martini glass.
4. Add a lemon twist as a garnish.

NUTRITION INFO (per serving):
Cals: 230, Carbs: 21g, Protein: 0g, Fat: 0g

219. Italian Bellini and Prosciutto:

Time: 10 mins
Servings: 2

Ingredients:
- 2 ripe peveryes, peel off and pitted
- 4 oz pevery puree
- 8 oz Prosecco (Italian sparkling wine)
- 4 slices of prosciutto

Instructions:
1. The ripe peveryes Must be pureed in a blender up to smooth.
2. In two champagne flutes, evenly distribute the pevery puree.
3. Pour the Prosecco into every flute gradually.
4. Prosciutto slice on the side Must be served.

NUTRITION INFO (per serving):
Cals: 160, Carbs: 12g, Protein: 3g, Fat: 3g

220. French Pernod and Croque Monsieur:

Time: 30 mins

Servings: 4

Ingredients:

- 8 slices of white bread
- 4 slices of cooked ham
- 4 slices of Gruyère cheese
- 2 tbsp Dijon mustard
- 2 tbsp butter
- 2 cups of milk
- 2 tbsp all-purpose flour
- 2 tbsp finely grated Parmesan cheese
- Salt and pepper as needed
- Pernod (anise-flavored liqueur)

Instructions:

1. Turn on the oven to 400 °F (200 °C).
2. Four pieces of bread Must be covered in Dijon mustard.
3. Add a piece of ham and Gruyère cheese on the top of every slice.
4. To make sandwiches, top with the remaining slices of bread.
5. Melt the butter in a saucepan over medium heat. For one to two mins, combine in the flour.
6. As the sauce begins to thicken, stir in the milk gradually. Add salt, pepper, and Parmesan cheese.
7. Then, top the sandwiches with more Parmesan cheese after drizzling the sauce over them.
8. Bake the sandwiches in the oven for roughly 15 mins, or up to they are crispy and golden brown.
9. Serve alongside a glass of Pernod.

NUTRITION INFO (per serving):
Cals: 450, Carbs: 30g, Protein: 22g, Fat: 25g

221. Spanish Sherry and Gazpacho:

Time: 15 mins

Servings: 4

Ingredients:

- 6 ripe tomatoes, chop-up
- 1 cucumber, peel off and chop-up
- 1 red bell pepper, chop-up
- 1 mini red onion, chop-up
- 2 garlic cloves, chop-up
- 3 cups of tomato juice
- 2 tbsp red wine vinegar
- 2 tbsp olive oil
- Salt and pepper as needed
- Spanish sherry (such as Fino or Manzanilla)

Instructions:

1. Chop the tomatoes, cucumber, red bell pepper, red onion, and garlic cloves. Combine in a blender.
2. After blending, transfer the finished product to a big basin.
3. Olive oil, red wine vinegar, and tomato juice Must all be combined.
4. As needed, add salt and pepper to the food.
5. Before serving, the gazpacho Must be chilled in the fridge for at least an hr.
6. Pour Spanish sherry over every serving before placing it in bowls or glasses.

NUTRITION INFO (per serving):
Cals: 120, Carbs: 12g, Protein: 2g, Fat: 7g

222. Mexican Tequila Sunrise Fiesta:

Time: 5 mins

Servings: 1

Ingredients:

- 2 oz tequila
- 4 oz orange juice
- 1/2 oz grenadine syrup
- Ice cubes
- Orange slice and maraschino cherry (for garnish)

Instructions:

1. Ice cubes Must be added to a highball glass.
2. Over the ice, pour the tequila and orange juice.
3. Pour the grenadine syrup into the glass slowly so that it can settle to the bottom.
4. Add an orange slice and a maraschino cherry as garnish.

NUTRITION INFO (per serving):
Cals: 200, Carbs: 23g, Protein: 1g, Fat: 0g

223. Caribbean Painkiller Party:

Time: 5 mins

Servings: 1

Ingredients:

- 2 oz dark rum
- 4 oz pineapple juice

- 1 oz orange juice
- 1 oz cream of coconut
- Freshly finely grated nutmeg (for garnish)
- Pineapple slice and cherry (for garnish)

Instructions:
1. Dark rum, pineapple juice, orange juice, and cream of coconut Must all be added to a cocktail shaker.
2. Shake the shaker vigorously after adding ice cubes.
3. Pour the Mixture through a strainer into an ice-filled glass.
4. A pineapple slice, a cherry, and freshly finely grated nutmeg Must be added as garnish.

NUTRITION INFO (per serving):
Cals: 260, Carbs: 23g, Protein: 1g, Fat: 8g

224. Turkish Rakı and Kebabs:

Time: 40 mins
Servings: 4

Ingredients for Kebabs:
- 1 lb lamb or chicken, slice into cubes
- 1 red bell pepper, slice into chunks
- 1 green bell pepper, slice into chunks
- 1 red onion, slice into chunks
- 2 tbsp olive oil
- 1 tbsp lemon juice
- 2 garlic cloves, chop-up
- 1 tsp ground cumin
- Salt and pepper as needed
- Skewers

Ingredients for Rakı:
1. Turkish rak, an alcoholic beverage with anise flavor
2. icy water
3. Directions for making kebabs:
4. Olive oil, lemon juice, chop-up garlic, ground cumin, salt, and pepper Must all be combined in a bowl.
5. Chicken or lamb cubes Must be added to the marinade, and it Must marinate for at least 30 mins.
6. Get the grill or the broiler ready.
7. Alternate between threading bell peppers and onions with the marinated meat on skewers.
8. The kebabs Must be grilled or broiled up to the meat is thoroughly cooked and the veggies are soft.
9. Guidelines for Rak:
10. Turkish rak Must be poured into tiny glasses up to they are about one-fourth full.
11. To make the rak white and foggy, fill the glasses with cold water.
12. Enjoy the kebabs with the Rak on the side after serving.

NUTRITION INFO for Kebabs (per serving):
Cals: 300 (approximate, depending on meat choice), Carbs: 5g, Protein: 25g, Fat: 20g

225. Greek Metaxa and Taramasalata:

Time: 15 mins
Servings: 4

Ingredients for Taramasalata:
- 4 oz tarama (fish roe paste)
- 1 cup of breadcrumbs
- 1/2 cup of olive oil
- 1/4 cup of lemon juice
- 1 mini red onion, finely grated
- 2-3 tbsp Greek Metaxa (brandy)
- Freshly ground black pepper
- Pita bread or cucumber slices (for serving)

Instructions for Taramasalata:
1. The breadcrumbs, finely grated red onion, and tarama Must be combined in a mixer.
2. Olive oil and lemon juice Must be added gradually while blending.
3. Greek Metaxa Must be added after blending the ingredients up to it is creamy and smooth.
4. Add freshly ground black pepper as needed when seasoning.
5. Serve the taramasalata with cucumber slices or pita bread.

NUTRITION INFO for Taramasalata (per serving):
Cals: 300 (approximate), Carbs: 20g, Protein: 5g, Fat: 23g

226. Russian Moscow Mule Parade:

Time: 5 mins
Servings: 1

Ingredients:
- 2 oz vodka
- 4 oz ginger beer
- 1/2 oz fresh lime juice
- Ice cubes
- Lime slices (for garnish)
- Fresh mint (for garnish)

Instructions:
1. Ice cubes Must be added to a copper mug or highball glass.
2. Over the ice, add vodka and freshly squeezed lime juice.
3. Add more ginger beer and gently stir.
4. Lime slices and fresh mint are garnishes.

NUTRITION INFO (per serving):
Cals: 220, Carbs: 16g, Protein: 0g, Fat: 0g

227. Indian Mango Lassi and Samosas:

Time: 30 mins

Servings: 4

Ingredients for Mango Lassi:
- 2 ripe mangoes, peel off and pitted
- 1 cup of plain yogurt
- 1/2 cup of milk
- 2 tbsp honey or sugar
- 1/2 tsp ground cardamom
- Ice cubes
- Ingredients for Samosas:
- 1 cup of all-purpose flour
- 1/4 cup of vegetable oil
- 1/2 tsp cumin seeds
- 1/2 tsp ground coriander
- 1/2 tsp ground turmeric
- 1/2 tsp chili powder
- 1/2 cup of peas
- 1/2 cup of boiled and diced potatoes
- Salt as needed
- Oil for frying

Instructions for Mango Lassi:
1. Ripe mangoes, plain yogurt, milk, honey (or sugar), and ground cardamom Must all be blended up to smooth in a blender.
2. When completely combined, add the ice cubes and blend one more.
3. Pour the cooled mango lassi into glasses.

NUTRITION INFO for Mango Lassi (per serving):
Cals: 180 (approximate), Carbs: 34g, Protein: 4g, Fat: 4g

228. Thai Singha Beer and Tom Yum:

Time: 30 mins

Servings: 4

Ingredients for Tom Yum:
- 4 cups of chicken or vegetable broth
- 1 stalk lemongrass, bruised
- 3-4 kaffir lime leaves
- 1-inch piece of galangal or ginger, split
- 2 cloves garlic, chop-up
- 2 red chilies, split (adjust to spice preference)
- 1 cup of mushrooms (such as straw mushrooms or shiitake), split
- 1 cup of cooked shrimp or chicken (non-compulsory)
- 2 tbsp fish sauce
- 2 tbsp lime juice
- Fresh cilantro leaves and split scallions for garnish

Instructions for Tom Yum:
1. Bring the vegetable or chicken broth to a boil in a pot.
2. Include garlic, ginger or galangal, lemongrass, and kaffir lime leaves. For 5 to 10 mins, simmer.
3. Cook the mushrooms, along with the red chile slices, up to they are fork-tender.
4. Add cooked chicken or shrimp to the soup, if desired.
5. Lime juice and fish sauce are used to season the soup.
6. Add split scallions and fresh cilantro leaves as a garnish.
7. Thai Singha Beer Must be served on the side.

NUTRITION INFO for Tom Yum (per serving):
Cals: 120 (excluding shrimp or chicken), Carbs: 10g, Protein: 8g, Fat: 6g

229. Japanese Suntory Toki and Sushi:

Time: 30 mins

Servings: 2-4

Ingredients for Sushi:
- Sushi rice (cooked according to box/pkg instructions)
- Nori (seaweed) sheets
- Sushi-grade fish (such as tuna, salmon, or shrimp), split
- Avocado, cucumber, and carrot, split into thin strips
- Soy sauce, pickled ginger, and wasabi (for serving)

Instructions for Sushi:
1. On a spotless surface, spread a nori sheet and a bamboo sushi rolling mat.
2. To avoid sticking, wet your hands before spreading a thin layer of sushi rice on the nori and leaving a thin border at the top.

3. Slices of fish, avocado, cucumber, and carrot Must be arranged in a line along the middle of the rice.
4. Roll the sushi carefully on the bamboo mat, sealing the roll by applying light pressure.
5. Use a sharp knife to slice the roll into bite-sized pieces.
6. Serve alongside wasabi, pickled ginger, and soy sauce.
7. Enjoy with a serving of Suntory Toki whisky.

NUTRITION INFO for Sushi (per serving, depending on ingredients):
Cals: Varies based on ingredients
Carbs: Varies based on ingredients
Protein: Varies based on ingredients
Fat: Varies based on ingredients

230. Chinese Plum Wine and Spring Rolls:

Time: 45 mins
Servings: 4

Ingredients:
- 8 spring roll wrappers
- 1 cup of cooked shrimp or chicken (thinly split)
- 1 cup of shredded cabbage
- 1 cup of julienned carrots
- 1 cup of bean sprouts
- 2 cloves garlic, chop-up
- 2 tbsp soy sauce
- 1 tsp sesame oil
- 1 tsp cornstarch (combined with 2 tbsp water to make a slurry)
- Oil for frying

Instructions for
1. Garlic Must be sautéed in oil in a pan up to aromatic.
2. Cook the chicken or shrimp till almost finished.
3. Add bean sprouts, julienned carrots, and shredded cabbage. For a few mins, stir-fry.
4. Soy sauce and sesame oil are good seasonings. To thicken the filling, stir in the cornstarch slurry.
5. Let the filling to cool before wrapping it in the spring roll wrappers and water-sealing the edges.
6. The spring rolls Must be fried in hot oil up to they are crisp and golden.
7. Tips for making plum wine dip:
8. Chinese plum wine, soy sauce, honey or brown sugar, and finely grated ginger Must all be combined in a mini bowl.
9. Along with the Plum Wine Dip, serve the spring rolls.

NUTRITION INFO for Spring Rolls (per serving, assuming 2 rolls):
Cals: 250 (approximate), Carbs: 25g, Protein: 15g, Fat: 10g

231. Korean Makgeolli and Japchae:

Time: 45 mins
Servings: 4

Ingredients:
- 8 oz Korean sweet potato noodles (dangmyeon)
- 1/2 lb beef (sirloin or ribeye), thinly split
- 1 onion, thinly split
- 2 cups of spinach
- 1 carrot, julienned
- 1 red bell pepper, julienned
- 2 cloves garlic, chop-up
- 2 tbsp soy sauce
- 1 tbsp sesame oil
- 1 tbsp sugar
- Sesame seeds and split scallions (for garnish)

Ingredients:
1. 2 glasses of Korean rice wine, Makgeolli
2. To be followed by Japchae:
3. Follow the directions on the box/pkg to prepare the sweet potato noodles. Drain, then set apart.
4. Garlic and steak Must be cooked together in a pan.
5. Add carrots, red bell pepper, and onions. Stir-fry the vegetables up to they are soft.
6. Add the spinach, soy sauce, sesame oil, sugar, and cooked sweet potato noodles. Combine thoroughly.
7. Add split scallions and sesame seeds as a garnish.
8. Advice for Makgeolli:
9. Makgeolli Must be served cold in individual cups of.

NUTRITION INFO for Japchae (per serving):
Cals: 300 (approximate), Carbs: 45g, Protein: 15g, Fat: 7g

232. Vietnamese Bia Hoi and Bun Thit Nuong:

Time: 1 hr
Servings: 4

Ingredients for Bun Thit Nuong:
- 1 lb pork Muster, thinly split

79

- 4 cups of cooked vermicelli noodles
- 1 cucumber, julienned
- 1 carrot, julienned
- Bean sprouts, lettuce, and fresh herbs (mint, cilantro, Thai basil) for serving
- Crushed peanuts and fried shallots (for garnish)
- Lime wedges (for serving)

Instructions for Bun Thit Nuong:
1. Split pork Must be marinated in a Mixture of sugar, soy sauce, fish sauce, and chop-up garlic. Give it at least 30 mins to marinate.
2. Grill the marinated pork up to it is done and just beginning to brown.
3. On serving dishes, arrange the prepared vermicelli noodles, grilled pork, cucumber, and carrot.
4. Bean sprouts, lettuce, and fresh herbs Must be served on the side.
5. Add fried shallots and crushed peanuts as garnish.
6. Serve with Nuoc Cham dipping sauce and lime wedges.
7. Nuoc Cham preparation instructions: Combine fish sauce, warm water, sugar, lime juice, chop-up garlic, and thinly split red chilies in a bowl. Stir the sugar up to it melts.
8. Serve chilled Bia Hoi in beer glasses, according to the recipe.

NUTRITION INFO for Bun Thit Nuong (per serving):
Cals: 400 (approximate, depending on pork portion), Carbs: 40g, Protein: 25g, Fat: 15g

233. Moroccan Mint Tea and Pastilla:

Time: 1 hr
Servings: 4

Ingredients for Moroccan Mint Tea:
- 4 cups of water
- 4 tsp loose green tea or 4 green tea bags
- 4-6 sprigs of fresh mint
- Sugar or honey as needed
- Ingredients for Pastilla:
- 1 lb cooked chicken, shredded
- 1/2 cup of almonds, blanched and slivered
- 1/4 cup of powdered sugar
- 1 tsp ground cinnamon
- 1/2 tsp ground ginger
- Pinch of saffron threads
- 1/4 cup of chop-up fresh parsley
- 1/4 cup of chop-up fresh cilantro
- 6 eggs, beaten
- 8 sheets of phyllo dough
- Butter for brushing

Instructions for Moroccan Mint Tea:
1. Bring water to a boil in a teapot.
2. The teapot Must now contain green tea and fresh mint. Steep for a few mins.
3. Add sugar or honey as needed to sweeten the tea.
4. Pastilla instructions:
5. Shredded chicken, almonds, powdered sugar, cinnamon, ginger, saffron threads, chop-up parsley, and cilantro Must all be combined in a bowl.
6. The beaten eggs Must be scrambled in a different pan up to they are done but still wet.
7. Combine the chicken Mixture with the scrambled eggs.
8. Set the oven's temperature to 375°F (190°C).
9. In a baking dish, arrange half of the phyllo dough sheets, coating every layer with dilute butter.
10. Over the phyllo dough, distribute the chicken and egg Mixture.
11. Brush every layer of the remaining phyllo dough with more dilute butter before covering.
12. The pastilla Must be baked in the oven up to the phyllo dough is crisp and golden brown.
13. Combined with Moroccan Mint Tea, serve the pastilla.

NUTRITION INFO for Pastilla (per serving):
Cals: 350 (approximate), Carbs: 25g, Protein: 20g, Fat: 20g

234. Hawaiian Blue Lagoon Luau:

Time: 10 mins
Servings: 1

Ingredients:
- 1 1/2 oz coconut rum
- 1 oz blue curaçao
- 4 oz pineapple juice
- Ice cubes
- Pineapple slice and maraschino cherry (for garnish)

Instructions:
1. Pineapple juice, blue curaçao, and coconut rum Must all be added to a shaker.
2. Shake the shaker vigorously after adding ice cubes.

3. Pour the Mixture through a strainer into a tall, ice-filled glass.
4. Add a pineapple slice and a maraschino cherry as garnish.

NUTRITION INFO (per serving):
Cals: 240, Carbs: 30g, Protein: 0g, Fat: 0g

235. Swiss Swiss Mule Magic:

Time: 5 mins
Servings: 1

Ingredients:
- 2 oz Swiss gin
- 1/2 oz lime juice
- 4 oz ginger beer
- Ice cubes
- Lime wheel and fresh mint (for garnish)

Instructions:
1. Ice cubes Must be added to a copper mug or highball glass.
2. Over the ice, add Swiss gin and lime juice.
3. Add more ginger beer and gently stir.
4. Lime wheel and fresh mint are garnishes.

NUTRITION INFO (per serving):
Cals: 170, Carbs: 12g, Protein: 0g, Fat: 0g

236. Italian Sgroppino and Bruschetta:

Time: 20 mins
Servings: 4

Ingredients for Sgroppino:
- 1/2 cup of lemon sorbet
- 1/2 cup of vodka
- 1/4 cup of Prosecco (Italian sparkling wine)
- Fresh mint (for garnish)
- Ingredients for Bruschetta:
- 4 slices of Italian bread (ciabatta or baguette)
- 2 cups of cherry tomatoes, halved
- 2 cloves garlic, chop-up
- 1/4 cup of fresh basil leaves, chop-up
- 2 tbsp balsamic glaze
- 2 tbsp olive oil
- Salt and pepper as needed

Instructions for Sgroppino:
1. Combine vodka, Prosecco, and lemon sorbet in a blender.
2. Blend up to foamy and well-combined.
3. Pour into cold glasses, then top with mint leaves.
4. How to prepare bruschetta:
5. Set the oven's temperature to 400°F (200°C).
6. Olive oil Must be used after placing the bread pieces on a baking sheet.
7. The bread Must be baked up to crisp and brown.
8. Cherry tomatoes, chop-up basil, chop-up garlic, extra virgin olive oil, salt, and pepper Must all be combined in a bowl.
9. Place the toasted bread slices on top of the tomato Mixture.
10. Sgroppino Must be served with Bruschetta.

NUTRITION INFO for Bruschetta (per serving, assuming 1 slice):
Cals: 180 (approximate), Carbs: 20g, Protein: 4g, Fat: 9g

237. French Kir Royale Breton Bonanza:

Time: 5 mins
Servings: 1

Ingredients:
- 1/2 oz crème de cassis (blackcurrant liqueur)
- 4 oz Champagne or sparkling wine
- Fresh blackberries or raspberries (for garnish)

Instructions:
1. In a Champagne flute, pour the crème de cassis.
2. Add more sparkling wine or Champagne.
3. Fresh raspberries or blackberries make lovely garnishes.

NUTRITION INFO (per serving):
Cals: 100, Carbs: 7g, Protein: 0g, Fat: 0g

238. Spanish Tinto de Verano Love

Time: 5 mins
Servings: 1

Ingredients:
- 1 cup of red wine
- 1/2 cup of lemon soda
- 1 slice of lemon
- Ice cubes

Instructions:
1. Ice cubes Must be added to a glass.
2. Over the ice, pour red wine.
3. Wine is added with lemon soda.
4. Gently stir the ingredients together.
5. Add a lemon slice as a garnish.

NUTRITION INFO: (Approximate values per serving)
Cals: 150 kcal, Carbs: 20g, Alcohol: 12g

239. Mexican Horchata and Tacos

Time: 20 mins

Servings: 4

Ingredients for Horchata:

- 1 cup of long-grain white rice
- 4 cups of water
- 1/2 cup of sugar
- 1/2 cup of milk
- 1 tsp vanilla extract
- Ground cinnamon (for garnish)
- Ingredients for Tacos:
- 8 mini corn tortillas
- 1 lb ground beef or chicken
- 1 tbsp taco seasoning
- Shredded lettuce
- Diced tomatoes
- Shredded cheese
- Salsa

Instructions for Tacos:

1. Cook the ground beef or chicken in a pan up to browned.
2. Add taco seasoning and adhere to the directions on the box/pkg.
3. Use a microwave or a griddle to warm the corn tortillas.
4. Place the cooked meat, lettuce, tomatoes, cheese, and salsa inside every tortilla.

NUTRITION INFO for Horchata: (Approximate values per serving)
Cals: 150 kcal, Carbs: 32g, Protein: 2g

240. Caribbean Rum Swizzle Soiree

Time: 10 mins

Servings: 1

Ingredients:

- 2 oz dark rum
- 1 oz lime juice
- 1 oz pineapple juice
- 1/2 oz grenadine
- 1 dash of Angostura bitters
- Ice cubes
- Pineapple slice and cherry for garnish

Instructions:

1. Ice cubes Must be put in a shaker.
2. To the shaker, add the rum, lime juice, pineapple juice, grenadine, and bitters.
3. For about 15 seconds, shake vigorously.
4. Strain into an ice-filled, cooled glass.
5. Add a cherry and a pineapple slice as garnish.

NUTRITION INFO: (Approximate values per serving)
Cals: 180 kcal, Carbs: 10g, Alcohol: 14g

241. Turkish Salep and Turkish Delight

Time: 15 mins

Servings: 2

Ingredients for Salep:

- 2 cups of milk
- 2 tbsp salep powder
- 2 tbsp sugar
- A pinch of ground cinnamon (non-compulsory)

Instructions for Salep:

1. The milk Must be heated in a pan over medium heat.
2. As it thickens, add sugar and salep powder and stir continuously.
3. If preferred, include a pinch of ground cinnamon.
4. Pour heated liquid into mugs and serve.
5. How to prepare Turkish Delight:
6. A square dish Must be greased or lined with parchment paper.
7. Combine cornstarch and water well in a saucepan.
8. Cook over medium heat, continually stirring, up to it thickens and turns into a sticky, transparent Mixture. Add sugar and lemon juice.
9. Combine well after adding the rosewater and food coloring (if using).
10. Smooth the top after pouring the contents into the dish.
11. On top, scatter chop-up pistachios.
12. Overnight or for a few hrs, let it cool and solidify.
13. Serve after Cutting into little squares.

NUTRITION INFO for Salep: (Approximate values per serving)
Cals: 200 kcal, Carbs: 40g, Protein: 6g

242. Greek Ouzo and Dolmades

Time: 30 mins

Servings: 4

Ingredients:

- 1 jar of grape leaves in brine, drained and rinsed
- 1 cup of long-grain rice
- 1/2 cup of chop-up onion
- 1/4 cup of chop-up fresh dill
- 1/4 cup of chop-up fresh mint
- 1/4 cup of chop-up pine nuts or walnuts
- 2 tbsp olive oil
- Juice of 1 lemon
- Salt and pepper as needed

Instructions for Ouzo:

1. Olive oil Must be used to sauté the chop-up onion up to it turns transparent.
2. Add the rice, pine nuts or walnuts, dill, and mint. Cook for a little while.
3. Cook the rice with the addition of water according to the directions on the rice box/pkg.
4. Add salt, pepper, and lemon juice for seasoning.
5. Let the Mixture to cool a bit.
6. To make a tiny roll, take a grape leaf, put a tbsp of the rice Mixture in the middle, and fold the leaf over.
7. Repetition is required with the remaining grape leaves and filling.
8. Serve the dolmades cold or at room temperature.

NUTRITION INFO for Dolmades: (Approximate values per serving)
Cals: 180 kcal, Carbs: 30g, Protein: 4g, Fat: 6g

243. Russian Black Russian and Piroshki

Time: 45 mins

Servings: 2

Ingredients for Black Russian:

- 2 oz vodka
- 1 oz coffee liqueur (e.g., Kahlua)
- Ice cubes
- Ingredients for Piroshki:
- 1 lb ground beef
- 1/2 cup of diced onion
- 1/2 cup of diced boiled potatoes
- 2 tbsp vegetable oil
- Salt and pepper as needed
- Store-bought or homemade dough for piroshki
- Instructions for Black Russian:
- Fill a glass with ice cubes.
- Pour vodka and coffee liqueur over the ice.
- Stir well before serving.

Instructions for Piroshki:

1. Cook the diced onion in vegetable oil in a pan up to translucent.
2. Brown the ground beef after adding it. Add salt and pepper as needed.
3. Combine well before adding the diced boiled potatoes to the beef Mixture.
4. The dough Must be rolled out and slice into circles with a diameter of about 4 inches.
5. Every circle Must have a tbsp of the meat filling in the center.
6. To create a semi-circle, fold the dough over the filling and pinch the sides to seal.
7. The piroshki Must be baked at 375°F (190°C) in a preheated oven up to golden brown.

NUTRITION INFO for Piroshki: (Approximate values per serving)
Cals: 350 kcal, Carbs: 20g, Protein: 20g, Fat: 20g

244. Indian Kingfisher Beer and Pakoras

Time: 30 mins

Servings: 4

Ingredients for Pakoras:

- 1 cup of chickpea flour (besan)
- 1/2 cup of water
- 1 cup of combined vegetables (e.g., potatoes, onions, spinach)
- 1 tsp cumin seeds
- 1 tsp garam masala
- 1/2 tsp turmeric powder
- Oil for frying
- Salt as needed

Ingredients for Beer:

1. 1 bottle of light beer (such as Kingfisher)
2. An ice cube
3. Directions for making pakoras:
4. To produce a smooth batter, combine chickpea flour, water, cumin seeds, garam masala, turmeric powder, and salt in a bowl.
5. Combine thoroughly after adding the blended veggies to the batter.
6. For frying, heat oil in a deep pan.
7. Spoonfuls of the vegetable batter Must be dropped into the hot oil and fried up to crispy and golden brown.
8. The pakoras Must be taken out of the oil and dried on paper towels.

NUTRITION INFO for Pakoras: (Approximate values per serving)
Cals: 150 kcal, Carbs: 20g, Protein: 5g, Fat: 6g

245. Thai Chang Beer and Green Curry

Time: 30 mins

Servings: 2

Ingredients for Green Curry:

- 1 lb chicken (or tofu for vegetarian option), slice into bite-sized pieces
- 1 can (14 oz) coconut milk
- 2 tbsp green curry paste
- 1 cup of combined vegetables (e.g., bell peppers, bamboo shoots, green beans)
- 1 tbsp fish sauce (or soy sauce for vegetarian option)
- 1 tbsp palm sugar (or brown sugar)
- Fresh basil leaves
- Cooked jasmine rice
- Ingredients for Beer:
- 2 bottles of Chang beer (or any other Thai beer)
- Ice cubes

Instructions for Green Curry:

1. Green curry paste and a tiny amount of coconut milk are heated in a saucepan while being stirred up to fragrant.
2. Cook the chicken (or tofu) after adding it up to it loses its pink color.
3. Add the remaining coconut milk, then boil the Mixture.
4. Add palm sugar, fish sauce (or soy sauce), and combined veggies. Simmer the vegetables up to they are done.
5. Fresh basil leaves are a nice garnish.
6. Serve jasmine rice alongside the green curry.

NUTRITION INFO for Green Curry: (Approximate values per serving)
Cals: 400 kcal, Carbs: 15g, Protein: 25g, Fat: 25g

246. Japanese Yamazaki Whisky and Tempura

Time: 40 mins

Servings: 2

Ingredients for Tempura:

- Assorted vegetables (e.g., sweet potatoes, bell peppers, zucchini, carrots)
- Shrimp or seafood (non-compulsory)
- 1 cup of all-purpose flour
- 1/2 cup of cornstarch
- 1 tsp baking powder
- 1 cup of ice-cold water
- Oil for frying
- Tempura dipping sauce (store-bought or homemade)

Ingredients for Whisky:

1. 2 ozs of Yamazaki (or other Japanese whiskey)
2. An ice cube
3. How to prepare tempura:
4. Make bite-sized slices in the seafood and vegetables.
5. All-purpose flour, cornstarch, and baking powder Must be combined in a bowl.
6. The dry components Must only be blended with ice-cold water, therefore occasional lumps are acceptable.
7. For frying, heat oil in a deep pan.
8. Dip the shrimp and veggies in the tempura batter before frying them till crisp and golden.
9. Towel-dry the tempura after draining it.
10. Serve the dipping sauce alongside the tempura.

NUTRITION INFO for Tempura: (Approximate values per serving)
Cals: 250 kcal, Carbs: 35g, Protein: 5g, Fat: 10g

247. Chinese Baijiu and Kung Pao Chicken

Time: 30 mins

Servings: 4

Ingredients for Kung Pao Chicken:

- 1 lb chicken breast, slice into bite-sized pieces
- 1/2 cup of roasted peanuts
- 1/2 cup of diced bell peppers
- 1/2 cup of diced onions
- 3-4 dried red chilies (adjust to your spice preference)
- 2 cloves garlic, chop-up
- 1-inch piece of ginger, chop-up
- 2 tbsp vegetable oil
- 2 tbsp soy sauce
- 1 tbsp Chinese black vinegar (or balsamic vinegar)
- 1 tbsp sugar
- 1 tbsp cornstarch (for thickening)
- Cooked white rice

Ingredients for Baijiu:

1. 2 ozs of Chinese white spirit (Baijiu)

2. An ice cube
3. How to prepare Kung Pao chicken:
4. To create the sauce, combine the soy sauce, sugar, and Chinese black vinegar in a bowl.
5. In a wok or skillet, heat vegetable oil over high heat.
6. Dried red chiles, ginger, and garlic, all chop-up, Must be stir-fried up to aromatic.
7. Chicken pieces Must be added and stir-fried up to done and browned.
8. Stir-fry the bell peppers and onions in diced form for a few mins more.
9. Combine well after adding the sauce to the chicken and vegetables.
10. Make a slurry of cornstarch and a tiny amount of water in a separate, minier bowl.
11. To thicken the sauce, add the cornstarch slurry to the pan.
12. Add the toasted peanuts and combine everything.
13. Serve white rice alongside the Kung Pao Chicken.

NUTRITION INFO for Kung Pao Chicken: (Approximate values per serving)
Cals: 350 kcal, Carbs: 15g, Protein: 25g, Fat: 20g

248. Korean Cass Beer and Bulgogi

Time: 40 mins
Servings: 2

Ingredients for Cass Beer:

- 2 bottles of Korean Cass Beer (or any other light beer)
- Ice cubes
- Ingredients for Bulgogi:
- 1 lb thinly split beef (sirloin or ribeye)
- 1/4 cup of soy sauce
- 2 tbsp brown sugar
- 1 tbsp sesame oil
- 2 cloves garlic, chop-up
- 1-inch piece of ginger, finely grated
- 2 green onions, split
- 1 tbsp vegetable oil
- Sesame seeds (for garnish)
- Cooked white rice (for serving)
- Instructions for Cass Beer:
- Chill the Cass Beer in the refrigerator.
- Fill a glass with ice cubes.
- Pour the beer into the glass and serve cold.

Instructions for Bulgogi:
1. To create the marinade, combine the soy sauce, brown sugar, sesame oil, finely grated ginger, chop-up garlic, and green onion slices in a bowl.
2. Give the thinly split beef a good 30 mins to marinate in the marinade.
3. Vegetable oil is heated at a high temperature in a skillet.
4. Stir-fry the meat with the marinade up to it is cooked through and caramelized.
5. Add sesame seeds as a garnish.
6. Serve white rice beside the bulgogi.

NUTRITION INFO for Bulgogi: (Approximate values per serving)
Cals: 300 kcal, Carbs: 10g, Protein: 25g, Fat: 15g

249. Vietnamese Ca Phe Sua Da and Banh Xeo

Time: 30 mins
Servings: 2

Ingredients for Ca Phe Sua Da:

- 2 cups of brewed Vietnamese coffee (strong, dark roast)
- 2 tbsp sweetened condensed milk
- Ice cubes
- Ingredients for Banh Xeo (Vietnamese Savory Pancake):
- 1 cup of rice flour
- 1 cup of coconut milk
- 1/2 cup of water
- 1/2 lb shrimp, peel off and deveined
- 1/2 lb pork belly or thinly split pork loin
- 1 cup of bean sprouts
- 1/2 cup of split green onions
- Fresh herbs (mint, cilantro, and perilla leaves)
- Dipping sauce (Nuoc Cham)

Instructions for Ca Phe Sua Da:
1. Ice cubes Must be put in two glasses.
2. Over the ice, pour brewed Vietnamese coffee.
3. Every glass Must have a spoonful of sweetened condensed milk.
4. Before serving, thoroughly stir.
5. Guidelines for Banh Xeo:
6. To make the pancake batter, stir together the rice flour, coconut milk, and water in a bowl.
7. A tiny amount of oil Must be heated over medium heat in a non-stick skillet.
8. Sauté the pork and shrimp up to done.

9. A ladleful of pancake batter Must be poured into the skillet, and it Must be swirled to coat the bottom.
10. One side of the pancake Must be topped with a few bean sprouts and thinly split green onions.
11. The pancake Must be folded in half and cooked up to crispy.
12. Serve the Banh Xeo with dipping sauce and fresh herbs.

NUTRITION INFO for Banh Xeo: (Approximate values per serving)
Cals: 400 kcal, Carbs: 30g, Protein: 25g, Fat: 20g

250. Moroccan Mint Tea and Briouats

Time: 30 mins

Servings: 4

Ingredients for:

- 4 cups of water
- 2 tbsp green tea leaves (or 4 green tea bags)
- 4-6 sprigs of fresh mint
- Sugar (as needed)
- Ingredients for Briouats (Moroccan Savory Pastries):
- 1/2 lb ground beef or lamb
- 1/2 cup of lightly chop-up onions
- 1/4 cup of chop-up fresh parsley
- 1/4 cup of chop-up fresh cilantro
- 1/2 tsp ground cinnamon
- 1/4 tsp ground cumin
- Salt and pepper as needed
- Filo dough sheets
- Butter, dilute
- Vegetable oil for frying

Instructions:

1. Bring water to a boil in a teapot.
2. After adding green tea, let it steep for a few mins (or use tea bags).
3. Add sugar and fresh mint as needed.
4. Through a sieve, pour the tea into the cups of.
5. Advice for Briouats:
6. Cook the ground beef (or lamb) and onions in a skillet up to the meat is well-browned and thoroughly cooked.
7. Sprinkle in salt, pepper, ground cumin, ground cinnamon, chop-up cilantro, and chop-up parsley. Combine well, then let it to cool.
8. Strips of filo dough about 2 inches wide Must be slice.
9. Dilute butter Must be brushed over every strip.
10. At one end of the strip, place a tbsp of the meat Mixture before folding the strip into a triangle.
11. Up up to the end of the strip, keep folding the triangle and sealing it with additional dilute butter.
12. For frying, warm up some vegetable oil in a Big pan.
13. The briouats Must be fried up to crisp and golden.

NUTRITION INFO for Briouats: (Approximate values per serving)
Cals: 250 kcal, Carbs: 15g, Protein: 10g, Fat: 18g

251. Hawaiian Lava Flow Luau

Time: 15 mins

Servings: 2

Ingredients:

- 2 oz light rum
- 2 oz coconut cream
- 1/2 cup of fresh or refrigerate strawberries
- 1 ripe banana
- 2 cups of crushed ice
- Pineapple slices and cherries for garnish

Instructions:

1. Light rum, coconut cream, fresh or refrigerate strawberries, and the ripe banana Must all be combined in a blender.
2. Blend in the ice cubes after adding them.
3. Put glasses with the Mixture inside.
4. Slices of pineapple and cherries are used as garnish.

NUTRITION INFO: (Approximate values per serving)
Cals: 300 kcal, Carbs: 40g, Protein: 2g, Fat: 15g

252. Swiss Chocolate Martini Magic

Time: 10 mins

Servings: 2

Ingredients:

- 3 oz chocolate liqueur
- 3 oz vodka
- 1 oz coffee liqueur (e.g., Kahlua)
- Ice cubes
- Chocolate shavings (for garnish)

Instructions:

1. Ice cubes Must be put in a shaker.

2. Vodka, coffee liqueur, and chocolate liqueur Must be added to the shaker.
3. For about 15 seconds, shake vigorously.
4. Pour the contents into martini glasses that have been cooled.
5. Add chocolate shavings as a garnish.

NUTRITION INFO: (Approximate values per serving)
Cals: 250 kcal, Carbs: 20g, Alcohol: 24g

253. Italian Limoncello Spritz and Caprese

Time: 10 mins
Servings: 2

Ingredients for Limoncello Spritz:

- 3 oz Limoncello liqueur
- 3 oz Prosecco (Italian sparkling wine)
- 1 oz club soda
- Ice cubes
- Lemon slices and mint leaves for garnish

Instructions for Caprese Salad:
1. Slice some ripe tomatoes and new mozzarella cheese.
2. On a serving plate, arrange the mozzarella, tomatoes, and fresh basil.
3. Add balsamic glaze (if used) and extra virgin olive oil.
4. As needed, add salt and pepper to the food.

NUTRITION INFO for Caprese Salad: (Approximate values per serving)
Cals: 250 kcal, Carbs: 5g, Protein: 15g, Fat: 18g

254. French Kir Normand Bonanza

Time: 10 mins
Servings: 2

Ingredients:

- 4 oz dry white wine (e.g., Sauvignon Blanc)
- 2 oz blackcurrant liqueur (e.g., Crème de Cassis)
- Ice cubes
- Apple slices and blackberries for garnish

Instructions:
1. Ice cubes Must be added to two wine glasses.
2. Over the ice, pour dry white wine.
3. To every glass, add blackcurrant liqueur.
4. Gently blend by stirring.
5. Blackberries and apple slices make lovely garnishes.

NUTRITION INFO: (Approximate values per serving)
Cals: 150 kcal, Carbs: 10g, Alcohol: 16g

255. Spanish Cava and Patatas Bravas

Time: 45 mins
Servings: 2

Ingredients for Cava:

- 2 cups of Spanish Cava (or any other sparkling wine)
- Ice cubes

Ingredients for Patatas Bravas:
1. 2 big, peel off, and cubed potatoes
2. frying with olive oil
3. 1/fourth cup of tomato sauce
4. Smoked paprika, 1 tsp
5. Cayenne pepper, 1/2 tsp. (modify to your taste)
6. pepper and salt as desired
7. (Store-bought or home-made) garlic aioli
8. split parsley (for decoration)
9. Cava needs these directives:
10. Cava from Spain Must be chilled in the fridge.
11. Ice cubes Must be added to two wine glasses.
12. Cava Must be poured into glasses before serving.
13. Patatas Bravas preparation guidelines:
14. Olive oil is heated over medium-high heat in a skillet.
15. Potato cubes Must be fried up to crisp and golden.
16. The potatoes Must be taken out of the skillet and dried with paper towels.
17. To make the bravas sauce, combine tomato sauce, smoked paprika, cayenne, salt, and pepper in a separate bowl.
18. Add the bravas sauce to the fried potatoes and toss to coat.
19. Garnish the Patatas Bravas with chop-up parsley and serve with garlic aioli.

NUTRITION INFO for Patatas Bravas: (Approximate values per serving)
Cals: 300 kcal, Carbs: 30g, Protein: 5g, Fat: 18g

256. Mexican Tequila Sunset Fiesta

Time: 10 mins
Servings: 2

Ingredients:

- 3 oz tequila
- 2 oz orange juice

87

- 2 oz grenadine syrup
- Ice cubes
- Orange slices and maraschino cherries for garnish

Instructions:
1. Ice cubes Must be put in two glasses.
2. Every glass Must contain tequila and orange juice.
3. To produce a sunset impression, slowly pour grenadine syrup into the glass over the back of a spoon.
4. Orange slices and maraschino cherries are used as garnish.

NUTRITION INFO: (Approximate values per serving)
Cals: 200 kcal, Carbs: 15g, Alcohol: 18g

257. Caribbean Hurricane Party

Time: 15 mins

Servings: 2

Ingredients:
- 3 oz dark rum
- 2 oz light rum
- 2 oz passion fruit juice
- 2 oz orange juice
- 1 oz lime juice
- 1 oz simple syrup
- Ice cubes
- Orange slices and maraschino cherries for garnish

Instructions:
1. Ice cubes Must be put in two glasses.
2. Combine dark rum, light rum, passion fruit juice, lime juice, orange juice, and simple syrup in a shaker.
3. For about 15 seconds, shake vigorously.
4. Into the glasses, strain the Mixture.
5. Orange slices and maraschino cherries are used as garnish.

NUTRITION INFO: (Approximate values per serving)
Cals: 250 kcal, Carbs: 20g, Alcohol: 24g

258. Turkish Mastic Raki and Turkish Delight

Time: 10 mins

Servings: 2

Ingredients:
- 1 cup of cornstarch
- 1 cup of water
- 1 1/2 cups of sugar
- 1 tsp rosewater (or any other flavoring)
- Food coloring (non-compulsory)
- Powdered sugar and crushed pistachios (for coating)
- Instructions for Mastic Raki:
- Chill the Turkish Raki in the freezer.
- Fill two glasses with ice cubes.
- Pour the Raki into the glasses and serve.

Instructions:
1. Combine cornstarch and water well in a saucepan.
2. Over low heat, while constantly stirring, add sugar.
3. Add the rosewater and food coloring, if desired, when the Mixture begins to thicken and come together (after about 10 mins).
4. Fill a greased dish with the Mixture, then let it to cool and set.
5. Turkish Delight Must be slice into squares and covered in powdered sugar and chop-up pistachios.

NUTRITION INFO for Turkish Delight:
(Approximate values per serving)
Cals: 180 kcal, Carbs: 45g, Protein: 0g, Fat: 0g

259. Greek Tsipouro and Saganaki

Time: 15 mins

Servings: 2

Ingredients for Tsipouro:
- 4 oz Greek Tsipouro (or any other pomace brandy)
- Ice cubes
- Ingredients for Saganaki:
- 1/2 lb Kefalotyri cheese (or any other hard, salty cheese)
- 1/4 cup of all-purpose flour
- 2 tbsp olive oil
- 1 lemon, slice into wedges

Instructions :
1. Slice the cheese into substantial pieces.
2. Using all-purpose flour, dredge the cheese slices and shake off any excess.
3. Olive oil is heated over medium-high heat in a skillet.
4. The cheese slices Must be fried up to crisp and brown on all sides.

5. Saganaki Must be served right away with lemon wedges.

NUTRITION INFO for Saganaki: (Approximate values per serving)
Cals: 300 kcal, Carbs: 5g, Protein: 20g, Fat: 22g

260. Russian White Russian and Blinchiki

Time: 20 mins

Servings: 2

Ingredients for White Russian:
- 2 oz vodka
- 1 oz coffee liqueur (e.g., Kahlua)
- 1 oz heavy cream
- Ice cubes

Instructions for Blinchiki:
1. The crepe batter is made by combining flour, eggs, milk, dilute butter, and a dash of salt in a basin.
2. A nonstick skillet Must be heated to medium.
3. A ladleful of the batter Must be added to the skillet, and it Must be swirled to coat the bottom.
4. Cook the crepe up to the bottom is golden brown and the edges begin to lift.
5. Cook the opposite side of the crepe by flipping it.
6. Continue by using the remaining batter.
7. Every crepe Must be filled with your preferred contents before being folded into quarters or rolled up.

NUTRITION INFO for Blinchiki: (Approximate values per serving)
Cals: 150 kcal, Carbs: 20g, Protein: 6g, Fat: 6g

261. Indian Kingfisher Beer and Tandoori Chicken

Time: 1 hr 30 mins

Servings: 2

Ingredients:
- 1 lb chicken drumsticks or thighs, skinless and bone-in
- 1 cup of plain yogurt
- 2 tbsp Tandoori masala spice combine
- 1 tbsp lemon juice
- 1 tbsp vegetable oil
- 2 cloves garlic, chop-up
- 1-inch piece of ginger, finely grated
- Salt and pepper as needed
- Fresh cilantro leaves (for garnish)

Instructions for Tandoori Chicken:
1. To create the marinade, combine the plain yogurt, lemon juice, vegetable oil, chop-up garlic, finely grated ginger, salt, and pepper in a bowl.
2. To help the marinade permeate, lightly score the chicken pieces.
3. Place the chicken in the refrigerator to marinate for at least one hr, preferably overnight. Coat the chicken with the marinade.
4. Heat the oven or grill to a high setting.
5. The marinated chicken Must be cooked thoroughly and browned.
6. Before serving, garnish with fresh cilantro leaves.

NUTRITION INFO for Tandoori Chicken: (Approximate values per serving)
Cals: 400 kcal, Carbs: 6g, Protein: 30g, Fat: 25g

262. Thai Singha Beer and Green Papaya Salad

Time: 20 mins

Servings: 2

Ingredients:
- 2 cups of shredded green papaya
- 1/2 cup of cherry tomatoes, halved
- 2 cloves garlic, chop-up
- 2-3 Thai bird chilies, lightly chop-up (adjust to your spice preference)
- 1-2 tbsp fish sauce (or soy sauce for vegetarian option)
- 1-2 tbsp lime juice
- 1 tbsp palm sugar (or brown sugar)
- 2 tbsp roasted peanuts, crushed

Instructions:
1. Shredded green papaya, cherry tomatoes, garlic, and Thai bird chilies are combined in a sizable bowl.
2. To create the dressing, combine palm sugar, lime juice, and fish sauce in a separate mini bowl.
3. Combine the papaya Mixture with the dressing after pouring it over it.
4. Fresh cilantro leaves are used as a garnish, followed by crushed toasted peanuts.
5. How to prepare Singha Beer:
6. Put the Singha beer in the fridge to chill.
7. Ice cubes Must be put in two glasses.
8. Serving chilled, pour the beer into the cups of.

NUTRITION INFO for Green Papaya Salad: (Approximate values per serving)
Cals: 150 kcal, Carbs: 15g, Protein: 4g, Fat: 8g

263. Japanese Toki Highball Parade

Time: 5 mins

Servings: 2

Ingredients:

- 3 oz Japanese Toki whisky (or any other Japanese whisky)
- 6 oz soda water
- Ice cubes
- Lemon slices (for garnish)

Instructions:
1. Ice cubes Must be added to two highball glasses.
2. Every glass Must be filled with Japanese Toki whiskey.
3. Add soda water to finish.
4. Gently blend by stirring.
5. Slices of lemon are a garnish.

NUTRITION INFO: (Approximate values per serving)
Cals: 120 kcal, Carbs: 0g, Alcohol: 14g

264. Chinese Tsingtao Beer and Dim Sum

Time: 30 mins

Servings: 2

Ingredients:

- Assorted Dim Sum (e.g., steamed dumplings, spring rolls, bao buns, siu mai)
- Soy sauce and chili sauce (for dipping)
- Instructions for Tsingtao Beer:
- Chill the Tsingtao beer in the refrigerator.
- Fill two glasses with ice cubes.
- Pour the beer into the glasses and serve cold.

Instructions:
1. According to the directions on the packaging, steam or cook the dim sum.
2. On a serving platter, arrange the dim sum.
3. Serve with dipping sauces like soy and chili.

NUTRITION INFO for Dim Sum: (Approximate values per serving)
Cals: Varies based on Dim Sum selection
Carbs: Varies based on Dim Sum selection
Protein: Varies based on Dim Sum selection
Fat: Varies based on Dim Sum selection

265. Korean Hite Beer and Korean Fried Chicken

Time: 1 hr

Servings: 2

Ingredients:

- 1 lb chicken wings or drumettes
- 1/2 cup of all-purpose flour
- 1/4 cup of cornstarch
- 1 tsp baking powder
- 1/2 tsp salt
- 1/2 cup of cold water
- Oil for frying
- 1/4 cup of Korean gochujang sauce (or any other spicy sauce)
- 1 tbsp soy sauce
- 1 tbsp honey
- Sesame seeds and chop-up scallions (for garnish)

Instructions for Korean Fried Chicken:
1. Combine all-purpose flour, cornstarch, baking soda, and salt in a basin.
2. Combine the dry ingredients with the cold water only up to incorporated (a few lumps are acceptable).
3. For frying, heat oil in a deep pan.
4. Chicken pieces are dipped in batter before being fried till golden and crispy.
5. To prepare the glaze, combine the honey, soy sauce, and Korean gochujang sauce in a separate bowl.
6. Stir the glaze into the fried chicken up to it is evenly distributed.
7. Add chop-up scallions and sesame seeds as a garnish.

NUTRITION INFO for Korean Fried Chicken: (Approximate values per serving)
Cals: 350 kcal, Carbs: 20g, Protein: 25g, Fat: 18g

266. Vietnamese Bia Hoi and Goi Cuon

Time: 30 mins

Servings: 2

Ingredients for Goi Cuon (Vietnamese Spring Rolls):

- Rice paper wrappers
- Cooked shrimp, peel off and deveined
- Rice vermicelli noodles, cooked

- Lettuce leaves
- Fresh herbs (mint, cilantro, and perilla leaves)
- Bean sprouts
- Chop-up peanuts
- Dipping sauce (Nuoc Cham)

Instructions for Goi Cuon:
1. A rice paper wrapper Must be briefly dipped in warm water to make it more malleable.
2. On a spotless surface, spread out the melted rice paper.
3. A lettuce leaf and a few rice vermicelli noodles Must be placed in the center of the rice paper.
4. On top of the noodles, scatter cooked shrimp, fresh herbs, and bean sprouts.
5. As you roll the rice paper into a spring roll form, fold the sides over the filling.
6. Continue by using the remaining ingredients.
7. Serve the Goi Cuon with dipping sauce and chop-up peanuts.

NUTRITION INFO for Goi Cuon: (Approximate values per serving)
Cals: 150 kcal, Carbs: 15g, Protein: 10g, Fat: 5g

267. Moroccan Mint Tea and Kefta Tagine

Time: 30 mins

Servings: 2

Ingredients for Moroccan Mint Tea:
- 4 cups of water
- 2 tbsp green tea leaves (or 4 green tea bags)
- 4-6 sprigs of fresh mint
- Sugar (as needed)

Instructions for Moroccan Mint Tea:
1. Bring water to a boil in a teapot.
2. After adding green tea, let it steep for a few mins (or use tea bags).
3. Add sugar and fresh mint as needed.
4. Through a sieve, pour the tea into the cups of.
5. How to make kefta tagine:
6. To make the kefta Mixture, combine the ground beef (or lamb), chop-up garlic, lightly chop-up onion, chop-up parsley, chop-up cilantro, ground cumin, ground paprika, and ground cinnamon in a bowl.
7. Create little meatballs out of the Mixture.
8. Heat some olive oil in a deep skillet or tagine over medium heat.
9. The meatballs Must be evenly browned.
10. Water (or beef broth) and chop-up tomatoes Must be added to the tagine.
11. For about 20 mins, simmer the tagine with the lid on to let the flavors blend.
12. Olives and preserved lemons (if using) are garnishes.

NUTRITION INFO for Kefta Tagine: (Approximate values per serving)
Cals: 400 kcal, Carbs: 15g, Protein: 25g, Fat: 28g

268. Hawaiian Blue Hawaii Luau

Time: 10 mins

Servings: 1

Ingredients:
- 2 oz rum
- 1 oz blue curaçao liqueur
- 2 oz pineapple juice
- 1 oz coconut cream
- Pineapple slice and maraschino cherry for garnish
- Ice cubes

Instructions:
1. Ice cubes Must be put in a shaker.
2. To the shaker, add the rum, blue curaçao, pineapple juice, and coconut cream.
3. Thoroughly shake up to cooled.
4. Pour the strained contents into an ice-filled, chilled glass.
5. Add a pineapple slice and a maraschino cherry as garnish.

NUTRITION INFO (per serving):
Cals: 280, Carbs: 31g, Fat: 5g, Protein: 1g

269. Swiss Alpine Negroni Magic

Time: 5 mins

Servings: 1

Ingredients:
- 1 oz gin
- 1 oz Campari
- 1 oz sweet vermouth
- Orange slice for garnish
- Ice cubes

Instructions:
1. Ice cubes are placed in a combining glass.
2. Over ice, combine the gin, Campari, and sweet vermouth.
3. To blend, thoroughly stir.
4. Pour the strained contents into an ice-filled, chilled glass.

5. Add an orange slice as a garnish.

NUTRITION INFO (per serving):
Cals: 200, Carbs: 16g, Fat: 0g, Protein: 0g

270. Italian Aperol Spritz and Carpaccio

Time: 15 mins

Servings: 2

Ingredients:
- 3 oz Aperol liqueur
- 6 oz Prosecco
- Club soda
- Orange slice for garnish
- 8 oz beef carpaccio
- Arugula and shaved Parmesan for serving

Instructions:
1. Ice cubes Must be added to two wine glasses.
2. Aperol 1.5 oz Must be poured into every glass.
3. Every glass Must contain 3 ozs of Prosecco.
4. Add club soda to the top of every glass.
5. Add an orange slice as a garnish.
6. Place the Aperol Spritz, beef carpaccio, arugula, and Parmesan shavings on a platter.

NUTRITION INFO (per serving - Aperol Spritz):
Cals: 120, Carbs: 10g, Fat: 0g, Protein: 0g

271. French Lillet Royale Bonanza

Time: 5 mins

Servings: 1

Ingredients:
- 2 oz Lillet Blanc
- 4 oz champagne
- Lemon twist for garnish
- Ice cubes

Instructions:
1. Ice cubes Must be added to a champagne glass.
2. Fill the flute with the Lillet Blanc.
3. Pour more champagne into the glass.
4. Add a lemon twist as a garnish.

NUTRITION INFO (per serving):
Cals: 140, Carbs: 4g, Fat: 0g, Protein: 0g

272. Spanish Kalimotxo Love

Time: 5 mins

Servings: 1

Ingredients:
- 4 oz red wine
- 4 oz cola
- Lemon or lime wedge for garnish
- Ice cubes

Instructions:
1. Ice cubes Must be added to a glass.
2. Fill the glass with the red wine.
3. Fill the glass with the cola.
4. To combine the ingredients, gently stir.
5. Add a wedge of lemon or lime as garnish.

NUTRITION INFO (per serving):
Cals: 180, Carbs: 21g, Fat: 0g, Protein: 0g

273. Mexican Mexican Mule Fiesta

Time: 5 mins

Servings: 1

Ingredients:
- 2 oz tequila
- 4 oz ginger beer
- 1 oz lime juice
- Lime slice and mint sprig for garnish
- Ice cubes

Instructions:
1. Ice cubes Must be added to a copper cup of.
2. Put the lime juice and tequila in the cup of.
3. Pour more ginger beer into the mug.
4. To combine the ingredients, gently stir.
5. Add a lime slice and a mint sprig as garnish.

NUTRITION INFO (per serving):
Cals: 160, Carbs: 14g, Fat: 0g, Protein: 0g

274. Caribbean Blue Hawaiian Party

Time: 10 mins

Servings: 1

Ingredients:
- 1.5 oz light rum
- 1 oz blue curaçao liqueur
- 2 oz pineapple juice
- 1 oz coconut cream
- Pineapple slice and maraschino cherry for garnish
- Ice cubes

Instructions:
1. Ice cubes Must be put in a shaker.

2. To the shaker, add the rum, blue curaçao, pineapple juice, and coconut cream.
3. Thoroughly shake up to cooled.
4. Pour the strained contents into an ice-filled, chilled glass.
5. Add a pineapple slice and a maraschino cherry as garnish.

NUTRITION INFO (per serving):
Cals: 280, Carbs: 31g, Fat: 5g, Protein: 1g

275. Turkish Bouncea and Baklava

Time: 1 hr
Servings: 4

Ingredients:

- 16 oz bouncea (a traditional Turkish fermented drink)
- 4 pieces of baklava (assorted flavors)

Instructions:

1. Bouncea Must be added 4 oz every serving glass.
2. Serve a tray of various baklava alongside the bouncea.

NUTRITION INFO (per serving - bouncea):
Cals: 100, Carbs: 25g, Fat: 0g, Protein: 0g

276. Greek Tsipouro and Souvlaki

Time: 1 hr
Servings: 4

Ingredients:

- 8 oz tsipouro (Greek pomace brandy)
- 1 lb pork or chicken, slice into cubes for souvlaki
- Olive oil
- Lemon juice
- Fresh oregano
- Salt and pepper as needed

Instructions:

1. Cubes of pork or chicken Must be marinated for at least 30 mins in a Mixture of olive oil, lemon juice, fresh oregano, salt, and pepper.
2. Onto skewers, thread the marinated meat.
3. Cook the souvlaki completely on a grill over a barbecue or stovetop.
4. Every serving glass Must contain 2 oz of tsipouro.
5. Pair the freshly grilled souvlaki with the tsipouro.

NUTRITION INFO (per serving - tsipouro):
Cals: 160, Carbs: 0g, Fat: 0g, Protein: 0g

277. Russian Moscow Mule Parade

Time: 5 mins
Servings: 1

Ingredients:

- 2 oz vodka
- 4 oz ginger beer
- 1 oz lime juice
- Lime slice and mint sprig for garnish
- Ice cubes

Instructions:

1. Ice cubes Must be added to a copper cup of.
2. In the mug, combine the vodka and lime juice.
3. Pour more ginger beer into the mug.
4. To combine the ingredients, gently stir.
5. Add a lime slice and a mint sprig as garnish.

NUTRITION INFO (per serving):
Cals: 160, Carbs: 14g, Fat: 0g, Protein: 0g

278. Indian Mango Lassi

Time: 10 mins
Servings: 2

Ingredients:

- 1 ripe mango, peel off and pitted
- 1 cup of plain yogurt
- 1/2 cup of milk
- 2 tbsp honey or sugar (adjust as needed)
- 1/2 tsp ground cardamom (non-compulsory)
- Ice cubes
- Mint leaves for garnish

Instructions:

1. The ripe mango, yogurt, milk, honey (or sugar), and ground cardamom (if using) Must all be combined in a blender.
2. Blend till creamy and smooth.
3. When the lassi is cold and foamy, add ice cubes to the blender and process once more.
4. Pour glasses with the mango lassi.
5. Use fresh mint leaves as a garnish.

NUTRITION INFO (per serving):
Cals: 180, Carbs: 37g, Fat: 2g, Protein: 6g

279. Indian Bhel Puri

Time: 15 mins
Servings: 4

Ingredients:

- 2 cups of puffed rice (murmura)
- 1/2 cup of sev (crispy chickpea noodles)
- 1/2 cup of chop-up onions
- 1/2 cup of chop-up tomatoes
- 1/4 cup of chop-up cucumber
- 1/4 cup of boiled and cubed potatoes
- 2 tbsp tamarind chutney
- 2 tbsp green chutney
- 1 tbsp chaat masala
- 1 tbsp roasted cumin powder
- 1/4 cup of chop-up coriander leaves

Instructions:

1. The puffed rice, sev, chop-up onions, tomatoes, cucumber, and boiling potatoes Must all be combined in a sizable combining dish.
2. You may adjust the flavour by adding tamarind and green chutney.
3. Over the Mixture, sprinkling chaat masala and toasted cumin powder.
4. Combine everything by tossing it together thoroughly.
5. Add chop-up coriander leaves as a garnish.

NUTRITION INFO (per serving):
Cals: 180, Carbs: 32g, Fat: 4g, Protein: 5g

280. Thai Singha Beer and Som Tum

Time: 20 mins

Servings: 2

Ingredients:

- 2 cups of shredded green papaya
- 1/4 cup of shredded carrot
- 2-3 cherry tomatoes, halved
- 2 cloves garlic
- 2-3 Thai bird's eye chilies (adjust to spice preference)
- 2 tbsp fish sauce
- 1 tbsp palm sugar (or brown sugar)
- 1 tbsp tamarind pulp
- 1 tbsp lime juice
- 2 tbsp roasted peanuts
- 1 tbsp dried shrimp (non-compulsory)
- Fresh cilantro for garnish

Instructions:

1. Thai chilies and garlic Must be well smashed in a mortar and pestle.
2. Cherry tomatoes, shredded carrots, and green papaya Must all be added to the mortar.
3. To unleash the flavors of the veggies, lightly bruise them with the pestle.
4. To make the dressing, combine the fish sauce, lime juice, palm sugar, and tamarind pulp in a mini bowl.
5. The dressing Must be added to the papaya Mixture, then thoroughly combined.
6. Toss the salad once more after adding the dried shrimp and lightly smashed roasted peanuts.
7. Singha Beer Must be served alongside the Som Tum.

NUTRITION INFO (per serving - Som Tum):
Cals: 120, Carbs: 20g, Fat: 4g, Protein: 5g

281. Japanese Hibiki Whisky and Sushi

Time: 30 mins

Servings: 2

Ingredients:

- Assorted sushi rolls (e.g., California roll, tuna roll, salmon roll, etc.)
- Soy sauce for dipping
- Pickled ginger for serving
- Wasabi for serving
- 2 oz Hibiki Japanese whisky per serving
- Ice cubes

Instructions:

1. The sushi rolls Must be arranged on a serving dish.
2. Wasabi, pickled ginger, and soy sauce Must be served on the side.
3. Every whisky glass Must have ice cubes, and 2 ozs of Hibiki Japanese whisky Must be added.
4. Sips of the silky Hibiki whisky go well with the sushi.

NUTRITION INFO (per serving - Hibiki Whisky):
Cals: 120, Carbs: 0g, Fat: 0g, Protein: 0g

282. Chinese Lychee Martini and Dumplings

Time: 45 mins

Servings: 2

Ingredients:

- 4 oz vodka
- 2 oz lychee liqueur
- 2 oz canned lychee syrup
- 4 fresh or refrigerate lychees for garnish

- Ice cubes
- Assorted Chinese dumplings (steamed or pan-fried) for serving
- Soy sauce and chili oil for dipping

Instructions:
1. Combine vodka, lychee syrup, and lychee liqueur in a shaker with ice cubes.
2. Thoroughly shake up to cooled.
3. Pour cold martini glasses with the lychee martini inside.
4. Every glass Must have a lychee, either fresh or refrigerate.
5. Chinese dumplings can be steamed or fried and served alongside the lychee martini.
6. Give the dumplings soy sauce and chile oil to dip in.

NUTRITION INFO (per serving - Lychee Martini):
Cals: 200, Carbs: 15g, Fat: 0g, Protein: 0g

283. Korean Soju and Jajangmyeon

Time: 30 mins
Servings: 2

Ingredients:
- 2 packs of instant Jajangmyeon (black bean noodles) or homemade if preferred
- 1 tbsp vegetable oil
- 1/2 cup of diced onion
- 1/2 cup of diced zucchini
- 1/2 cup of diced potato
- 1/2 cup of diced carrot
- 2 tbsp black bean paste (chunjang)
- 2 cups of water
- 2 tbsp cornstarch combined with 2 tbsp water (for thickening sauce)
- 2 tbsp vegetable oil
- 2 tbsp split cucumber for garnish
- 1 tbsp sesame oil for garnish
- 2-4 cups of cold soju

Instructions:
1. Prepare handmade Jajangmyeon or cook the instant Jajangmyeon as directed on the packaging.
2. Vegetable oil Must be heated to medium heat in a big skillet.
3. Add diced onions, potatoes, carrots, and zucchini. Stir-fry them for a while to soften them.
4. Stir the vegetables with the black bean paste (chunjang) to properly distribute the coating.
5. Add water, cover, and simmer up to the vegetables are tender.
6. To thicken the sauce, stir in the cornstarch Mixture.
7. Individual bowls of the Jajangmyeon Must be served with split cucumber and a sprinkle of sesame oil as garnishes.
8. Take pleasure in the Jajangmyeon with a glass of cool soju.

NUTRITION INFO (per serving - Jajangmyeon):
Cals: 400, Carbs: 50g, Fat: 10g, Protein: 5g

284. Vietnamese Bia Hoi and Ca Phe Trung

Time: 10 mins
Servings: 2

Ingredients:
- 2 cups of fresh Bia Hoi (Vietnamese draft beer)
- 2 Big eggs
- 4 tbsp condensed milk
- 2 tbsp Vietnamese coffee grounds
- Ice cubes

Instructions:
1. The Vietnamese egg coffee, Ca Phe Trung, is made by whipping egg yolks and condensed milk up to foamy.
2. Place a drip filter or a Vietnamese coffee machine with the coffee grounds in a different cup of.
3. Coffee will spill into the cup of when you pour hot water over the coffee grinds.
4. Stir thoroughly after adding the egg yolk and condensed milk Mixture to the coffee.
5. Pour the Bia Hoi into two glasses that have been filled with ice cubes.
6. Ca Phe Trung Must be served alongside the Bia Hoi.

NUTRITION INFO (per serving - Ca Phe Trung):
Cals: 200, Carbs: 18g, Fat: 10g, Protein: 8g

285. Moroccan Mint Tea and Maakouda

Time: 30 mins
Servings: 4

Ingredients:
- 4 cups of water
- 4 tsp loose green tea or 4 green tea bags
- 1/4 cup of fresh mint leaves
- Sugar (non-compulsory), as needed
- 2 Big potatoes, boiled and mashed

- 1/4 cup of chop-up fresh parsley
- 1/4 cup of chop-up fresh cilantro
- 1 mini onion, lightly chop-up
- 1 tsp ground cumin
- 1/2 tsp paprika
- Salt and pepper as needed
- Vegetable oil for frying

Instructions:
1. Bring the water to a boil in a teapot.
2. Fresh mint leaves and green tea Must be added to the teapot.
3. Give the tea about five mins to steep.
4. Tea can be given sugar if desired. Stir up to sugar is dissolved.
5. Pour the tea into glasses or tea cups of.
6. The cooked and mashed potatoes, chop-up parsley, chop-up cilantro, lightly chop-up onion, ground cumin, paprika, salt, and pepper Must all be combined in a combining dish.
7. All of the ingredients Must be thoroughly combined.
8. Create tiny patties (maakouda) out of the ingredients.
9. Vegetable oil Must be heated in a frying pan over medium heat.
10. The maakouda patties Must be fried up to crispy and browned on all sides.
11. Serve the delectable maakouda patties alongside the Moroccan mint tea.

NUTRITION INFO (per serving - Maakouda):
Cals: 180, Carbs: 25g, Fat: 6g, Protein: 4g

286. Hawaiian Piña Colada Luau

Time: 10 mins
Servings: 2

Ingredients:
- 2 cups of refrigerate pineapple chunks
- 1 cup of coconut cream
- 2 oz white rum
- Pineapple slices and maraschino cherries for garnish
- Ice cubes

Instructions:
1. Refrigerate pineapple chunks, coconut cream, and white rum Must all be blended together.
2. Blend till creamy and smooth.
3. For a thicker texture or a greater kick, you can add extra rum or coconut cream, as desired.
4. Into two ice-filled glasses, pour the Pia Colada.
5. Slices of pineapple and maraschino cherries are used as garnish.

NUTRITION INFO (per serving):
Cals: 400, Carbs: 40g, Fat: 24g, Protein: 2g

287. Swiss Glacier Martini Magic

Time: 5 mins
Servings: 1

Ingredients:
- 2 oz vodka
- 1 oz blue curaçao liqueur
- 1 oz lemon juice
- Ice cubes
- Lemon twist for garnish

Instructions:
1. Ice cubes Must be put in a shaker.
2. In the shaker, combine the vodka, blue curaçao, and lemon juice.
3. Thoroughly shake up to cooled.
4. Pour the Mixture through a strainer into a martini glass.
5. Add a lemon twist as a garnish.

NUTRITION INFO (per serving):
Cals: 190, Carbs: 8g, Fat: 0g, Protein: 0g

288. Italian Bellini and Prosciutto

Time: 10 mins
Servings: 2

Ingredients:
- 2 ripe peveryes, peel off and pitted
- 4 oz pevery schnapps or pevery liqueur
- Chilled prosecco or sparkling wine
- Prosciutto slices for serving

Instructions:
1. The ripe peveryes Must be pureed in a blender up to smooth.
2. The pevery puree Must be combined well with the pevery schnapps or liquor.
3. Every champagne glass Must contain 2 ozs of the pevery combination.
4. Refill the glass with sparkling wine or prosecco that has been chilled.
5. Slices of prosciutto Must be served alongside the Bellini.

NUTRITION INFO (per serving - Bellini):
Cals: 180, Carbs: 18g, Fat: 0g, Protein: 1g

289. French Pernod and Croque Monsieur

Time: 30 mins
Servings: 2

Ingredients:

- 4 slices of bread
- 2 tbsp Dijon mustard
- 4 slices ham
- 4 slices Swiss cheese
- 2 tbsp butter
- 1/4 cup of finely grated Gruyere cheese
- Pernod for serving

Instructions:

1. On two slices of bread, spread Dijon mustard.
2. Every piece of mustard-coated bread Must be topped with a slice of ham and a slice of Swiss cheese.
3. Add the final two slices of bread on top.
4. On the sandwich's exterior sides, butter it.
5. The sandwiches Must be cooked in a pan over medium heat up to golden brown and the cheese has dilute.
6. Every sandwich Must have finely grated Gruyere cheese on top, which Must be cooked up to it melts.
7. Serve a side of Pernod beside the Croque Monsieur.

NUTRITION INFO (per serving - Croque Monsieur):
Cals: 550, Carbs: 27g, Fat: 33g, Protein: 31g

290. Spanish Sherry and Gazpacho

Time: 15 mins
Servings: 4

Ingredients:

- 4 Big tomatoes, diced
- 1 cucumber, peel off and diced
- 1 red bell pepper, diced
- 1 mini red onion, diced
- 2 garlic cloves, chop-up
- 3 cups of tomato juice
- 1/4 cup of red wine vinegar
- 1/4 cup of extra-virgin olive oil
- Salt and pepper as needed
- Sherry for serving

Instructions:

1. Combine the diced tomatoes, cucumber, red bell pepper, red onion, and chop-up garlic in a blender or mixer.
2. Up to smooth, blend.
3. Blend together tomato juice, red wine vinegar, and extra virgin olive oil.
4. Add salt and pepper, then blend once more to incorporate.
5. Before serving, the gazpacho Must be chilled in the fridge for at least an hr.
6. Sherry Must be served alongside the gazpacho.

NUTRITION INFO (per serving - Gazpacho):
Cals: 160, Carbs: 15g, Fat: 10g, Protein: 3g

291. Mexican Tequila Sunrise Fiesta

Time: 5 mins
Servings: 1

Ingredients:

- 2 oz tequila
- 4 oz orange juice
- 1/2 oz grenadine syrup
- Orange slice and maraschino cherry for garnish
- Ice cubes

Instructions:

1. Ice cubes Must be added to a glass.
2. Over the ice, pour the tequila and orange juice.
3. To achieve the sunrise look, slowly pour the grenadine syrup into the glass over the back of a spoon.
4. Add an orange slice and a maraschino cherry as garnish.
5. Just before drinking, stir lightly.

NUTRITION INFO (per serving):
Cals: 200, Carbs: 18g, Fat: 0g, Protein: 1g

292. Caribbean Painkiller Party

Time: 5 mins
Servings: 1

Ingredients:

- 2 oz dark rum
- 4 oz pineapple juice
- 1 oz orange juice
- 1 oz cream of coconut
- Freshly finely grated nutmeg for garnish
- Ice cubes

Instructions:
1. Ice cubes Must be put in a shaker.
2. To the shaker, add dark rum, pineapple juice, orange juice, and cream of coconut.
3. Thoroughly shake up to cooled.
4. Pour the strained Mixture into an ice-filled glass.
5. Add freshly finely grated nutmeg as a garnish.

NUTRITION INFO (per serving):
Cals: 300, Carbs: 26g, Fat: 6g, Protein: 1g

293. Turkish Rakı and Kebabs

Time: 45 mins

Servings: 4

Ingredients:
- 1 lb lamb or chicken, cubed for kebabs
- 1/4 cup of olive oil
- 2 tbsp lemon juice
- 2 cloves garlic, chop-up
- 1 tsp ground cumin
- 1 tsp paprika
- Salt and pepper as needed
- Rakı for serving

Instructions:
1. The marinade is made by combining the olive oil, lemon juice, chop-up garlic, ground cumin, paprika, salt, and pepper in a bowl.
2. Cubed lamb or chicken Must be added to the marinade and combined to coat thoroughly.
3. For at least 30 mins to marinate, cover the bowl and place in the refrigerator.
4. Onto skewers, thread the marinated meat.
5. On a grill over an open flame or a stovetop, cook the kebabs up to done.
6. Rak is traditionally served alongside kebabs.

NUTRITION INFO (per serving - Kebabs):
Cals: 300, Carbs: 2g, Fat: 18g, Protein: 30g

294. Greek Metaxa and Taramasalata

Time: 15 mins

Servings: 4

Ingredients:
- 1/2 cup of taramasalata (fish roe dip)
- 4 pita bread or slices of baguette
- 2 tbsp olive oil
- Fresh dill and lemon wedges for garnish
- Metaxa for serving

Instructions:
1. On pita bread or pieces of baguette, spread taramasalata.
2. Olive oil Must be drizzled on the taramasalata.
3. Add lemon wedges and fresh dill as garnish.
4. Serve Metaxa beside the taramasalata.

NUTRITION INFO (per serving - Taramasalata):
Cals: 180, Carbs: 8g, Fat: 15g, Protein: 3g

295. Russian Moscow Mule Parade

Time: 5 mins

Servings: 1

Ingredients:
- 2 oz vodka
- 4 oz ginger beer
- 1 oz lime juice
- Lime slice and mint sprig for garnish
- Ice cubes

Instructions:
1. Ice cubes Must be added to a copper cup of.
2. In the mug, combine the vodka and lime juice.
3. Pour more ginger beer into the mug.
4. To combine the ingredients, gently stir.
5. Add a lime slice and a mint sprig as garnish.

NUTRITION INFO (per serving):
Cals: 160, Carbs: 14g, Fat: 0g, Protein: 0g

296. Indian Mango Lassi and Samosas

Time: 1 hr

Servings: 4

Ingredients:
- 2 ripe mangoes, peel off and pitted
- 2 cups of plain yogurt
- 1/4 cup of milk
- 2 tbsp honey or sugar (adjust as needed)
- 1/2 tsp ground cardamom (non-compulsory)
- 1 box/pkg refrigerate samosas (meat or vegetable) or homemade if preferred
- Tamarind chutney and mint chutney for serving

Instructions:
1. The ripe mangoes, plain yogurt, milk, honey (or sugar), and ground cardamom (if used) Must all be blended together.
2. Blend till creamy and smooth.
3. The mango lassi Must be chilled in the fridge up to ready to serve.

4. Prepare handmade samosas or cook the samosas per the box/pkg's directions.
5. Serve the hot, crispy samosas alongside the mango lassi.
6. Give the samosas tamarind and mint chutney to dip in.

NUTRITION INFO (per serving - Mango Lassi):
Cals: 200, Carbs: 30g, Fat: 5g, Protein: 8g

297. Thai Singha Beer and Tom Yum

Time: 30 mins

Servings: 4

Ingredients:

- 4 cups of chicken or vegetable broth
- 1 stalk lemongrass, bruised
- 3 kaffir lime leaves
- 2 Thai bird's eye chilies, split (adjust to spice preference)
- 2 tbsp fish sauce
- 1 tbsp tamarind paste
- 1 cup of combined seafood (shrimp, squid, mussels) or chicken/tofu
- 1/2 cup of split mushrooms
- 1/4 cup of coconut milk (non-compulsory)
- Fresh cilantro and lime wedges for garnish
- Singha Beer for serving

Instructions:
1. Bring the vegetable or chicken broth to a boil in a pot.
2. Split Thai bird's eye chilies, lemongrass, and kaffir lime leaves Must all be added to the soup.
3. For the flavors to really meld, boil the Mixture for around 10 mins.
4. Add the split mushrooms, fish sauce, tamarind paste, and combined seafood (or chicken/tofu).
5. Cook up to the chicken is tender or the seafood is thoroughly cooked.
6. Add coconut milk to the soup if desired to make it creamier.
7. With lime wedges and fresh cilantro as garnishes, serve the tom yum in separate bowls.
8. Enjoy a chilled Singha Beer alongside the tom yum.

NUTRITION INFO (per serving - Tom Yum):
Cals: 120, Carbs: 8g, Fat: 5g, Protein: 12g

298. Japanese Suntory Toki and Sushi

Time: 30 mins

Servings: 2

Ingredients:

- Assorted sushi rolls (e.g., California roll, tuna roll, salmon roll, etc.)
- Soy sauce for dipping
- Pickled ginger for serving
- Wasabi for serving
- 4 oz Suntory Toki Japanese whisky per serving
- Ice cubes

Instructions:
1. The sushi rolls Must be arranged on a serving dish.
2. Wasabi, pickled ginger, and soy sauce Must be served on the side.
3. Every whisky tumbler Must contain 4 ozs of Suntory Toki Japanese whisky with ice cubes.
4. Take sips of the silky Suntory Toki whisky while enjoying the sushi.

NUTRITION INFO (per serving - Suntory Toki Whisky):
Cals: 160, Carbs: 0g, Fat: 0g, Protein: 0g

299. Chinese Plum Wine and Spring Rolls

Time: 45 mins

Servings: 4

Ingredients:

- 1 lb ground pork or chicken
- 1 cup of shredded cabbage
- 1/2 cup of shredded carrots
- 2-3 cloves garlic, chop-up
- 2 tbsp soy sauce
- 1 tbsp oyster sauce
- 1 tsp sesame oil
- Spring roll wrappers
- Plum wine for serving

Instructions:
1. Cook the ground chicken or pork in a pan up to it is browned.
2. Shredded carrots, chop-up garlic, and cabbage Must all be added to the pan. Cook the vegetables up to they are tender.
3. Add the sesame oil, soy sauce, and oyster sauce. Combine thoroughly and heat for an additional min.
4. A spring roll wrapper Must be placed flat on a tidy surface.
5. Onto the wrapper's middle, spoon the contents.

6. To create a spring roll, roll the wrapper while folding the sides inward. With a little water, seal the edges.
7. For the remaining wrappers and filling, repeat the procedure.
8. The spring rolls Must be deep-fried up to crispy and golden.
9. Alongside the spring rolls, serve Chinese Plum Wine.

NUTRITION INFO (per serving - Spring Rolls):
Cals: 200, Carbs: 15g, Fat: 10g, Protein: 12g

300. Korean Makgeolli and Japchae

Time: 1 hr
Servings: 4

Ingredients:
- 8 oz Korean sweet potato noodles (dangmyeon)
- 1/2 lb beef (sirloin or ribeye), thinly split
- 1/2 cup of split onions
- 1/2 cup of split carrots
- 1/2 cup of split bell peppers
- 1/2 cup of split mushrooms
- 2-3 cloves garlic, chop-up
- 3 tbsp soy sauce
- 2 tbsp sesame oil
- 1 tbsp sugar
- 1 tbsp vegetable oil
- 4 cups of makgeolli (Korean rice wine)

Instructions:
1. Follow the directions on the box/pkg to prepare the sweet potato noodles. Drain, then set apart.
2. Split beef Must be combined with soy sauce, sesame oil, and sugar in a bowl. Give it at least 15 mins to marinate.
3. Vegetable oil Must be heated over medium-high heat in a sizable pan or wok.
4. Cook the marinated meat completely in a stir-fry. Take out of the pan and place aside.
5. The chop-up garlic and slice veggies Must be stir-fried in the same skillet up to they are soft.
6. Re-add the steak and cooked sweet potato noodles to the pan. Combine all of the ingredients.
7. If necessary, season with more soy sauce and sesame oil.
8. Serve the Makgeolli beside the Japchae.

NUTRITION INFO (per serving - Japchae):
Cals: 350, Carbs: 40g, Fat: 12g, Protein: 18g

301. Vietnamese Bia Hoi and Bun Thit Nuong

Time: 45 mins
Servings: 4

Ingredients:
- 1 lb pork Muster or loin, thinly split
- 4-6 cups of cooked vermicelli noodles
- 1 cup of shredded lettuce
- 1 cup of bean sprouts
- 1/2 cup of julienned cucumber
- 1/4 cup of chop-up peanuts
- 2-3 sprigs of mint
- 2-3 sprigs of cilantro
- 2 tbsp chop-up green onions
- Nuoc Cham (Vietnamese dipping sauce) for serving
- 4 cups of Bia Hoi (Vietnamese draft beer)

Instructions:
1. Grill the thinly split pork up to it is totally done and has developed a light sear.
2. Prepare a bed of cooked vermicelli noodles in a bowl.
3. Add grilled pork, bean sprouts, julienned cucumber, and lettuce shredded to the noodles.
4. Add chop-up peanuts, mint, cilantro, and green onion to the dish as a garnish.
5. Bun Thit Nuong Must be served with Nuoc Cham on the side for dipping.
6. Pair the dish with a cold draft of Vietnamese beer called Bia Hoi.

NUTRITION INFO (per serving - Bun Thit Nuong):
Cals: 400, Carbs: 30g, Fat: 15g, Protein: 25g

302. Moroccan Mint Tea and Pastilla

Time: 1 hr
Servings: 4

Ingredients:
- 1 lb chicken or pigeon, cooked and shredded
- 1/2 cup of ground almonds
- 1/2 cup of powdered sugar
- 1/2 tsp ground cinnamon
- 1/4 tsp ground ginger
- 1/4 tsp ground nutmeg
- 1/4 tsp ground cloves
- 1/4 tsp saffron threads
- 3 tbsp butter, dilute
- 8-10 sheets of phyllo dough

- 1 tbsp powdered sugar for dusting
- Fresh mint leaves for garnish
- 4 cups of Moroccan Mint Tea

Instructions:
1. Set the oven's temperature to 375°F (190°C).
2. Shredded chicken or pigeon, ground almonds, powdered sugar, cinnamon, ginger, nutmeg, cloves, saffron threads, and dilute butter are combined in a basin. Combine thoroughly.
3. Butter a pie plate or baking pan. Spread dilute butter over one sheet of phyllo dough before placing it in the dish. Layer three or four more sheets on top of one another and repeat.
4. Over the phyllo dough, distribute half of the chicken or pigeon Mixture.
5. Brush every sheet of phyllo dough with dilute butter before adding a second layer of three to four sheets.
6. Over the phyllo dough, spread the remaining chicken or pigeon Mixture.
7. Add a final layer of 3–4 phyllo dough sheets on top, coating every one with dilute butter.
8. When the phyllo dough is golden and crisp, bake the Pastilla in the preheated oven for about 30 mins.
9. After taking it out of the oven, let it cool a little before dusted with powdered sugar.
10. Use fresh mint leaves as a garnish.
11. Serve Moroccan Mint Tea alongside the pastilla.

NUTRITION INFO (per serving - Pastilla):
Cals: 450, Carbs: 25g, Fat: 25g, Protein: 30g

303. Hawaiian Blue Lagoon Luau

Time: 10 mins

Servings: 1

Ingredients:
- 2 oz coconut rum
- 1 oz blue curaçao liqueur
- 4 oz pineapple juice
- Pineapple slice and maraschino cherry for garnish
- Ice cubes

Instructions:
1. Ice cubes Must be put in a shaker.
2. The shaker Must be filled with pineapple juice, blue curaçao, and coconut rum.
3. Thoroughly shake up to cooled.
4. Pour the strained Mixture into an ice-filled glass.
5. Add a pineapple slice and a maraschino cherry as garnish.

NUTRITION INFO (per serving):
Cals: 250, Carbs: 30g, Fat: 0g, Protein: 0g

304. Swiss Swiss Mule Magic

Time: 5 mins

Servings: 1

Ingredients:
- 2 oz Swiss herbal liqueur (e.g., Appenzeller)
- 1/2 oz fresh lime juice
- 4 oz ginger beer
- Lime slice and mint sprig for garnish
- Ice cubes

Instructions:
1. Ice cubes Must be added to a glass or copper cup of.
2. Fill the mug with fresh lime juice and Swiss herbal liqueur.
3. Pour more ginger beer into the mug.
4. To combine the ingredients, gently stir.
5. Add a lime slice and a mint sprig as garnish.

NUTRITION INFO (per serving):
Cals: 200, Carbs: 20g, Fat: 0g, Protein: 0g

305. Italian Sgroppino and Bruschetta

Time: 15 mins

Servings: 4

Ingredients:
- 1/2 cup of vodka
- 1 cup of lemon sorbet or lemon gelato
- 1 cup of Prosecco or sparkling wine
- Fresh mint leaves for garnish
- Split baguette or Italian bread
- Cherry tomatoes, halved
- Fresh basil leaves
- Extra-virgin olive oil
- Balsamic glaze (non-compulsory)

Instructions:
1. Combine vodka and lemon sorbet or gelato in a blender. Up to smooth, blend.
2. Add Prosecco or sparkling wine gradually to the blender, then process up to foamy.
3. Sgroppino Must be poured into chilled glasses.
4. Use fresh mint leaves as a garnish.
5. Toast Italian or baguette bread to make bruschetta.

6. Split cherry tomatoes and fresh basil leaves are placed on top of every slice.
7. Balsamic glaze and extra-virgin olive oil may be added as garnishes.
8. Serve Bruschetta alongside the Italian Sgroppino.

NUTRITION INFO (per serving - Sgroppino):
Cals: 180, Carbs: 25g, Fat: 0g, Protein: 1g

306. French Kir Royale Breton Bonanza

Time: 5 mins
Servings: 1

Ingredients:
- 2 oz Crème de Cassis (blackcurrant liqueur)
- 5 oz sparkling wine or Champagne
- Blackberries for garnish
- Ice cubes

Instructions:
1. Ice cubes Must be added to a Champagne flute.
2. Fill the flute with crème de cassis.
3. Fill the rest of the flute with Champagne or sparkling wine.
4. Gently stir the flavors together.
5. Fresh blackberries make a nice garnish.

NUTRITION INFO (per serving):
Cals: 150, Carbs: 20g, Fat: 0g, Protein: 0g

307. Spanish Tinto de Verano Love

Time: 5 mins
Servings: 1

Ingredients:
- 2 oz red wine (Spanish Rioja or Tempranillo)
- 2 oz lemon-lime soda or sparkling water
- Lemon and lime slices for garnish
- Ice cubes

Instructions:
1. Add ice cubes to a wine glass.
2. Put a little red wine in the glass.
3. Fill the rest of the glass with sparkling water or lemon-lime soda.
4. Gently stir the ingredients together.
5. Slices of lime and lemon may be garnished.

NUTRITION INFO (per serving):
Cals: 120, Carbs: 10g, Fat: 0g, Protein: 0g

308. Mexican Horchata and Tacos

Time: 1 hr (+ soaking time for rice)
Servings: 4

Ingredients:
- 1 cup of long-grain white rice
- 4 cups of water
- 1/2 cup of milk (or almond milk for a dairy-free version)
- 1/4 cup of granulated sugar (adjust as needed)
- 1 tsp vanilla extract
- 1 tsp ground cinnamon
- Corn tortillas
- Cooked filling of choice (e.g., shredded chicken, seasoned beef, beans, or grilled vegetables)
- Toppings of choice (e.g., shredded lettuce, diced tomatoes, shredded cheese, salsa, guacamole)
- Lime wedges for serving

Instructions:
1. Rice and water Must be put in a blender. To soften the rice, let it soak for at least one hr (or overnight).
2. Rice and water Must be thoroughly blended.
3. Discard the rice particles after straining the rice Mixture through a fine-mesh screen into a pitcher or big dish.
4. Add the milk, sugar, cinnamon ground, and vanilla essence.
5. Before serving, let the horchata cool in the fridge for at least 30 mins.
6. Warm up the corn tortillas for the tacos in the oven or a skillet.
7. Every tortilla Must be filled with your preferred prepared filling.
8. Add toppings like salsa, guacamole, shredded lettuce, chop-up tomatoes, and shredded cheese.
9. Serve tacos beside the horchata.

NUTRITION INFO (per serving - Horchata):
Cals: 150, Carbs: 30g, Fat: 2g, Protein: 2g

309. Caribbean Rum Swizzle Soiree

Time: 5 mins
Servings: 1

Ingredients:
- 2 oz dark rum
- 1 oz lime juice
- 1 oz pineapple juice
- 1 oz orange juice
- 1/2 oz grenadine syrup
- Lime slice and pineapple wedge for garnish

- Ice cubes

Instructions:
1. Ice cubes Must be put in a shaker.
2. To the shaker, add dark rum, lime, pineapple, orange, and grenadine syrup.
3. Thoroughly shake up to cooled.
4. Pour the strained Mixture into an ice-filled glass.
5. Add a lime slice and a pineapple wedge as garnish.

NUTRITION INFO (per serving):
Cals: 250, Carbs: 20g, Fat: 0g, Protein: 0g

310. Turkish Salep and Turkish Delight

Time: 15 mins

Servings: 2

Ingredients:
- 2 cups of milk
- 2 tbsp salep powder
- 2 tbsp sugar
- 1/2 tsp ground cinnamon
- Crushed pistachios for garnish
- Turkish Delight for serving

Instructions:
1. The milk Must be heated in a saucepan over medium heat up to it is warm but not boiling.
2. Salep powder, sugar, and more whisking up to the Mixture becomes thick.
3. Add cinnamon powder and well stir.
4. Place crushed pistachios on top of the Salep after it has been poured into serving cups of.
5. Turkish Delight Must be served alongside the Salep.

NUTRITION INFO (per serving - Salep):
Cals: 200, Carbs: 30g, Fat: 6g, Protein: 8g

311. Greek Ouzo and Dolmades

Time: 30 mins

Servings: 4

Ingredients:
- 1 jar of grape leaves in brine, drained and rinsed
- 1 cup of cooked white rice
- 1/2 cup of chop-up onions
- 1/2 cup of chop-up tomatoes
- 1/4 cup of chop-up fresh dill
- 1/4 cup of chop-up fresh mint
- 1/4 cup of chop-up pine nuts
- 1/4 cup of olive oil
- 1/4 cup of lemon juice
- Salt and pepper as needed
- Ouzo for serving

Instructions:
1. Cooked white rice, diced tomatoes, onions, fresh dill, mint, pine nuts, olive oil, lemon juice, salt, and pepper Must all be combined in a bowl.
2. Flatten a grape leaf on a tidy surface.
3. A tbsp of the rice Mixture Must be placed in the leaf's middle.
4. To create a dolma, fold the leaf's sides inside and roll it up tightly.
5. For the remaining grape leaves and rice combination, repeat the procedure.
6. The dolmades Must be steamed for ten mins, or up to well heated.
7. Ouzo Must be served alongside the dolmades.

NUTRITION INFO (per serving - Dolmades):
Cals: 250, Carbs: 20g, Fat: 10g, Protein: 6g

312. Russian Black Russian and Piroshki

Time: 45 mins

Servings: 4

Ingredients:
- 1 lb ground beef or pork
- 1 cup of diced onions
- 1/2 cup of diced carrots
- 1/2 cup of diced potatoes
- 1/4 cup of chop-up dill pickles
- 2 tbsp vegetable oil
- 1 tsp salt
- 1/2 tsp black pepper
- 1 box/pkg store-bought or homemade pizza dough
- 1 egg, beaten (for egg wash)
- Black Russian cocktail (recipe below) for serving

Instructions:
1. Vegetable oil Must be heated in a pan over medium heat.
2. To the pan, add diced potatoes, diced carrots, and diced onions. Cook the vegetables up to they are tender.
3. Cook the ground beef or pork in the pan up to well-done and browned.
4. Add salt, black pepper, and split dill pickles after stirring. Combine thoroughly.
5. Set the oven's temperature to 375°F (190°C).

6. Pizza dough Must be rolled out and slice into circles or squares that are 4 inches in diameter.
7. Every dough circle or square Must have a spoonful of the meat Mixture placed in the center of it.
8. To create a piroshki, fold the dough over the filling and press the edges together to seal.
9. For a golden crust, brush the piroshki with beaten egg.
10. The piroshki Must be baked in the preheated oven for around 20 mins, or up to golden brown.
11. Serve the Black Russian cocktail alongside the piroshki.

NUTRITION INFO (per serving - Piroshki):
Cals: 350, Carbs: 20g, Fat: 15g, Protein: 25g

313. Black Russian Cocktail:

Time: 5 mins
Servings: 1

Ingredients:
- 2 oz vodka
- 1 oz coffee liqueur (e.g., Kahlúa)
- Ice cubes
- Coffee beans for garnish (non-compulsory)

Instructions:
1. Place ice cubes in a rocks glass.
2. Vodka and coffee liqueur Must be added to the glass.
3. To combine the ingredients, gently stir.
4. If desired, add coffee beans as a garnish.

NUTRITION INFO (per serving - Black Russian):
Cals: 180, Carbs: 15g, Fat: 0g, Protein: 0g

314. Indian Kingfisher Beer and Pakoras

Time: 30 mins
Servings: 4

Ingredients:
- 1 cup of chickpea flour (besan)
- 1/4 cup of rice flour
- 1/2 tsp baking soda
- 1/2 tsp cumin seeds
- 1/2 tsp red chili powder
- 1/4 tsp turmeric powder
- 1 tsp garam masala
- 1/2 cup of water
- 1 Big potato, thinly split
- 1 medium onion, thinly split
- 1 cup of combined vegetables (e.g., spinach leaves, cauliflower florets, bell pepper slices)
- Vegetable oil for frying
- Kingfisher beer for serving

Instructions:
1. Chickpea and rice flours, baking soda, cumin seeds, red chili powder, turmeric powder, garam masala, and water Must all be combined in a bowl. Stir the Mixture up to it becomes smooth.
2. A deep fryer or pan with vegetable oil is heated.
3. Split potatoes, onions, and a variety of other veggies Must all be thoroughly coated in batter.
4. In the hot oil, fry the coated vegetables up to they are crisp and brown.
5. After removing the pakoras from the oil, drain the extra oil on paper towels.
6. Kingfisher beer Must be served alongside the pakoras.

NUTRITION INFO (per serving - Pakoras):
Cals: 200, Carbs: 25g, Fat: 10g, Protein: 5g

315. Thai Chang Beer and Green Curry

Time: 45 mins
Servings: 4

Ingredients:
- 1 lb chicken, beef, or tofu, slice into bite-sized pieces
- 2 tbsp green curry paste
- 1 can (14 oz) coconut milk
- 1 cup of split bamboo shoots
- 1 cup of split bell peppers
- 1 cup of Thai basil leaves
- 2 tbsp fish sauce (or soy sauce for a vegetarian version)
- 1 tbsp brown sugar
- Cooked jasmine rice for serving
- Thai Chang Beer for serving

Instructions:
1. Heat a little amount of coconut milk in a pan or wok over medium heat.
2. Stir in the green curry paste and cook up to aromatic.
3. Brown any chicken, beef, or tofu that has been added to the pan.
4. Add the remaining coconut milk, then boil the Mixture.
5. Add Thai basil leaves, split bell peppers, fish sauce, brown sugar, and slices of bamboo shoots.

6. Let the spices to meld in the curry by letting it boil for about 15 mins.
7. Serve jasmine rice with the green curry.
8. Enjoy the curry with a side of Thai Chang beer.

NUTRITION INFO (per serving - Green Curry):
Cals: 350, Carbs: 15g, Fat: 20g, Protein: 25g

316. Japanese Yamazaki Whisky and Tempura

Time: 30 mins
Servings: 4

Ingredients:
- Assorted vegetables (e.g., sweet potatoes, bell peppers, zucchini, mushrooms)
- Assorted seafood (e.g., shrimp, squid, scallops)
- 1 cup of all-purpose flour
- 1/4 cup of cornstarch
- 1 tsp baking powder
- 1 cup of cold sparkling water
- Ice cubes
- Vegetable oil for frying
- Yamazaki Whisky for serving

Instructions:
1. To make the tempura batter, combine all-purpose flour, cornstarch, baking powder, and cold sparkling water in a basin.
2. A deep fryer or pan with vegetable oil is heated.
3. Lightly coat the seafood and veggies with tempura batter by dipping them in.
4. In the hot oil, fry the coated fish and vegetables up to crisp and golden.
5. Take the tempura out of the oil and drain any extra oil on paper towels.
6. Serve Yamazaki Whisky alongside the tempura.

NUTRITION INFO (per serving - Tempura):
Cals: 250, Carbs: 30g, Fat: 10g, Protein: 8g

317. Chinese Baijiu and Kung Pao Chicken

Time: 30 mins
Servings: 4

Ingredients:
- 1 lb chicken breast or thigh, diced
- 1/2 cup of roasted peanuts
- 1/2 cup of diced bell peppers
- 1/2 cup of diced zucchini
- 1/4 cup of diced onions
- 2-3 dried red chili peppers
- 2 cloves garlic, chop-up
- 1/4 cup of soy sauce
- 2 tbsp baijiu (Chinese liquor)
- 1 tbsp black vinegar (or balsamic vinegar)
- 1 tbsp sugar
- 1 tbsp cornstarch, dissolved in 2 tbsp water
- Cooked white rice for serving
- Baijiu for serving

Instructions:
1. A mini amount of vegetable oil Must be heated on high in a wok or pan.
2. Garlic cloves and dried red chile peppers Must be stir-fried up to aromatic.
3. Cook the chicken diced in the wok up to browned.
4. Add the diced bell peppers, zucchini, onions, and toasted peanuts after combining. Cook the vegetables up to they are soft.
5. Combine soy sauce, baijiu, black vinegar, and sugar in a bowl. Combine well after adding the sauce to the wok.
6. To thicken the sauce, stir in the cornstarch Mixture.
7. Use white rice to accompany the Kung Pao Chicken.
8. With the dish, sip some Baijiu.

NUTRITION INFO (per serving - Kung Pao Chicken):
Cals: 350, Carbs: 15g, Fat: 15g, Protein: 30g,

318. Korean Cass Beer and Bulgogi

Time: 1 hr (+ marinating time)
Servings: 4

Ingredients:
- 1 lb beef (sirloin or ribeye), thinly split
- 1/4 cup of soy sauce
- 2 tbsp sesame oil
- 2 tbsp brown sugar
- 2 cloves garlic, chop-up
- 1 tbsp finely grated ginger
- 1 tbsp sesame seeds
- 1/2 onion, thinly split
- 2 green onions, chop-up
- Vegetable oil for cooking
- Cass beer for serving

Instructions:

1. The bulgogi marinade is made by combining soy sauce, sesame oil, brown sugar, finely grated ginger, chop-up garlic, and sesame seeds in a bowl.
2. Combine in the thinly split meat with the marinade.
3. For at least an hr (or overnight for additional flavor), cover the bowl and place the beef in the refrigerator to marinate.
4. Vegetable oil is heated over high heat in a pan or grill.
5. The marinated meat Must be stir-fried up to well-done and caramelized.
6. Add chop-up green onions and thinly split onions to the pan. To soften the onions, cook for a few more mins.
7. Bulgogi Must be served with a side of Cass beer.

NUTRITION INFO (per serving - Bulgogi):
Cals: 300, Carbs: 15g, Fat: 15g, Protein: 25g

319. Vietnamese Ca Phe Sua Da and Banh Xeo

Time: 1 hr

Servings: 4

Ingredients:

- 1 cup of rice flour
- 1/4 cup of cornstarch
- 1 tsp turmeric powder
- 1 cup of coconut milk
- 1 cup of water
- 1/2 lb pork belly or shrimp, cooked and split
- 1/2 cup of bean sprouts
- 1/4 cup of split green onions
- Fresh herbs (e.g., cilantro, mint, basil)
- Nuoc Cham (Vietnamese dipping sauce) for serving
- Ca Phe Sua Da (Vietnamese iced coffee) for serving

Instructions:

1. The banh xeo batter is made by combining rice flour, cornstarch, turmeric powder, coconut milk, and water in a bowl. Stir the Mixture up to it becomes smooth.
2. A little vegetable oil and a non-stick pan on medium heat.
3. Banh xeo batter Must be poured into the pan and swirled to coat the bottom.
4. On one half of the pancake, place bean sprouts, slice green onions, and split pork belly or shrimp.
5. To create a half-moon shape, fold the second side of the pancake over the filling.
6. Banh xeo Must be cooked up to both sides are crispy and brown.
7. Fresh herbs are a nice garnish.
8. Serve the Banh Xeo with Nuoc Cham on the side for dipping and Ca Phe Sua Da as a cool beverage.

NUTRITION INFO (per serving - Banh Xeo):
Cals: 250, Carbs: 30g, Fat: 10g, Protein: 15g

320. Moroccan Mint Tea and Briouats

Time: 15 mins

Servings: 4

Ingredients:

- 4 cups of water
- 4 tsp loose green tea leaves
- 4 tbsp sugar (adjust as needed)
- 1 bunch fresh mint leaves
- 1 box/pkg of phyllo dough
- 1 cup of cooked ground meat (beef or lamb)
- 1/4 cup of chop-up onions
- 2 cloves garlic, chop-up
- 1 tsp ground cinnamon
- 1/2 tsp ground cumin
- Salt and pepper as needed
- Vegetable oil for frying

Instructions:

1. Boil some water in a teapot for the Moroccan Mint Tea. After adding the green tea, let it to steep for a while. Add sugar and mint leaves that are fresh. Serve warm.
2. Combine cooked ground beef, chop-up onions, chop-up garlic, ground cumin, ground cinnamon, and salt and pepper in a bowl to make the Briouats.
3. Phyllo dough Must be slice into strips.
4. Place a tbsp of the meat Mixture at one end of a strip of phyllo dough.
5. In order to enclose the meat Mixture, fold the phyllo dough diagonally into a triangle.
6. When you get to the end of the strip, keep folding the triangle.
7. Add a little water to the end to seal it.
8. In a pan, heat vegetable oil over medium-low heat.
9. The Briouats Must be fried up to crispy and golden.

10. Along with the Moroccan Mint Tea, serve the briouats.

NUTRITION INFO (per serving - Briouats):
Cals: 250, Carbs: 15g, Fat: 10g, Protein: 20g

321. Hawaiian Lava Flow Luau

Time: 10 mins

Servings: 1

Ingredients:

- 2 oz light rum
- 2 oz coconut cream
- 4 oz pineapple juice
- 2 oz strawberry puree
- Pineapple slice and strawberry for garnish
- Ice cubes

Instructions:

1. Ice cubes Must be put in a shaker.
2. To the shaker, add light rum, coconut cream, and pineapple juice.
3. Thoroughly shake up to cooled.
4. In a glass, pour the strawberry puree.
5. To produce a tiered look, carefully pour the shaken Mixture over the strawberry puree.
6. Slices of pineapple and strawberries are used as garnish.

NUTRITION INFO (per serving):
Cals: 300, Carbs: 35g, Fat: 10g, Protein: 1g

322. Swiss Chocolate Martini Magic

Time: 5 mins

Servings: 1

Ingredients:

- 1 1/2 oz vodka
- 1 1/2 oz chocolate liqueur
- 1 oz coffee liqueur (e.g., Kahlúa)
- 1 oz cream or milk
- Chocolate shavings or cocoa powder for garnish
- Ice cubes

Instructions:

1. Ice cubes Must be put in a shaker.
2. Vodka, coffee, chocolate, and cream or milk Must all be added to the shaker.
3. Thoroughly shake up to cooled.
4. Pour the Mixture through a strainer into a martini glass.
5. Add cocoa powder or chocolate shavings as a garnish.

NUTRITION INFO (per serving):
Cals: 300, Carbs: 20g, Fat: 5g, Protein: 0g

323. Italian Limoncello Spritz and Caprese

Time: 5 mins

Servings: 1

Ingredients:

- 2 oz Limoncello liqueur
- 3 oz Prosecco or sparkling wine
- 1 oz soda water
- Lemon slices and fresh basil for garnish
- Fresh mozzarella
- Tomato slices
- Fresh basil leaves
- Extra-virgin olive oil
- Balsamic glaze (non-compulsory)

Instructions:

1. Add ice cubes to a wine glass.
2. Prosecco and Limoncello liqueur Must be added to the glass.
3. Add more soda water to the glass.
4. Gently stir the flavors together.
5. Lemon slices and fresh basil are garnishes.
6. Slices of fresh mozzarella and tomato Must be arranged on a platter for caprese.
7. Place some fresh basil between the pieces.
8. Balsamic glaze and extra-virgin olive oil may be added as garnishes.
9. Serve Caprese alongside the Limoncello Spritz.

NUTRITION INFO (per serving - Limoncello Spritz):
Cals: 200, Carbs: 20g, Fat: 0g, Protein: 0g

324. French Kir Normand Bonanza

Time: 5 mins

Servings: 1

Ingredients:

- 2 oz crème de cassis (blackcurrant liqueur)
- 4 oz sparkling apple cider
- Apple slices and blackberries for garnish
- Ice cubes

Instructions:

1. Ice cubes Must be added to a Champagne flute.
2. Fill the flute with crème de cassis.
3. Put some sparkling apple cider in the flute.
4. Gently stir the flavors together.

5. Blackberries and apple slices make lovely garnishes.

NUTRITION INFO (per serving):
Cals: 150, Carbs: 20g, Fat: 0g, Protein: 0g

325. Spanish Cava and Patatas Bravas

Time: 45 mins

Servings: 4

Ingredients:
- 4 Big potatoes, peel off and slice into cubes
- Olive oil for frying
- 1/2 cup of tomato sauce or tomato puree
- 1/4 cup of mayonnaise
- 1 tbsp hot sauce (adjust as needed)
- 1 tsp paprika
- Salt and pepper as needed
- Fresh parsley for garnish

Instructions:
1. Over medium heat, warm up the olive oil in a Big pan.
2. Potato cubes Must be fried in hot oil up to golden and crispy.
3. To drain off extra oil, take the potatoes out of the oil and place them on paper towels.
4. Combine tomato sauce or tomato puree, mayonnaise, and spicy sauce in a bowl. Salt, pepper, and paprika are stirred in.
5. Serve the Patatas Bravas beside the hot tomato sauce.

NUTRITION INFO (per serving - Patatas Bravas):
Cals: 250, Carbs: 30g, Fat: 15g, Protein: 3g

326. Mexican Tequila Sunset Fiesta

Time: 5 mins

Servings: 1

Ingredients:
- 2 oz tequila
- 4 oz orange juice
- 1/2 oz grenadine syrup
- Orange slice and maraschino cherry for garnish
- Ice cubes

Instructions:
1. Ice cubes are placed in a tall glass.
2. Fill the glass with orange juice and tequila.
3. To combine the ingredients, gently stir.
4. Pour the grenadine syrup into the glass slowly to give it a sunset effect as it settles to the bottom.
5. Add an orange slice and a maraschino cherry as garnish.

NUTRITION INFO (per serving):
Cals: 200, Carbs: 25g, Fat: 0g, Protein: 0g

327. Caribbean Hurricane Party

Time: 10 mins

Servings: 1

Ingredients:
- 2 oz light rum
- 2 oz dark rum
- 2 oz passion fruit juice
- 1 oz orange juice
- 1 oz lime juice
- 1 tbsp grenadine syrup
- Orange slice and maraschino cherry for garnish
- Ice cubes

Instructions:
1. Ice cubes Must be put in a shaker.
2. The shaker Must be filled with light rum, dark rum, passion fruit juice, orange juice, lime juice, and grenadine syrup.
3. Thoroughly shake up to cooled.
4. Pour the Mixture through a strainer into an ice-filled hurricane glass.
5. Add an orange slice and a maraschino cherry as garnish.

NUTRITION INFO (per serving):
Cals: 250, Carbs: 25g, Fat: 0g, Protein: 0g

328. Turkish Mastic Raki and Turkish Delight

Time: 5 mins

Servings: 1

Ingredients:
- 2 oz raki (anise-flavored spirit)
- Ice-cold water
- Turkish Delight for serving
- Instructions:
- Pour raki into a glass.
- Add ice-cold water to the glass to dilute the raki to your preferred strength (usually 1 part raki to 2 parts water).
- Serve the Turkish Mastic Raki with Turkish Delight on the side.

NUTRITION INFO (per serving - Turkish Mastic Raki):
Cals: 100, Carbs: 0g, Fat: 0g, Protein: 0g

329. Greek Tsipouro and Saganaki

Time: 15 mins
Servings: 4

Ingredients:
- 1/2 lb Greek graviera cheese or kefalograviera cheese, split
- 1/2 cup of all-purpose flour
- 1/4 cup of olive oil
- 2 tbsp lemon juice
- 1 tbsp dried oregano
- Lemon wedges for serving
- Tsipouro for serving

Instructions:
1. Shake off any excess flour before dredging the cheese slices in all-purpose flour.
2. Over a medium-high flame, warm the olive oil in the pan.
3. Slices of cheese Must be fried in hot oil up to both sides are crispy and golden.
4. Cheese Must be taken out of the oil and dried on paper towels to absorb any extra oil.
5. Over the fried cheese pieces, smear dry oregano.
6. Lemon juice Must be poured over the Saganaki.
7. Lemon wedges and a side of tsipouro Must be served with the saganaki.

NUTRITION INFO (per serving - Saganaki):
Cals: 200, Carbs: 10g, Fat: 15g, Protein: 10g

330. Russian White Russian and Blinchiki

Time: 15 mins
Servings: 1

Ingredients:
- 1 1/2 oz vodka
- 3/4 oz coffee liqueur (e.g., Kahlúa)
- 3/4 oz heavy cream
- Ice cubes
- Ground cinnamon or cocoa powder for garnish
- Blinchiki (Russian crepes) for serving

Instructions:
1. Place ice cubes in a rocks glass.
2. Vodka and coffee liqueur Must be added to the glass.
3. To combine the ingredients, gently stir.
4. Place the heavy cream on top of the beverage with care.
5. Sprinkle some chocolate powder or ground cinnamon on top as a garnish.
6. Blinchiki Must be served with the White Russian.

NUTRITION INFO (per serving - White Russian):
Cals: 250, Carbs: 20g, Fat: 10g, Protein: 0g

331. Indian Kingfisher Beer and Tandoori Chicken

Time: 1 hr (+ marinating time)
Servings: 4

Ingredients:
- 1 lb chicken drumsticks or thighs
- 1 cup of plain yogurt
- 2 tbsp tandoori masala
- 1 tbsp lemon juice
- 1 tbsp vegetable oil
- Salt as needed
- Kingfisher beer for serving

Instructions:
1. To make the marinade, combine plain yogurt, tandoori masala, lemon juice, vegetable oil, and salt in a basin.
2. Apply the marinade to the chicken drumsticks or thighs, and then chill for at least two hrs (or overnight for additional flavor).
3. Set the oven's temperature to 425°F (220°C).
4. Place the marinated chicken on a foil-lined baking sheet.
5. For 35 to 40 mins, or up to the chicken is cooked through and the edges are blackened, bake the chicken in a preheated oven.
6. Serve a side of Kingfisher beer with the tandoori chicken.

NUTRITION INFO (per serving - Tandoori Chicken):
Cals: 300, Carbs: 5g, Fat: 15g, Protein: 30g

332. Thai Singha Beer and Green Papaya Salad

Time: 20 mins
Servings: 2

Ingredients:
- 2 cups of shredded green papaya
- 1/4 cup of cherry tomatoes, halved

- 2 tbsp crushed peanuts
- 2 tbsp dried shrimp (non-compulsory)
- 2 cloves garlic, chop-up
- 2 Thai bird's eye chilies, chop-up (adjust to spiciness preference)
- 2 tbsp fish sauce
- 1 tbsp palm sugar (or brown sugar)
- 1 tbsp lime juice
- Singha beer for serving

Instructions:
1. Thai bird's eye chilies and garlic are combined to create a paste in a mortar and pestle.
2. To the paste, add lime juice, palm sugar, and fish sauce. To prepare the dressing, thoroughly stir.
3. Shredded green papaya, cherry tomatoes slice in half, crushed peanuts, and dried shrimp (if used) Must all be combined in a bowl.
4. Toss the papaya Mixture with the dressing after pouring it over it.
5. Serve Singha beer alongside the green papaya salad.

NUTRITION INFO (per serving - Green Papaya Salad):
Cals: 150, Carbs: 20g, Fat: 6g, Protein: 5g

333. Japanese Toki Highball Parade

Time: 5 mins
Servings: 1

Ingredients:
- 2 oz Japanese whisky (e.g., Suntory Toki)
- Ice-cold soda water
- Lemon or lime twist for garnish
- Ice cubes

Instructions:
1. Ice cubes Must be added to a highball glass.
2. Japanese whisky Must be poured into the glass.
3. Pour in some soda water that is icy cold.
4. Combine the liquid with gentle stirring.
5. Add a lemon or lime twist as a garnish.

NUTRITION INFO (per serving):
Cals: 100, Carbs: 0g, Fat: 0g, Protein: 0g

334. Chinese Tsingtao Beer and Dim Sum

Time: 30 mins
Servings: 4

Ingredients:
- Assorted dim sum (e.g., dumplings, spring rolls, buns)
- Tsingtao beer for serving

Instructions:
1. As directed on the packaging, steam or pan-fry the various dim sum up to they are fully cooked.
2. The prepared dim sum Must be arranged on a serving dish.
3. Serve Tsingtao beer alongside the dim sum.

NUTRITION INFO (per serving - Assorted Dim Sum):
Cals: Varies depending on the type and quantity of dim sum
Carbs: Varies depending on the type and quantity of dim sum
Fat: Varies depending on the type and quantity of dim sum
Protein: Varies depending on the type and quantity of dim sum

335. Korean Hite Beer and Korean Fried Chicken

Time: 1 hr
Servings: 4

Ingredients:
- 2 lbs chicken wings or drumettes
- 1 cup of all-purpose flour
- 1/2 cup of cornstarch
- 1 tsp baking powder
- 1 cup of water or club soda
- Salt and pepper as needed
- Vegetable oil for frying
- Korean fried chicken sauce (e.g., spicy gochujang sauce, sweet and sticky soy sauce)
- Hite beer for serving

Instructions:
1. To create the batter, combine the all-purpose flour, cornstarch, baking powder, liquid soap (or water), salt, and pepper in a basin.
2. Dip the drumettes or chicken wings into the batter, thoroughly covering them.
3. A deep fryer or pan with vegetable oil is heated.
4. In the hot oil, fry the coated chicken till golden and crispy.
5. To drain off extra oil, take out the fried chicken from the oil and place it on paper towels.
6. Choose your favorite Korean fried chicken sauce before adding it to the fried chicken.

7. Hite beer Must be served alongside the Korean fried chicken.

NUTRITION INFO (per serving - Korean Fried Chicken):
Cals: 350, Carbs: 20g, Fat: 15g, Protein: 25g

336. Vietnamese Bia Hoi and Goi Cuon

Time: 30 mins
Servings: 4

Ingredients:
- 8 rice paper wrappers
- 8 Big cooked shrimp, peel off and deveined
- 2 cups of cooked vermicelli noodles
- 1 cup of fresh herbs (e.g., mint, cilantro, Thai basil)
- 1 cup of bean sprouts
- 1/2 cup of split cucumber
- 1/4 cup of crushed peanuts
- Hoisin peanut dipping sauce for serving
- Bia Hoi (fresh Vietnamese draft beer) for serving

Instructions:
1. A rice paper wrapper Must be briefly dipped in warm water to make it more malleable.
2. On a spotless surface, spread out the damp rice paper.
3. A cooked shrimp Must be placed in the center of the rice paper.
4. On top of the shrimp, scatter a few cooked vermicelli noodles.
5. On top of the noodles, sprinkle fresh herbs, bean sprouts, and cucumber slices.
6. Sprinkle the vegetables with crushed peanuts.
7. The rice paper is rolled tightly after being folded over the filling on the sides.
8. To make more rolls, repeat the process with the remaining ingredients.
9. Vietnamese spring rolls (Goi Cuon) Must be served with Hoisin peanut dipping sauce and Bia Hoi on the side.

NUTRITION INFO (per serving - Goi Cuon):
Cals: 200, Carbs: 30g, Fat: 5g, Protein: 10g

337. Moroccan Mint Tea and Kefta Tagine

Time: 1 hr
Servings: 4

Ingredients:
- 1 lb ground beef or lamb
- 1/2 cup of chop-up onions
- 2 cloves garlic, chop-up
- 2 tsp ground cumin
- 2 tsp ground paprika
- 1 tsp ground coriander
- 1/2 tsp ground cinnamon
- Salt and pepper as needed
- 1 can (14 oz) diced tomatoes
- 1 cup of beef or vegetable broth
- 1/2 cup of chop-up fresh parsley or cilantro
- Cooked couscous or rice for serving
- Moroccan mint tea for serving

Instructions:
1. To make the kefta Mixture, combine the ground beef or lamb with the chop-up onions, chop-up garlic, cumin, paprika, coriander, cinnamon, salt, and pepper in a bowl.
2. Make little meatballs out of the kefta Mixture.
3. The meatballs Must be browned over medium heat in a sizable skillet or tagine.
4. To the skillet or tagine, add diced tomatoes and beef or veggie broth.
5. Once the meatballs are thoroughly cooked and the sauce has thickened, cover and simmer for around 30 mins.
6. Add freshly chop-up cilantro or parsley.
7. Along with cooked rice or couscous and Moroccan mint tea, serve the kefta tagine.

NUTRITION INFO (per serving - Kefta Tagine):
Cals: 350, Carbs: 10g, Fat: 25g, Protein: 20g

338. Hawaiian Blue Hawaii Luau

Time: 5 mins
Servings: 1

Ingredients:
- 1 1/2 oz light rum
- 3/4 oz blue curaçao liqueur
- 2 oz pineapple juice
- 1 oz coconut cream
- Pineapple slice and maraschino cherry for garnish
- Ice cubes

Instructions:
1. Ice cubes Must be put in a shaker.
2. The shaker Must be filled with light rum, blue curaçao liqueur, pineapple juice, and coconut cream.
3. Thoroughly shake up to cooled.

4. Pour the Mixture through a strainer into an ice-filled, chilled glass.
5. Add a pineapple slice and a maraschino cherry as garnish.

NUTRITION INFO (per serving):
Cals: 300, Carbs: 30g, Fat: 10g, Protein: 0g

339. Swiss Alpine Negroni Magic

Time: 5 mins
Servings: 1

Ingredients:
- 1 oz gin
- 1 oz sweet vermouth
- 1 oz Campari
- Orange slice or twist for garnish
- Ice cubes

Instructions:
1. Ice cubes are placed in a combining glass.
2. Combining glass with gin, sweet vermouth, and Campari added.
3. Stir thoroughly up to thoroughly blended and cold.
4. Pour the Mixture through a strainer into an ice-filled, chilled glass.
5. Add an orange slice or twist as a garnish.

NUTRITION INFO (per serving):
Cals: 150, Carbs: 10g, Fat: 0g, Protein: 0g

340. Italian Aperol Spritz and Carpaccio

Time: 5 mins
Servings: 1

Ingredients:
- 2 oz Aperol
- 3 oz Prosecco or sparkling wine
- 1 oz soda water
- Orange slice for garnish
- Ice cubes
- Thinly split raw beef (e.g., beef tenderloin)
- Arugula
- Shaved Parmesan cheese
- Extra-virgin olive oil
- Lemon juice
- Salt and pepper as needed

Instructions:
1. Add ice cubes to a wine glass.
2. Fill the glass with Prosecco and Aperol.
3. Add more soda water to the glass.
4. Gently stir the flavors together.
5. Add an orange slice as a garnish.
6. Lay out thinly split raw meat on a platter for carpaccio.
7. Arugula and shaved Parmesan cheese are placed on top of the steak.
8. Lemon juice and extra virgin olive oil Must be drizzled on.
9. As needed, add salt and pepper to the food.
10. Serve the carpaccio beside the aperitif.

NUTRITION INFO (per serving - Aperol Spritz):
Cals: 150, Carbs: 15g, Fat: 0g, Protein: 0g

341. French Lillet Royale Bonanza

Time: 5 mins
Servings: 1

Ingredients:
- 2 oz Lillet Blanc (French aperitif wine)
- 1 oz blackcurrant liqueur (e.g., crème de cassis)
- Champagne or sparkling wine
- Lemon twist for garnish
- Ice cubes

Instructions:
1. Add ice cubes to a wine glass.
2. In the glass, add Lillet Blanc and blackcurrant liqueur.
3. Add more Champagne or sparkling wine to the glass.
4. Gently stir the flavors together.
5. Add a lemon twist as a garnish.

NUTRITION INFO (per serving):
Cals: 150, Carbs: 15g, Fat: 0g, Protein: 0g

342. Spanish Kalimotxo Love

Time: 5 mins
Servings: 1

Ingredients:
- 2 oz red wine (e.g., Rioja)
- 2 oz cola
- Lemon or lime wedge for garnish
- Ice cubes

Instructions:
1. Ice cubes Must be added to a glass.
2. Put a little red wine in the glass.

3. Add more cola to the glass.
4. Gently stir the flavors together.
5. Add a wedge of lemon or lime as garnish.

NUTRITION INFO (per serving):
Cals: 100, Carbs: 10g, Fat: 0g, Protein: 0g

343. Mexican Mexican Mule Fiesta

Time: 5 mins
Servings: 1

Ingredients:
- 2 oz tequila
- 1 oz lime juice
- Ginger beer
- Lime wedge and mint sprig for garnish
- Ice cubes

Instructions:
1. Add ice cubes to a wine glass.
2. In the glass, add Lillet Blanc and blackcurrant liqueur.
3. Add more Champagne or sparkling wine to the glass.
4. Gently stir the flavors together.
5. Add a lemon twist as a garnish.

NUTRITION INFO (per serving):
Cals: 150, Carbs: 10g, Fat: 0g, Protein: 0g

344. Caribbean Blue Hawaiian Party

Time: 10 mins
Servings: 1

Ingredients:
- 1 1/2 oz light rum
- 3/4 oz blue curaçao liqueur
- 2 oz pineapple juice
- 1 oz coconut cream
- Pineapple slice and maraschino cherry for garnish
- Ice cubes

Instructions:
1. Ice cubes Must be put in a shaker.
2. The shaker Must be filled with light rum, blue curaçao liqueur, pineapple juice, and coconut cream.
3. Thoroughly shake up to cooled.
4. Pour the Mixture through a strainer into an ice-filled, chilled glass.
5. Add a pineapple slice and a maraschino cherry as garnish.

NUTRITION INFO (per serving):
Cals: 250, Carbs: 30g, Fat: 10g, Protein: 0g

345. Turkish Bouncea and Baklava

Time: 1 hr
Servings: 4

Ingredients:
- 2 cups of millet or wheat flour
- 1 cup of sugar
- 6 cups of water
- 1/2 tsp ground cinnamon
- 1/2 tsp ground cloves
- Crushed walnuts for serving
- Turkish baklava for serving

Instructions:
1. Combine millet or wheat flour, sugar, water, ground cloves, and cinnamon in a big pot.
2. Stirring continually while cooking the Mixture over medium heat will cause it to thicken.
3. The pot Must be taken from the heat and let to cool to room temperature.
4. Incorporate the chilled Mixture into serving cups of or bowls.
5. Crushed walnuts Must be added on top.
6. Turkish baklava Must be served alongside the bouncea.

NUTRITION INFO (per serving - Bouncea):
Cals: 200, Carbs: 40g, Fat: 2g, Protein: 2g

346. Greek Tsipouro and Souvlaki

Time: 30 mins (+ marinating time)
Servings: 4

Ingredients:
- 1 lb pork or chicken, slice into mini cubes
- 1/4 cup of olive oil
- 1/4 cup of lemon juice
- 2 cloves garlic, chop-up
- 1 tbsp dried oregano
- Salt and pepper as needed
- Tsipouro (Greek grape pomace brandy) for serving

Instructions:
1. To make the marinade, combine the olive oil, lemon juice, chop-up garlic, dried oregano, salt, and pepper in a bowl.

2. Cubed pork or chicken Must be added to the marinade and well coated.
3. For at least two hrs (or overnight for additional flavor), cover the bowl and place in the refrigerator.
4. Skewers with marinated chicken or pork Must be used.
5. The skewers Must be cooked through and slightly browned after being grilled on a grill or stovetop.
6. Tsipouro Must be served alongside the souvlaki.

NUTRITION INFO (per serving - Souvlaki):
Cals: 250, Carbs: 0g, Fat: 15g, Protein: 25g

347. Russian Moscow Mule Parade

Time: 5 mins
Servings: 1

Ingredients:
- 2 oz vodka
- 1/2 oz lime juice
- Ginger beer
- Lime wedge and mint sprig for garnish
- Ice cubes

Instructions:
1. Ice cubes Must be added to a copper cup of.
2. Fill the mug with vodka and lime juice.
3. Pour more ginger beer into the mug.
4. Gently stir the flavors together.
5. Add a lime slice and a mint sprig as garnish.

NUTRITION INFO (per serving):
Cals: 150, Carbs: 10g, Fat: 0g, Protein: 0g

348. Indian Mango Lassi and Bhel Puri

Time: 15 mins
Servings: 2

Ingredients:
- 2 ripe mangoes, peel off and pitted
- 1 cup of plain yogurt
- 1/2 cup of milk
- 2 tbsp sugar (adjust to sweetness preference)
- Pinch of ground cardamom
- Crushed ice
- Bhel Puri Mixture (puffed rice, chop-up vegetables, tamarind chutney, etc.) for serving

Instructions:
1. Ripe mangoes, plain yogurt, milk, sugar, and crushed cardamom Must all be blended together up to smooth.
2. Up to the Lassi is foamy, add crushed ice to the combiner and process once more.
3. Incorporate serving glasses with the mango lassi.
4. Serve the mango lassi along with the Bhel Puri Mixture.

NUTRITION INFO (per serving - Mango Lassi):
Cals: 200, Carbs: 40g, Fat: 5g, Protein: 5g

349. Thai Singha Beer and Som Tum

Time: 20 mins
Servings: 2

Ingredients:
- 2 cups of shredded green papaya
- 1/4 cup of cherry tomatoes, halved
- 2 tbsp crushed peanuts
- 2 tbsp dried shrimp (non-compulsory)
- 2 cloves garlic, chop-up
- 2 Thai bird's eye chilies, chop-up (adjust to spiciness preference)
- 2 tbsp fish sauce
- 1 tbsp palm sugar (or brown sugar)
- 1 tbsp lime juice
- Singha beer for serving

Instructions:
1. Thai bird's eye chilies and garlic are combined to create a paste in a mortar and pestle.
2. To the paste, add lime juice, palm sugar, and fish sauce. To prepare the dressing, thoroughly stir.
3. Shredded green papaya, cherry tomatoes slice in half, crushed peanuts, and dried shrimp (if used) Must all be combined in a bowl.
4. Toss the papaya Mixture with the dressing after pouring it over it.
5. Serve Singha beer alongside the Som Tum (Green Papaya Salad).

NUTRITION INFO (per serving - Som Tum):
Cals: 150, Carbs: 20g, Fat: 6g, Protein: 5g

350. Japanese Hibiki Whisky and Sushi

Time: 30 mins (+ cooking rice and preparation time)
Servings: 2

Ingredients:
- Assorted sushi rolls (e.g., California roll, spicy tuna roll, salmon avocado roll)
- Freshly prepared sushi rice
- Wasabi and pickled ginger for serving
- Hibiki Japanese whisky for serving

Instructions:
1. Sushi rice Must be prepared and leted to cool to room temperature.
2. The sushi rolls Must be arranged on a serving dish.
3. Wasabi and pickled ginger Must be served alongside the sushi.
4. Fill glasses with Hibiki Japanese whiskey.
5. Along with the sushi rolls, serve the Hibiki Whisky.

351. Chinese Lychee Martini and Dumplings

Time: 10 mins

Servings: 1

Ingredients:
- 2 oz vodka
- 1 oz lychee liqueur or syrup
- 1 oz lemon juice
- Canned lychees for garnish (non-compulsory)
- Ice cubes
- Steamed or pan-fried dumplings for serving

Instructions:
1. Ice cubes Must be put in a shaker.
2. To the shaker, add vodka, lychee syrup or liqueur, and lemon juice.
3. Thoroughly shake up to cooled.
4. Pour the Mixture through a strainer into a martini glass.
5. If using, garnish with lychees in cans.
6. Dumplings can be steamed or pan-fried and served alongside the Lychee Martini.

NUTRITION INFO (per serving - Lychee Martini):
Cals: 180, Carbs: 15g, Fat: 0g, Protein: 0g

352. Korean Soju and Jajangmyeon

Time: 30 mins

Servings: 2

Ingredients:
- 8 oz jajangmyeon noodles (Korean black bean noodles)
- 1/2 cup of jajang sauce (Korean black bean sauce)
- 1/2 cup of diced pork or beef
- 1 cup of diced vegetables (e.g., onions, zucchini, potatoes)
- 2 tbsp vegetable oil
- 2 cups of water
- Soju for serving

Instructions:
1. Jajangmyeon noodles Must be prepared per the directions on the box/pkg and then placed aside.
2. Vegetable oil Must be heated over medium heat in a sizable pan or wok.
3. Cook the beef or pork cubed till thoroughly cooked and browned.
4. Vegetables Must be added to the pan and stir-fried for a few mins up to they are soft.
5. Water and jajang sauce are stirred in, and the sauce is simmered up to it thickens.
6. Jajangmyeon Must be served with a side of soju.

NUTRITION INFO (per serving - Jajangmyeon):
Cals: 400, Carbs: 40g, Fat: 15g, Protein: 25g

Printed in Great Britain
by Amazon